Renewed

DAY BY DAY

A DAILY DEVOTIONAL

BY A.W. TOZER

COMPILED BY G. B. SMITH

Christian Publications, Inc.

Harrisburg, Pennsylvania

Christian Publications, Inc.

25 S. 10th Street, P.O. Box 3404

Harrisburg, PA 17105

The mark of *CP* vibrant faith

Excerpts from *The Divine Conquest* by A. W. Tozer,
© 1950 Fleming H. Revell Company.
Used by permission

Library of Congress Catalog Card Number: 80-69301

ISBN: 0-87509-292-6

Printed in the United States of America

Preface

Dr. A. W. Tozer often told his friends that his primary spiritual concern was proclamation and promotion of "personal heart religion." His pulpit ministry and his writings during his lifetime reflected this concern.

Dr. Tozer was also plainly on record that he tried always to preach and write for "the plain persons whose hearts stir them up to seek after God for Himself!"

Such "stirring of heart" must always be in the realm of spiritual awakening—seeking to be more Christlike through willingness to know Him better!

This volume of 366 selected and edited daily readings from Dr. Tozer's books, editorials, and sermons is published for the spiritual help it may consistently bring to "God's good, plain people," who, as Dr. Tozer himself pointed out, "are a benediction wherever they are found!"

In tribute here to Dr. Tozer's own spiritual balance and God-given humility concerning his sermons and his writings, we quote his own assessment:

> "The work of a good book is to incite the reader to moral action, to turn his eyes toward God and urge him forward. Beyond that it cannot go!"

In one sense, we do not believe this is a typical book of daily "devotions," for you will find Dr. Tozer will often be rapping your spiritual knuckles as you read on from day to day!

God Is Always First—
and Will Surely Be Last

I am Alpha and Omega, the beginning and the ending, saith the Lord.
Revelation 1:8

God is always first, and God will surely be last!

In the plan of God, man is never permitted to utter the first word nor the last. That is the prerogative of the Deity, and one which He will never surrender to His creatures.

Man has no say about the time or the place of his birth; God determines that without consulting the man himself. One day the little man finds himself in consciousness and accepts the fact that he is. There his volitional life begins.

Before that he had nothing to say about anything.

After that he struts and boasts, and encouraged by the sound of his own voice he may declare his independence of God.

Have your fun, little man; you are only chattering in the interim between first and last. You had no voice at the first and you will have none at the last!

God reserves the right to take up at the last where He began at the first, and you are in the hands of God whether you will or not.

Adam became a living soul but that becoming was not of his own volition. It was God who willed it and who executed His will in making Adam a living soul. God was there first!

And when Adam sinned and wrecked his whole life, God was there still. Adam's whole future peace lay in this—that God was still there after he had sinned.

It would be great wisdom for us to begin to live in the light of this wonderful and terrible truth: God is the first and the last!

January 1

Jesus Christ Is All That the Godhead Is

But of him are ye in Christ Jesus, who of God is made unto us wisdom, and righteousness, and sanctification, and redemption. 1 Corinthians 1:30

I advise you not to listen to those who spend their time demeaning the person of Christ.

I advise you to look beyond the cloudiness of modern terms used by those who themselves are not sure who Jesus Christ was in reality.

You cannot trust the man who can only say, "I believe that God revealed Himself through Christ." Find out what he really believes about the person of the incarnate Son of God!

You cannot trust the man who will only say that Christ reflected more of God than other men do. Neither can you trust those who teach that Jesus Christ was the supreme religious genius, having the ability to catch and reflect more of God than any other man.

All of these approaches are insults to the Person of Jesus Christ. He was and is and can never cease to be God, and when we find Him and know Him, we are back at the ancient fountain again.

Christ is all that the Godhead is!

This is the wonder, the great miracle—that by one swift, decisive, considered act of faith and prayer, our souls go back to the ancient fountain of our being, and we start over again!

It is in Jesus Christ Himself that we find our source, our satisfaction. I think this is what John Newton perceived in the miracle of the new birth, causing him to sing, "Now rest my long-divided heart, fixed on this blissful center—rest!"

January 2

Holy Spirit: God in Contact with His Creatures

. . .The Spirit of truth, who proceedeth from the Father, he shall testify of me. John 15:26

If I read aright the record of Christian experience through the years, those who most enjoyed the power of the Spirit of God have had the least to say about Him by way of attempted definition.

The Bible saints who walked in the Spirit never tried to explain Him. In post-biblical times many who were filled and possessed by the Spirit were by the limitations of their literary gifts prevented from telling us much about Him. They had no gift for self-analysis, but lived from within in uncritical simplicity.

To them the Spirit was One to be loved and fellowshipped the same as the Lord Jesus Himself. They would have been lost completely in any metaphysical discussion of the nature of the Spirit, but they had no trouble in claiming the power of the Spirit for holy living and fruitful service.

This is as it should be. Personal experience must always be first in real life. Knowledge by acquaintance is always better than knowledge by description, and the first does not presuppose the second nor require it.

What we have in the Christian doctrine of the Holy Spirit is Deity present among us.

He is not God's messenger only—He is God!

He is God in contact with His creatures, doing in them and among them a saving and renewing work.

January 3

The Spirit of Man Makes Him a Human Being

For what man knoweth the things of a man, save the spirit of man which is in him? even so the things of God knoweth no man, but the Spirit of God. 1 Corinthians 2:11

Deep inside every man there is a private sanctum where dwells the mysterious essence of his being. It is the man's "I am," a gift from the I AM who created him.

The I AM which is God is underived and self-existent; the "I am" which is man is derived from God and dependent every moment upon His creative fiat for its continued existence. One is the Creator, high over all, ancient of days, dwelling in light unapproachable. The other is a creature and, though privileged beyond all others, is still but a creature, a pensioner on God's bounty and a suppliant before His throne!

The deep-in human entity of which we speak is called in the Scriptures "the spirit of man." Paul told the Corinthian church: "For what man knoweth the things of man, save the spirit of man which is in him? even so the things of God knoweth no man, but the Spirit of God."

As God's self-knowledge lies in the eternal Spirit, so man's self-knowledge is by his own spirit, and his knowledge of God is by the direct impression of the Spirit of God upon the spirit of man. This reveals the essential spirituality of mankind.

It also denies that man is a creature having a spirit and boldly declares that he is a spirit having a body!

That which makes man a human being is not his body but his spirit, in which the image of God originally lay.

January 4

Do Not Mistake the True Meaning of the Cross

But God forbid that I should glory, save in the cross of our Lord Jesus Christ, by whom the world is crucified unto me, and I unto the world. Galatians 6:14

All unannounced and mostly undetected there has come in modern times a new cross into popular evangelical circles.

It is like the old cross, but different: the likenesses are superficial, the differences fundamental!

From this new cross has sprung a new philosophy of the Christian life with encouragement for a new and entirely different evangelistic approach. The evangelist tries to show that Christianity makes no unpleasant demands; rather, it offers the same thing the world does, only on a higher level. The modern view is that the new cross does not slay the sinner, it redirects him!

The philosophy back of this kind of thing may be sincere, but it is as false as it is blind. It misses completely the whole meaning of the cross.

The old cross is a symbol of death. It stands for the abrupt, violent end of a human being. In Roman times, the man who took up his cross and started down the road was not coming back. He was not going out to have his life redirected: he was going out to have it ended! The cross did not try to keep on good terms with its victim. It struck cruel and hard, and when it had finished its work, the man was no more!

The race of Adam is under death sentence. God cannot approve any of the fruits of sin. In coming to Christ we do not bring our old life up onto a higher plane; we leave it at the cross. Thus God salvages the individual by liquidating him and then raising him again to newness of life!

January 5

The Bible: More Than a Volume of Facts

All scripture is given by inspiration of God, and is profitable for doctrine, for reproof, for correction, for instruction in righteousness. 2 Timothy 3:16

Charles G. Finney believed that Bible teaching without moral application could be worse than no teaching at all and could result in positive injury to the hearers. I used to feel that this might be an extreme position, but after years of observation have come around to it, or to a view almost identical with it.

There is scarcely anything so dull and meaningless as Bible doctrine taught for its own sake. Theology is a set of facts concerning God, man and the world. These facts may be and often are set forth as values in themselves; and there lies the snare both for the teacher and for the hearer.

The Bible is more than a volume of hitherto unknown facts about God, man and the universe. It is a book of exhortation based upon these facts. By far the greater portion of the book is devoted to an urgent effort to persuade people to alter their ways and bring their lives into harmony with the will of God as set forth in its pages.

Actually, no man is better for knowing that God in the beginning created the heaven and the earth. The devil knows that, and so did Ahab and Judas Iscariot. No man is better for knowing that God so loved the world of men that He gave His only begotten Son to die for their redemption. In hell there are millions who know that.

Theological truth is useless until it is obeyed. The purpose behind all doctrine is to secure moral action!

January 6

The Flock of God: Safe in Jesus Christ

Feed the flock of God which is among you. . . .And when the chief Shepherd shall appear, ye shall receive a crown of glory that fadeth not away. 1 Peter 5:2, 4

The people who want to know God and walk with God, those who have learned to recognize the voice of the good Shepherd, will always be at home in a Spirit-filled congregation.

It is sad indeed that some have never heard the voice of the Shepherd. His voice is as tender as a lullaby and as strong as the wind and as mighty as the sound of many waters. The people who have learned to hear and recognize the voice of Jesus—that healing, musical, solemn, beautiful voice of Jesus in His church—are always at home where everything centers around Him.

The true Christian church can be a conglomeration of everything under the sun. That is, we may have Calvinists and Arminians and Methodists and Baptists and all sorts of others, and yet we are all together on one thing—Jesus Christ is wisdom, righteousness, sanctification, and redemption! He is All in all, and the people of the Lord who have learned to hear the voice of the Shepherd gravitate towards that kind of church!

They may not be so sure about who else is present, but they know the Lord is present and they are sensitive to that.

Do you find your own heart sensitive to the Lord's presence or are you among those who are "samplers" and "nibblers"? God help you if you are, for the child of the king is a sheep who loves his Shepherd and he stays close to Him! That's the only safe place for a sheep. Stay close to Jesus and all of the wolves in the world cannot get a tooth in you!

January 7

True Worship: Fully Seeking the Lord We Adore

O come, let us worship and bow down. . . .Psalm 95:6

An old creed says that we worship one God, the Father Almighty, maker of heaven and earth and of all things visible and invisible.

If we could set forth all of God's attributes and tell all that He is, we would fall on our knees in adoring worship.

The Bible tells us that God dwells in light that is unapproachable, whom no man can see or has seen, and whom no man can see and live.

It says that God is holy and eternal and omnipotent and omniscient and sovereign, and that He has a thousand sovereign attributes. And all of these should humble us and bring us down!

I have come to believe that no worship is wholly pleasing to God until there is nothing in us displeasing to God. If there is anything within me that does not worship God, then there is nothing in me that worships God perfectly.

Note that I am not saying that God must have a perfection of worship or He will not accept any worship at all. I would not go so far; if I did, I would rule myself out. But, I do say that the ideal God sets before us is to worship as near to perfectly as we can. Faith and love and obedience and loyalty and high conduct of life—all of these must be taken as burnt offerings and offered to God!

True worship seeks union with its beloved, and an active effort to close the gap between the heart and the God it adores is worship at its best!

January 8

Believe the Right Thing about the Right Person

Now the God of hope fill you with all joy and peace in believing, that ye may abound in hope, through the power of the Holy Ghost. Romans 15:13

There is a nebulous idea accepted by many in our day that faith is an almighty power flowing through the universe which anyone may plug into at will! It is conceived vaguely as a subrational creative pulsation streaming down from somewhere Up There, ready at any time to enter our hearts and change our whole mental and moral constitution as well as our total outlook on man, God and the cosmos.

When it comes in, supposedly out go pessimism, fear, defeat and failure; in come optimism, confidence, personal mastery and unfailing success in war, love, sports, business and politics.

All of this is, of course, a gossamer of self-deception woven of the unsubstantial threads of fancy spun out of minds of tenderhearted persons who want to believe it! What is overlooked in all this is that faith is good only when it engages truth; when it is made to rest upon falsehood it can and often does lead to eternal tragedy.

For it is not enough that we believe; we must believe in the right thing about the right One!

To believe in God is more than to believe that He exists. To a right faith knowledge is necessary. We must know at least something of what God is like and what His will is for His human creatures. To know less than this is to be thrown back upon the necessity of accepting the affirmations of the soul and substituting "Thus saith my soul" for the biblical "Thus saith the Lord," and no man has any right to pick and choose among revealed truths.

January 9

Every One Must Pray as if He Alone Could Pray

And he spake a parable unto them to this end, that men ought always to pray, and not to faint. Luke 18:1

Thomas a' Kempis wrote that the man of God ought to be more at home in his prayer chamber than before the public. It is not too much to say that the preacher who loves to be before the public is hardly prepared spiritually to be before them. Right praying may easily make a man hesitant to appear before an audience.

The man who is really at home in the presence of God will find himself caught in a kind of inward contradiction. He is likely to feel his responsibility so keenly that he would rather do almost anything than face an audience; and yet the pressure upon his spirit may be so great that wild horses could not drag him away from his pulpit.

No man should stand before an audience who has not first stood before God. Many hours of communion should precede one hour in the pulpit. The prayer chamber should be more familiar than the public platform.

Schools teach everything about preaching except the important part, praying. The best any school can do is to recommend prayer and exhort to its practice. Praying itself must be the work of the individual. That it is the one religious work which gets done with the least enthusiasm cannot but be one of the tragedies of our times!

In true prayer, every man must be an original, for true prayer cannot be imitated nor can it be learned from someone else. Everyone must pray as if he alone could pray!

January 10

A Calamity: Accepting This World as Our Home

Love not the world, neither the things that are in the world. If any man love the world, the love of the Father is not in him. 1 John 2:15

Of all the calamities that have been visited upon the world, the surrender of the human spirit to this present world and its ways is the worst—without doubt!

No oriental monarch ever ruled his cowering subjects with any more cruel tyranny than things—visible things, audible things, tangible things—rule mankind.

That we who were made to communicate with angels and archangels and seraphim and with the God who made them all—that we should settle down here as a wild eagle of the air come down to scratch in the barnyard with the common hens—this I say is the worst of anything that has ever come to the world!

It seems incredible that we who were made for many worlds should accept this one world as our ultimate home.

Man was made in the image of God and is now a fallen being that has left its place in the celestial world and has plummeted down like a falling star. Now, in this world, he has all but forgotten the place from which he came.

That is why the devil sees to it that we seldom get alone with time to think and meditate on the reality of the other world. For when a man really gets alone, he senses often that this life in this world is not the answer—it is not the end.

Actually and simply, a Christian is one who dedicates himself to God to inhabit another and better world!

January 11

Satan Would Bind Us in Our Own Grave Clothes

. . .For this purpose the Son of God was manifested, that he might destroy the works of the devil. 1 John 3:8

It is part of the devil's business to keep the Christian's spirit imprisoned. He knows that the believing and justified Christian has been raised up out of the grave of his sins and trespasses. From that point on, Satan works that much harder to keep us bound and gagged, actually imprisoned in our own grave clothes!

He knows that if we continue in this kind of bondage we will never be able to claim our rightful spiritual heritage. He knows also that while we continue bound in this kind of enslavement we are not much better off than when we were spiritually dead.

This is one reason why the Christians in today's churches are behaving like a flock of frightened sheep— so intimidated by the devil that we can't even say "Amen!"

I am sure that it is not glorifying to our God that Christians should be so intimidated and silenced in our day. It was Jesus Christ, the Lord of glory, who came down and took our human body for Himself. He was a man, born of a woman, a man wearing our own nature— but He was also God!

He went out to the cross and they sacrificed Him there. The Father, God Almighty, accepted His sacrifice as the one, final fulfillment and consummation of all the sacrifices ever made on Jewish altars. After three days, He came out of the grave, then ascended as Victor over death and hell!

Believing this, we ought to be the most fearless, the happiest and most God-assured people in the whole world!

January 12

Learn to Love God for Himself Alone

We love him, because he first loved us. 1 John 4:19

The phrase, "the love of God," when used by Christians almost always refers to God's love for us. We must remember that it can also mean our love for God!

The first and great commandment is that we should love God with all the power of our total personality. Though all love originates in God and is for that reason God's own love, yet we are permitted to catch and reflect back that love in such manner that it becomes our love indeed!

The Christian's love for God has by some religious thinkers been divided into two kinds, the love of gratitude and the love of excellence. But we must carry our love to God further than love of gratitude and love of excellence.

There is a place in the religious experience where we love God for Himself alone, with never a thought of His benefits. There is, in the higher type of love, a suprarational element that cannot and does not attempt to give reasons for its existence—it only whispers, "I love!"

In the perfection of love, the heart does not reason from admiration to affection, but quickly rises to the height of blind adoration where reason is suspended and the heart worships in unreasoning blessedness. It can only exclaim, "Holy, holy, holy," while scarcely knowing what it means.

If this should all seem too mystical, too unreal, we offer no proof. But some will read and recognize the description of the sunlit peaks where they have been for at least brief periods and to which they long often to return. And such will need no proof!

January 13

Feeling Right: Not the Same as Being Right

The lord of that servant shall come. . .and appoint him his portion with the hypocrites. . . . Matthew 24:50, 51

It appears that too many Christians want to enjoy the thrill of feeling right but are not willing to endure the inconvenience of being right!

The glaring disparity between theology and practice among professing Christians is a more destructive evil in its effect upon the Christian religion than communism, Romanism and liberalism combined.

So wide is the gulf that separates theory from practice in the church that an inquiring stranger who chances upon both would scarcely dream that there was any relation between them.

An intelligent observer of our human scene who heard the Sunday morning sermon and later watched the Sunday afternoon conduct of those who had heard it would conclude that he had been examining two distinct and contrary religions!

Christians habitually weep and pray over beautiful truth, only to draw back from that same truth when it comes to the difficult job of putting it in practice.

The average church simply does not dare to check its practices against biblical precepts. It tolerates things that are diametrically opposed to the will of God. This can be explained only by assuming a lack of integration in the religious personality. The mind can approve and the emotions enjoy while the will drags its feet and refuses to go along!

And since Christ makes His appeal directly to the will, are we not justified in wondering whether or not these divided souls have ever made a true commitment to the Lord?

January 14

The World Changes—But Not the Human Race

. . .That ye henceforth walk not as other Gentiles walk, in the vanity of their mind. Ephesians 4:17

To a Christian, conditioned as he is to observing life from above and judging all things in the light of eternal values, the modern feverish devotion to the newest invention and the latest happening seems more than a little ridiculous!

One thing seems to be quite forgotten: the world moves and times change but people remain the same always. Just as a pendulum remains fixed at the top while it swings back and forth from one extreme to another, so the human race remains basically unchanged while it moves through its limited arc.

No responsible person will deny that some changes made by the race over the years have been improvements and so may have represented progress and advance. However, just what we are supposed to be advancing toward has not been made very clear by our leaders!

It would seem humanly difficult, indeed, to show that we are moving toward an end when we do not know what or where that end is, or even if such an end exists at all.

The only parallel we can think of at the moment is that of a deadly-serious and fanatically determined dachshund chasing breathlessly after its tail—a tail, incidentally, which is not there because it has previously been removed. Add a large number of other dachshunds, bespectacled and solemn, writing books to prove that the frustrated puppy's activity is progress, and you have the picture!

The Grace of God Cannot Be Extinguished

And the grace of our Lord was exceeding abundant with faith and love which is in Christ Jesus. 1 Timothy 1:14

Brethren, we should be keenly aware that the living God can no more hide His grace than the sun can hide its brightness!

We must keep in mind also that the grace of God is infinite and eternal. Being an attribute of God, it is as boundless as infinitude!

The Old Testament is indeed a book of law, but not of law only. Before the great flood Noah "found grace in the eyes of the Lord," and after the law was given God said to Moses, "Thou hast found grace in my sight."

There never was a time when the law did not represent the will of God for mankind nor a time when the violation of it did not bring its own penalty, though God was patient and sometimes "winked" at wrongdoing because of the ignorance of the people.

The great source and spring of Christian morality is the love of Christ Himself, not the law of Moses; nevertheless there has been no abrogation of the principles of morality contained in the law. The grace of God made sainthood possible in Old Testament days just as it does today!

God has promised that He will always be Himself. Men may flee from the sunlight to dark and musty caves of the earth, but they cannot put out the sun. So men may in any dispensation despise the grace of God, but they cannot extinguish it!

January 16

Man's Fall Created a Perpetual Moral Crisis

For as by one man's disobedience many were made sinners, so by the obedience of one shall many be made righteous. Romans 5:19

The fall of man has created a perpetual crisis. It will last until sin has been put down and Christ reigns over a redeemed and restored world.

Until that time the earth remains a disaster area and its inhabitants live in a state of extraordinary emergency.

Statesmen and economists talk hopefully of "a return to normal conditions," but conditions have not been normal since "the woman saw that the tree was good for food. . .and pleasant" and "to be desired to make one wise" and "took of the fruit thereof, and did eat, and gave also unto her husband with her; and he did eat."

It is not enough to say that we live in a state of moral crisis. That is true, but it is not all, for the Fall has affected every part of man's nature, moral, intellectual, psychological, spiritual and physical.

Man's whole being has been deeply injured; the sin in his heart has overflowed into his total life, affecting his relation to God, to his fellow men and to everyone and everything that touches him.

To me, it has always been difficult to understand those evangelical Christians who insist upon living in the crisis as if no crisis existed. They say they serve the Lord, but they divide their days so as to leave plenty of time to play and loaf and enjoy the pleasures of the world as well. They are at ease while the world burns; and they can furnish many convincing reasons for their conduct, even quoting Scripture if you press them a bit.

I wonder whether such Christians actually believe in the Fall of man!

January 17

The True Christian Is the Practicing Christian

According as his divine power hath given unto us all things that pertain unto life and godliness, through the knowledge of him that hath called us to glory and virtue. 2 Peter 1:3

The supreme purpose of the Christian religion is to make men like God in order that they may act like God. In Christ the verbs "to be" and "to do" follow each other in that order.

True religion leads to moral action. The only true Christian is the practicing Christian. Such a one is in very reality an incarnation of Christ as Christ is the incarnation of God; not in the same degree and fullness of perfection, for there is nothing in the moral universe equal to that awful mystery of godliness which joined God and man in eternal union in the person of the Man Christ Jesus; but as the fullness of the Godhead was and is in Christ, so Christ is in the nature of the one who believes in Him in the manner prescribed in the Scriptures.

Just as in eternity God acted like Himself and when incarnated in human flesh still continued in all His conduct to be true to His holiness, so does He when He enters the nature of a believing man. This is the method by which He makes the redeemed man holy.

The faith of Christ was never intended to be an end in itself nor to serve instead of something else. In the minds of some teachers faith stands in lieu of moral conduct and every inquirer after God must take his choice between the two. We are presented with the well-known either/or: either we have faith or we have works, and faith saves while works damn us. This error has lowered the moral standards of the church!

January 18

Obedience: The Final Test of Love for Christ

He that hath my commandments, and keepeth them, he it is that loveth me. . .and I will love him, and will manifest myself to him. John 14:21

The final test of love is obedience, not sweet emotions, not willingness to sacrifice, not zeal, but obedience to the commandments of Christ!

Our Lord drew a line plain and tight for everyone to see. On one side He placed those who keep His commandments and said, "These love Me." On the other side He put those who keep not His sayings, and said, "These love Me not."

The commandments of Christ occupy in the New Testament a place of importance that they do not have in current evangelical thought. The idea that our relation to Christ is revealed by our attitude to His commandments is now considered legalistic by many influential Bible teachers, and the plain words of our Lord are rejected outright or interpreted in a manner to make them conform to religious theories ostensibly based upon the epistles of Paul.

The Christian cannot be certain of the reality and depth of his love until he comes face to face with the commandments of Christ and is forced to decide what to do about them. Then he will know!

I think we should turn for a while from finespun theological speculations about grace and faith and humbly read the New Testament with a mind to obey what we see there. Love for Christ is a love of willing, as well as a love of feeling, and it is psychologically impossible to love Him adequately unless we will to obey His words!

January 19

Wisdom: Knowing the True Fear of the Lord

The fear of the Lord is the beginning of knowledge. . . . Proverbs 1:7

A truth fully taught in the Scriptures and verified in personal experience by countless numbers of holy men and women throughout the centuries might be condensed thus into a religious axiom:

"No one can know the true grace of God who
has not first known the fear of God!"

The first announcement of God's redemptive intention toward mankind was made to a man and a woman hiding in mortal fear from the presence of the Lord.

The Law of God was given to a man trembling in terror amid fire and smoke, quaking at the voice of thunder and sound of the divine trumpet.

Even the famous annunciation, "On earth peace, good will toward men," was given to shepherds who were "sore afraid" by reason of the sudden overwhelming presence of the heavenly host.

The presence of the divine always brought fear to the hearts of sinful men, a terror having no relation to mere fear of bodily harm.

I do not believe that any lasting good can come from religious activities that do not root in this quality of creature-fear. The animal in us is very strong and altogether self-confident. Until it has been defeated God will not show Himself to the eyes of our faith.

It is sad but true that the love of God affects a carnal heart not at all; or if at all, then adversely, for the knowledge that God loves us may simply confirm us in our self-righteousness!

Unsung but Singing: The Unappreciated Christian

Speaking to yourselves in psalms and hymns and spiritual songs, singing and making melody in your heart to the Lord. Ephesians 5:19

To value the esteem of mankind and for Christ's sake to renounce it is a form of crucifixion suffered by true Christians since the days of the apostles. It cannot be denied that the way of the cross is unpopular and that it brings a measure of reproach upon those who take it.

The learned historians tell of councils and persecutions and religious wars, but in the midst of all the mummery were a few who saw the Eternal City in full view and managed almost to walk on earth as if they had already gone to heaven. These were the joyous ones who got little recognition from the world of institutionalized religion, and might have gone altogether unnoticed except for their singing.

Unsung but singing: this is the short and simple story of many today whose names are not known beyond the small circle of their own company. Their gifts are not many nor great, but their song is sweet and clear!

John Milton lost his sight and mourned that loss in the third book of his *Paradise Lost*. But in spite of his affliction he refused to be desolate. If he could not see, he could still think and he could still pray. Like the nightingale he could sing in the darkness

> ". . .as the wakeful bird
> Sings darkling, and, in shadiest covert hid,
> Tunes her nocturnal note."

We are never sure where a true Christian may be found—and the busy world may actually not even know he is there—except that they hear him singing!

Getting Glory for God—or for Ourselves?

Whether therefore ye eat, or drink, or whatsoever ye do, do all to the glory of God. 1 Corinthians 10:31

I think that we ought to be mature enough to confess that many have been converted to Christ and have come into the church without wrestling with that basic human desire for honor and praise. As a result, some have actually spent a lifetime in religious work doing little more than getting glory for themselves!

Brethren, the glory can belong only to God! If we take the glory, God is being frustrated in the church.

The work of the ministry which the saints are to do will bring about the edifying of the Body of Christ—and this is not just in reference to the ordained ministry as we know it. It is the ministry of all Christians to have some share in the building up of the Body of Christ until we all come into the unity of the faith and of the knowledge of the Son of God unto a perfect man, with a measure of the stature of the fullness of Christ.

Surely in this sense God desires to use the Body of Christ for doing His final work—His eternal work.

But Christian believers and Christian congregations must be thoroughly consecrated to Christ's glory alone!

This means absolutely turning our backs on the modern insistence for human glory and recognition.

Natural gifts and talents are not enough in God's work. The mighty Spirit of God must have freedom to animate and quicken with His overtones of creativity and blessing.

You can write it down as a fact: no matter what a man does, no matter how successful he seems to be, if the Holy Spirit is not the chief energizer of his activity, it will all fall apart when he dies!

January 22

Our Lord the Object of Faith for Salvation

. . .Preaching peace by Jesus Christ: (he is Lord of all:). Acts 10:36

It is altogether doubtful whether any man can be saved who comes to Christ for His help but with no intention of obeying Him, for Christ's saviourhood is forever united to His lordship.

Look at the apostle's instruction and admonition:

"If thou shalt confess with thy mouth the Lord Jesus, and shalt believe in thine heart that God hath raised him from the dead, thou shalt be saved. . .for the same Lord over all is rich unto all that call upon him. For whosoever shall call upon the name of the Lord shall be saved." Romans 10:9-13

There the Lord is the object of faith for salvation! And when the Philippian jailer asked the way to be saved, Paul replied, "Believe on the Lord Jesus Christ, and thou shalt be saved" (Acts 16:31).

Paul did not tell him to believe on the Saviour with the thought that he could later take up the matter of His lordship and settle it at his own convenience. To Paul there could be no division of offices. Christ must be Lord or He will not be Saviour!

There is no intention here to teach that our first saving contact with Christ brings perfect knowledge of all He is to us. The contrary is true. Ages upon ages will hardly be long enough to allow us to experience all the riches of His grace.

As we discover new meanings in His titles and make them ours we will grow in the knowledge of our Lord and the many forms of love He wears exalted on His throne!

January 23

Walking a Tightrope between Two Kingdoms?

. . .For I do always those things that please him. John 8:29

We who follow Christ are aware of the fact that we inhabit at once two worlds, the spiritual and the natural.

As children of Adam we do live our lives on earth subject to the limitations of the flesh and the weaknesses and ills to which human nature is heir.

In sharp contrast to this is our life in the Spirit. There we enjoy a higher kind of life; we are children of God. We possess heavenly status and enjoy intimate fellowship with Christ!

This tends to divide our total life into two departments, as we unconsciously recognize two sets of actions, the so-called secular acts and the sacred.

This is, of course, the old "sacred-secular" antithesis and most Christians are caught in its trap. Walking the tightrope between two kingdoms they find no peace in either.

Actually, the sacred-secular dilemma has no foundation in the New Testament. Without doubt a more perfect understanding of Christian truth will deliver us from it.

The Lord Jesus Christ Himself is our perfect example and He lived no divided life. God accepted the offering of His total life and made no distinction between act and act. "I do always the things that please Him," was His brief summary of His own life as related to the Father.

We are called upon to exercise an aggressive faith, in which we offer all our acts to God and believe that He accepts them. Let us believe that God is in all our simple deeds and learn to find Him there!

January 24

Old Things Pass—All Things Become New

But we have this treasure in earthen vessels, that the excellency of the power may be of God, and not of us. 2 Corinthians 4:7

The Christian who has dedicated his life to God and has shouldered his cross need not be surprised at the conflict in which he at once finds himself engaged. Such conflict is logical; it results from the nature of God and of man and of Christianity!

He will, for instance, discover that the ways of God and the ways of men are not equal. He will find that the skills he learned in Adam's world are of very little use to him in the spiritual realm. His tried and proven methods for getting things done will fail him when he attempts to apply them to the work of the Spirit. The new Adam will not surrender to the old Adam nor gear His new creation to the methods of the world. God will not share His glory with another!

The true Church of God, the company of the forgiven and regenerated, is a marvel and an astonishment in the eyes of the old creation, a perpetual sign of the supernatural in the midst of natural things.

The Church is a sheet let down from heaven, an interposition of something unlike and dissimilar, a wonder and a perplexity which cannot be understood nor explained nor gotten rid of. That about her which yields itself to analysis by the historian or the psychologist is the very thing that does not signify, the earthen vessel in which the precious treasure is contained.

The treasure itself transcends the art of man to comprehend! Those who follow on to know the Lord discover that old things will pass away and all things will become new!

January 25

Faith Rests upon the Character of God

. . .So now also Christ shall be magnified in my body, whether it be by life, or by death. For to me to live is Christ, and to die is gain. Philippians 1:20, 21

The witness of the Christian church is most effective when she declares rather than explains, for the gospel is addressed not to reason but to faith. What can be proved requires no faith to accept and faith rests upon the character of God, not upon the demonstrations of laboratory or logic.

The power of Christianity appears in its antipathy toward, never in its agreement with, the ways of fallen men. At the heart of the Christian system lies the cross of Christ with its divine paradox and the truth of the cross is revealed in its contradictions.

The cross stands in bold opposition to the natural man. Its philosophy runs contrary to the processes of the unregenerate mind, so that Paul could say bluntly that the preaching of the cross is to them that perish foolishness. To try to find a common ground between the message of the cross and man's fallen reason can only result in an impaired reason, a meaningless cross and a powerless Christianity!

Note this also about the cross-carrying Christian: when he looks at the cross he is a pessimist, for he knows that the same judgment that fell on the Lord of glory condemns in that one act all nature and all the world of men. He rejects every human hope out of Christ because he knows that man's noblest effort is only dust building on dust.

Yet he is calmly, restfully optimistic, for the resurrection of Christ guarantees the ultimate triumph of good throughout the universe. Through Christ, all will be well at last and the Christian waits the consummation!

Knowing God: Goal of All Christian Doctrine

Give ear to my words, O Lord, consider my meditation. For thou art not a God that hath pleasure in wickedness; neither shall evil dwell with thee. Psalm 5:1, 4

Among Christians of all ages and of varying shades of doctrinal emphasis there has been fairly full agreement on one thing: they all believed that it was important that the Christian with serious spiritual aspirations should learn to meditate long and often on God!

Let a Christian insist upon rising above the poor average of current religious experience and he will soon come up against the need to know God Himself as the ultimate goal of all Christian doctrine.

Let him seek to explore the sacred wonders of the Triune Godhead and he will discover that sustained and intelligently directed meditation on the Person of God is imperative. To know God well he must think on Him unceasingly. Nothing that man has discovered about himself or God has revealed any shortcut to pure spirituality. It is still free, but tremendously costly!

Of course this presupposes at least a fair amount of sound theological knowledge. To seek God apart from His own self-disclosure in the inspired Scriptures is not only futile but dangerous. There must be also a knowledge of and complete trust in Jesus Christ as Lord and Redeemer.

Christ is not one of many ways to approach God, nor is He the best of several ways; He is the only way, "the way, the truth and the life."

To believe otherwise is to be something less than a Christian!

January 27

God's Will: Less of Me, More of Him

Being filled with the fruits of righteousness, which are by Jesus Christ, unto the glory and praise of God. Philippians 1:11

Some Christian believers seemingly are committed to endless dialogue about the deeper spiritual life, just as though it were some new kind of fun and games.

Actually, many people want to talk about it as a topic but no one seems to want to know and love God for Himself!

When do we learn that God IS the deeper life?

Jesus Christ Himself is the deeper life and as I plunge on into the knowledge of the triune God, my heart moves on into the blessedness of His fellowship.

This means that there is less of me and more of God— thus my spiritual life deepens, and I am strengthened in the knowledge of His will.

I think this is what Paul meant when he penned that great desire, "That I may know Him!" He was expressing more than the desire for acquaintance—he was yearning to be drawn into the full knowledge of fellowship with God which has been provided in the plan of redemption.

God originally created man in His own image so that man could know companionship with God in a unique sense and to a degree which is impossible for any other creature.

Because of his sin, man lost this knowledge, this daily partnership with God, and his heart has been darkened. But God has given sinful man another opportunity in salvation through the merits of a Redeemer, only because he was made in the image of God, and God has expressed His own everlasting love for man through the giving of His Son.

Discipleship: Saying Goodbye to World's Toys

Blessed is the man that endureth temptation: . . .he shall receive the crown of life, which the Lord hath promised. . . . James 1:12

There is one kind of human suffering which can be known only to the believing Christian, and that is voluntary suffering deliberately and knowingly incurred for the sake of Jesus Christ!

Such voluntary suffering displayed among us in these times is a luxury, a treasure of fabulous value, a source of riches beyond the power of the mind to conceive. And it is rare as well as precious, for there are few in this decadent age who will of their own choice go down into this dark mine looking for jewels.

But of their own choice it must be, for there is no other way to get down. God will not force us into this kind of suffering; He will not lay this cross upon us nor embarrass us with riches we do not want.

Some riches are reserved for those who apply to serve in the legion of the expendables, who love not their lives unto the death, who volunteer to suffer for Christ's sake and who follow up their application with lives that challenge the devil and invite the fury of hell.

Such as these have said goodbye to the world's toys; they have chosen to suffer affliction with the people of God. They have accepted toil and suffering as their earthly portion.

But where are they? Has this breed of Christian died out of the earth? Have the saints of God joined the mad scramble for security?

Are we now afraid to suffer and unwilling to die?

I hope not—but I wonder. And only God has the answer!

January 29

The Humble Man Says: "The Mistakes Are Mine"

Take my yoke upon you, and learn of me; for I am meek and lowly in heart; and ye shall find rest unto your souls. Matthew 11:29

A page in church history reveals that the godly Macarius of Optino was once told that his spiritual counsel had been helpful.

"This cannot be," Macarius wrote in reply. "Only the mistakes are mine. All good advice is the advice of the Spirit of God; His advice that I happen to have heard rightly and to have passed on without distorting it."

There is an excellent lesson here which we must not allow to go unregarded. It is the sweet humility of the man of God who was enabled to say, "Only the mistakes are mine."

He was fully convinced that his own efforts could result only in mistakes and that any good that came of his advice must be the work of the Holy Spirit operating within him.

Apparently this was more than a sudden impulse of self-depreciation, which the proudest of men may at times feel; it was rather a settled conviction that gave set and direction to his entire life. His long and humble ministry which brought spiritual aid to many reveals this clearly enough.

It is our belief that the evangelical movement will continue to drift farther and farther from the New Testament position unless its leadership passes from the modern religious star to the self-effacing saint who asks for no praise and seeks no place, happy only when the glory is attributed to God and himself forgotten!

Teach the Bible with High Moral Obligation

. . .Yield yourselves unto God, as those that are alive from the dead, and your members as instruments of righteousness unto God. Romans 6:13

Much that passes for New Testament Christianity is little more than objective truth sweetened with song, and made palatable by religious entertainment.

I take the risk of being misunderstood when I say that probably no other portion of the Scriptures can compare with the Pauline Epistles when it comes to making artificial saints. Peter warned that the unlearned and unstable would wrest Paul's writings to their own destruction, and we have only to visit the average Bible conference and listen to a few lectures to know what he meant!

The ominous thing is that the Pauline doctrines may be taught with complete faithfulness to the letter of the text without making the hearers one whit better. The teacher may and often does so teach the truth as to leave the hearers without a sense of moral obligation.

One reason for the divorce between truth and life may be lack of the Spirit's illumination. Another surely is the teacher's unwillingness to get himself into trouble. Any man with fair pulpit gifts can get on with the average congregation if he just "feeds" them and lets them alone. Give them plenty of objective truth and never hint that they are wrong and should be set right, and they will be content!

But the man who preaches truth and applies it to the lives of his hearers will feel the nails and the thorns. He will lead a hard life—but a glorious one!

January 31

God's Boundless Power Is All around Us

And what is the exceeding greatness of his power to us-ward who believe, according to the working of his mighty power, Which he wrought in Christ. . . . Ephesians 1:19, 20

God is spirit and His universe is basically spiritual!

Scientists change their beliefs radically from time to time and I do not want to quote them in confirmation of Christian truth, but there does appear to be a startling parallel between the atomic theory of matter and the biblical concept of the Eternal Word as the source and support of all created things.

Could it be that, as certain mystics have insisted, all things in heaven and on earth, visible and invisible, are in reality but the goings forth of the power of God?

Whatever God is He is infinitely. In Him lies all the power there is; any power at work anywhere is His. Even the power to do evil must first have come from Him since there is no other source from which it could come.

Lucifer, son of the morning, when he lifted up himself against the Most High, had only the abilities he had received from God. These he misused to become the devil he is.

I am well aware that this kind of teaching raises certain very difficult questions, but we should never retreat before truth simply because we cannot explain it.

The fact of sin introduces a confusing element into our thinking about God and the universe and requires that we suspend judgment on many things. The wise man will note that the things we cannot understand have nothing to do with our salvation.

We are saved by the truth we know, and true Christians know that the boundless power of our infinite God is all around us, preserving us and keeping us unto salvation ready to be revealed.

February 1

Faith Must Rest in the Adequacy of Christ

Because the foolishness of God is wiser than men; and the weakness of God is stronger than men. 1 Corinthians 1:25

Science and philosophy are more arrogant and bigoted than religion could ever possibly be, and still they try to brand evangelical Christians as bigots.

But I have never taken my Bible and gone into the laboratory and tried to tell the scientist how to conduct his experiments, and I would thank him if he didn't bring his test tube into the holy place and tell me how to conduct mine!

The scientist has nothing he can tell me about Jesus Christ, our Lord. There is nothing he can add, and I do not need to appeal to him.

Studying the philosophers may clarify my thinking and may help me broaden my outlook, but it is not necessary to my salvation. I have studied Plato and the rest of them from the time I was knee-high to a rubber worker in Akron, Ohio. But I have never found that Plato added anything, finally, to what Jesus Christ has said.

You know what Jesus said: "I am the Light that lighteth every man. I am the Bread that feedeth every man. I am the One who came from the heart of the Father, and I am the Eternal Word which was in the beginning with God, and which was and is God, and that's who I am."

So, we are assured in the Word that it is Jesus only and He is enough! It is not Jesus *plus* a lot of other religions. It is not Jesus *plus* a lot of other philosophies. He is the Eternal Word, and so we must listen to Him!

February 2

To Be Christlike: Walk in the Spirit

Howbeit when he, the Spirit of truth, is come. . .He shall glorify me: for he shall receive of mine, and shall shew it unto you. John 16:13, 14

If we are going to reproduce Christ on earth and be Christlike and show forth Christ, what is our greatest need?

We must have the Spirit of Christ!

If we are going to be the children of God, we must have the Spirit of the Father to breathe in our hearts and breathe through us. That is why we must have the Spirit of God! That is why the church must have the Spirit of Christ!

The Christian church is called to live above her own ability. She is called to live on a plane so high that no human being can live like that of his own ability and power. The humblest Christian is called to live a miracle, a life that is a moral and spiritual life with such intensity and such purity that no human being can do it—only Jesus Christ can do it. He wants the Spirit of Christ to come to His people—an invasion from above affecting us mentally, morally and spiritually!

The Holy Spirit brings the wonderful mystery that is God to us, and presents Him to the human spirit. The Spirit is our Teacher, and if He does not teach us, we never can know. He is our Illuminator, and if He does not turn on the light, we never can see. He is the Healer of our deaf ears, and if He does not touch our ears, we never can hear!

The Holy Ghost bestows upon us a beatitude beyond compare. He asks nothing except that we be willing to listen, willing to obey!

We Are Loved of God—for Jesus' Sake

But God commendeth his love toward us, in that, while we were yet sinners, Christ died for us. Romans 5:8

Never while the stars burn in their silence can it be said that God loves the sin in the sinner. Never can it be said that the holy God loves an unholy thing—and yet God loves sinners!

God loves sinners for that which He sees in them of His lost and fallen image, for God can never love anything but Himself, directly. He loves everything else for His own sake. So, you are loved of God—but you are loved of God for Jesus' sake!

God loves lost men, not because He is careless or morally lax, but because He once stood and said: "Let us make man in our image."

Man was made in the image of God, and while sin has ruined him and condemned him to death forever unless he be redeemed through the blood of Jesus Christ, mankind is a being only one degree removed from the angels.

But sin, God knows, is like a cancer in the very being of man. Although once made in the image of God, he is now a dying man, sick unto spiritual death, because of the poison of sin.

But extract and take out that sin and you have the image of God again! And Jesus Christ was the image of God because He was a man without sin.

God sees in Jesus Christ what you would have been! He sees that in His perfect humanity, not His deity—for you and I could never be divine in that sense. When Jesus Christ came to us, He was incarnated in the body of a man without embarrassment and without change, because man was an image of the God who made him.

Christ's Victory Rightfully Belongs to Us

. . .In all things it behoved him to be made like unto his brethren. . . .
Hebrews 2:17

"Is it possible to be a true Christian and still suffer in the doldrums of discouragement?"

This is a question that we are hearing often. Frankly, I cannot assure you whether Christians should know discouragement or not: I can only tell you that they all do!

Inwardly, they are often heavy-hearted, defeated, unhappy and a little bit frightened—yet they are Christians!

What we need, brethren, is to get the true scriptural vision of our victorious Lord, our victorious human brother. Paul wrote to the Philippians about Jesus Christ humbling Himself and becoming obedient even unto the death of the cross, and then: "Wherefore, God also hath highly exalted him and given him a name which is above every name" and "every tongue shall confess that Jesus Christ is Lord, to the glory of God, the Father."

Now, that is our victorious Lord, our victorious human brother.

Someone may say: "It is no great news to say that God is victorious."

But what we read in the New Testament is that God has joined His nature to the nature of man and has made a Man victorious, so that men might be victorious and overcoming in that Man!

God has made Him to be Head of the Church and He meanwhile waits for the time of His returning, guiding and keeping and instructing His Church. This He does by the Holy Spirit through the Word of God!

God Tells Us in the Bible What He Is Like

And there appeared unto them cloven tongues like as of fire, and it sat upon each of them. Acts 2:3

Just because God cannot tell us what He is, He very often tells us what He is like, and by these "like" figures He leads our faltering minds as close as they can come to that "Light which no man can approach unto."

Through the more cumbersome medium of the intellect the soul is prepared for the moment when it can, through the operation of the Holy Spirit, know God as He is in Himself. God has used a number of these similitudes to hint at His incomprehensible being, and judging from the Scriptures one would gather that His favorite similitude is fire.

In one place the Spirit speaks expressly, "For our God is a consuming fire."

With the coming of the Holy Spirit at Pentecost the same imagery was continued—for that which came upon the disciples in that upper room was nothing less than God Himself!

The God who had appeared to them as fire throughout all their long history was now dwelling in them as fire. He had moved from without to the interior of their lives. The Shekinah that had once blazed over the mercy seat now blazed on their foreheads as an external emblem of the fire that had invaded their natures.

This was Deity giving Himself to ransomed men and women.

The flame was the seal of a new union. They were now men and women of the Fire!

February 6

A Compromise: "The Church Must Change"

For the time will come when they will not endure sound doctrine. . .and they shall turn away their ears from the truth. . . .2 Timothy 4:3, 4

Any evangelism which by appeal to common interests and chatter about current events seeks to establish a common ground where the sinner can feel at home is as false as the altars of Baal ever were.

Every effort to smooth out the road for men and to take away the guilt and the embarrassment is worse than wasted: it is evil and dangerous to the souls of men!

One of the most popular of current errors, and the one out of which springs most of the noisy, blustering religious activity in evangelical circles, is the notion that as times change the church must change with them. Christians must adapt their methods by the demands of the people. If they want ten-minute sermons, give them ten-minute sermons! If they want truth in capsule form, give it to them! If they want pictures, give them plenty of pictures! If they like stories, tell them stories!

Meanwhile, the advocates of compromise insist that "The message is the same, only the method changes."

"Whom the gods would destroy they first make mad," the old Greeks said, and they were wiser than they knew. That mentality which mistakes Sodom for Jerusalem and Hollywood for the Holy City is too gravely astray to be explained otherwise than as a judicial madness visited upon professed Christians for affronts committed against the Spirit of God!

Encounter with God Brings Wonder and Awe

And when I saw him, I fell at his feet as dead. And he laid his right hand upon me, saying unto me, Fear not; I am the first and the last. Revelation 1:17

There is a point in true worship where the mind may cease to understand and goes over to a kind of delightful astonishment—probably to what Carlyle described as "transcendent wonder," a degree of wonder without limit and beyond expression!

That kind of worship is found throughout the Bible (though it is only fair to say that the lesser degrees of worship are found there also).

Abraham fell on his face in holy wonderment as God spoke to him. Moses hid his face before the presence of God in the burning bush. Paul could hardly tell whether he was in or out of the body when he was allowed to see the unspeakable glories of the third heaven. When John saw Jesus walking among His churches, he fell at His feet as dead.

These were in unusual circumstances—but the spiritual content of the experiences is unchanging and is found alike wherever true believers are found. It is always true that an encounter with God brings wonderment and awe!

The pages of Christian biography are sweet with the testimonies of enraptured worshipers who met God in intimate experience and could find no words to express all they felt and saw and heard!

Christian hymnody takes us where the efforts of common prose break down, and brings the wings of poetic feeling to the aid of the wondering saint. Open an old hymnal and turn to the sections on worship and the divine perfections and you will see the part that wonder has played in worship through the centuries.

February 8

True Faith Is Accompanied by Expectation

According to my earnest expectation and my hope. . .so now also Christ shall be magnified in my body, whether it be by life, or by death. Philippians 1:20

Expectation and faith, though alike, are not identical. An instructed Christian will not confuse the two.

True faith is never found alone; it is always accompanied by expectation. The man who believes the promises of God expects to see them fulfilled. Where there is no expectation there is no faith.

It is, however, quite possible for expectation to be present where no faith is. The mind is quite capable of mistaking strong desire for faith. Indeed faith, as commonly understood, is little more than desire compounded with cheerful optimism.

Real faith is not the stuff dreams are made of; rather it is tough, practical and altogether realistic. Faith sees the invisible but it does not see the nonexistent. Faith engages God, the one great Reality, who gave and gives existence to all things. God's promises conform to reality, and whoever trusts them enters a world not of fiction but of fact!

Expectation has always been present in the church in the times of her greatest power. When she believed, she expected, and her Lord never disappointed her. His blessings accorded with their expectations, "and blessed is she that believed: for there shall be a performance of those things which were told her from the Lord."

Prayer Is Never a Substitute for Obedience

Not every one that saith unto me, Lord, Lord, shall enter into the kingdom of heaven; but he that doeth the will of my Father which is in heaven. Matthew 7:21

Have you noticed how much praying for revival has been going on of late—and how little revival has resulted?

I believe our problem is that we have been trying to substitute praying for obeying, and it simply will not work!

A church, for instance, follows its traditions without much thought about whether they are scriptural or not. Or it surrenders to pressure from public opinion and falls in with popular trends which carry it far from the New Testament pattern. Then the leaders notice a lack of spiritual power among the people and become concerned about it. What to do? How can they bring down refreshing showers to quicken their fainting souls?

The answer is all ready for them. The books tell them how—pray!

The passing evangelist confirms what the books have said—pray!

So the pastor calls his people to pray. The tide of feeling runs high and it looks for a while as if the revival might be on the way. But it fails to arrive and the zeal for prayer begins to flag. Soon the church is back where it was before and a numb discouragement settles over everyone.

What has gone wrong? Simply this: Neither the leaders nor the people have made any effort to obey the Word of God. They felt that their only weakness was failure to pray, when actually in a score of ways they were falling short in the vital matter of obedience!

February 10

Our Heavenly Abode: Part of God's Goodness

. . .We have a building of God, an house not made with hands, eternal in the heavens. 2 Corinthians 5:1

The true Christian may safely look forward to a future state that is as happy as perfect love wills it to be!

No one who has felt the weight of his own sin or heard from Calvary the Saviour's mournful cry, "My God, my God, why hast thou forsaken me?" can ever allow his soul to rest on the feeble hope popular religion affords.

He will—indeed, he must—insist upon forgiveness and cleansing and the protection the vicarious death of Christ provides.

"God has made him who knew no sin to be sin for us, that we might be made the righteousness of God in him." So wrote Paul, and Luther's great outburst of faith shows what this can mean in a human soul: "O Lord," cried Luther, "Thou art my righteousness, I am Thy sin!"

Any valid hope of a state of righteousness beyond the incident of death must lie in the goodness of God and the work of atonement accomplished for us by Jesus Christ on the cross. The deep, deep love of God is the fountain out of which flows our future beatitude, and the grace of God in Christ is the channel by which it reaches us!

Even justice is on our side, for it is written, "If we confess our sins, he is faithful and just to forgive us our sins, and to cleanse us from all unrighteousness."

February 11

The Devil Hates Everything Dear to God

. . .For the devil sinneth from the beginning. For this purpose the Son of God was manifested, that he might destroy the works of the devil. 1 John 3:8

I have observed among spiritual persons in the Christian fellowship a tendency either to ignore the devil altogether or to make too much of him.

Both attitudes are wrong!

There is in the world an enemy whom we dare not ignore. We see him first in the third chapter of Genesis and last in the twentieth of Revelation, which is to say that he was present at the beginning of human history and will be there at its earthly close.

This enemy is not a creation of religious fancy, not a mere personification of evil for convenience, but a being as real as man himself. The Bible attributes to him qualities of personality too detailed to be figurative, and reveals him speaking and acting in situations hard and practical and far removed from the poetic imagination.

He is said to be a liar, a deceiver and a murderer who achieves his ends by guile and trickery. While he is not omnipresent (omnipresence being an attribute of God alone) he is ubiquitous, which for his purpose amounts to the same thing.

Satan hates God for His own sake, and everything that is dear to God he hates for the very reason that God loves it. Because man was made in God's image the hatred with which Satan regards him is particularly malevolent, and since the Christian is doubly dear to God he is hated by the powers of darkness with an aggravated fury.

In view of this, it cannot be less than folly for us Christians to disregard the reality and presence of such an enemy.

February 12

Divine Love: Necessity for the Church on Earth

To him that overcometh will I grant to sit with me in my throne. . . .He that hath an ear, let him hear what the Spirit saith unto the churches. Revelation 3:21, 22

The kind of Christianity that relies upon the influence of its own human and earthly power makes God sick, for the church of Jesus Christ is a heavenly institution.

For myself, if I could not have the divine power of God, I would walk out and quit the whole religious business. The church that wants God's power will have something to offer besides social clubs, knitting societies and all of the other side issues.

If any church is to be a church of Christ, the living, organic member of that redeemed Body of which Christ is the Head, then its teachers and its members must strive earnestly and sacrificially with constant prayer to do a number of things.

We must strive to make our beliefs and practices New Testament in their content. We must teach and believe New Testament truths, with nothing dragged in from the outside.

We must keep our little field of God's planting healthy, and there is only one way to do that: keep true to the Word of God! We must constantly go back to the grass roots and get the Word into the church.

We must live to gear ourselves into things eternal and to live the life of heaven here upon the earth, empowered by the Spirit of God with that same power that came on the earliest believers. We must put loyalty to Christ first at any cost. Anything less than that really is not a Christian church!

February 13

Bad Dispositions: "The Vice of the Virtuous"

Be not overcome of evil, but overcome evil with good. Romans 12:21

A bad disposition has been called "the vice of the virtuous," which brings us directly to the conclusion that it is time we Christians stop trying to excuse our un-Christlike dispositions and frankly admit our failure to live as we should!

Wesley said that we will not injure the cause of Christ by admitting our sins, but that we are sure to do so by denying them.

Dispositional sins are as many as the various facets of human nature. Just so there be no misunderstanding let us list a few of them: Sensitiveness, irritability, churlishness, faultfinding, peevishness, temper, resentfulness, cruelty, uncharitable attitudes; and of course there are many more.

These kill the spirit of the church and slow down any progress which the gospel may be making in the community. Many persons who had been secretly longing to find Christ have been turned away and embittered by manifestations of ugly dispositional flaws in the lives of the very persons who were trying to win them!

Unsaintly saints are the tragedy of Christianity. The low state of religion in our day is largely due to the lack of public confidence in religious people.

There is a remedy for inward evil. The power of Christ can enable the worst of us to live lives of purity and love. We have but to seek it and to lay hold of it in faith. God will not disappoint us!

February 14

Tragedy: Men Do Not Know That God Is Here

And Jacob awaked out of his sleep, and he said, Surely the Lord is in this place; and I knew it not. Genesis 28:16

The patriarch Jacob saw a vision of God and cried out in wonder, "Surely the Lord is in this place; and I knew it not."

Jacob had never been for one small division of a moment outside the circle of that all-pervading Presence. But he knew it not. That was his trouble, and it is ours.

Men do not know that God is here. What a difference it would make if they knew!

The Presence and the manifestation of the Presence are not the same. There can be the one without the other. God is here when we are wholly unaware of it. He is manifest only when and as we are aware of His Presence. On our part there must be surrender to the Spirit of God, for His work is to show us the Father and the Son.

If we cooperate with Him in loving obedience God will manifest Himself to us, and that manifestation will be the difference between a nominal Christian life and a life radiant with the light of His face.

It has been asked, "Why does God manifest His Presence to some and let multitudes of others struggle along in the half-light of imperfect Christian experience?" We can only reply that the will of God is the same for all—He has no favorites within His household. All he has ever done for any of His children He will do for all of His children. The difference lies not with God but with us!

Secular Men Confuse Truths with "Truth"

The Lord by wisdom hath founded the earth; by understanding hath he established the heavens. Proverbs 3:19

The celebrated prayer of the great German astronomer, Kepler, has been a benediction to many: "O God, I thank Thee that Thou has permitted me to think Thy thoughts after Thee!"

This prayer is theologically sound because it acknowledges the priority of God in the universe. Whatever new thing anyone discovers is already old, for it is but the present expression of a previous thought of God. The idea of the thing precedes the thing itself; and when things raise thoughts in the thinker's mind these are the ancient thoughts of God, however imperfectly understood.

Should an athiest, for instance, state that two times two equals four, he would be stating a truth and thinking God's thoughts after Him, even though he might deny that God exists.

In their search for facts, men have confused truths with truth. The words of Christ, "Ye shall know the truth and the truth shall make you free," have been wrenched from their context and used to stir people to the expectation of being made "free" by knowledge. Certainly this is not what Christ had in mind when He uttered the words.

It is the Son who is the Truth that makes men free. Not facts, not scientific knowledge, but eternal Truth delivers men, and that eternal Truth became flesh to dwell among us!

February 16

Live for Christ? Then Die with Him First

Now if we be dead with Christ, we believe that we shall also live with him.
Romans 6:8

Do you realize that many, many persons now take it for granted that it is possible to live for Christ without first having died with Christ?

This is a serious error and we dare not leave it unchallenged!

The victorious Christian has known two lives. The first was his life in Adam which was motivated by the carnal mind and can never please God in any way. It can never be converted; it can only die (Rom. 8:5-8).

The second life of the Christian is his new life in Christ (Rom. 6:1-14). To live a Christian life with the life of Adam is wholly impossible. Yet multitudes take for granted that it can be done and go on year after year in defeat. Worst of all, they accept this half-dead condition as normal!

Another aspect of this attitude is the effort of many to do spiritual work without spiritual power. David Brainerd once compared a man without the power of the Spirit of God trying to do spiritual work to a workman without fingers attempting to do manual labor. The figure is striking but it does not overstate the facts.

The Holy Spirit is not a luxury meant to make deluxe Christians, as an illuminated frontispiece and a leather binding makes a deluxe book. The Spirit is an imperative necessity. Only the Eternal Spirit can do eternal deeds!

The Christian Life Cannot Feed on Negatives

. . .Forgetting those things which are behind, and reaching forth unto those things which are before. Philippians 3:13

The Christian is saved from his past sins. With these he simply has nothing more to do; they are among the things to be forgotten as the night is forgotten at the dawning of the day.

The Christian is also saved from the wrath to come. With this also he has nothing to do. The wrath of God exists, but not for him. Sin and wrath have a cause and effect relationship, and because for the Christian sin is canceled, wrath is canceled also. To be engrossed still in what we have been saved from is to live in a state of negation.

We are not called to fellowship with nonexistence. We are called to things that exist in truth, to positive things, and it is as we become occupied with these that health comes to the soul.

Spiritual life cannot feed on negatives. The man who is constantly reciting the evils of his unconverted days is looking in the wrong direction. He is like a man trying to run a race while looking back over his shoulder!

There is an art of forgetting, and every Christian should become skilled in it. Forgetting the things which are behind is a positive necessity if we are to become more than mere babes in Christ.

And here's the good part: into the empty world vacated by our sins and failures rushes the blessed Spirit of God, bringing with Him everything new. New life, new hope, new enjoyments, new interests, new purposeful toil, and best of all a new and satisfying object toward which to direct our soul's enraptured gaze!

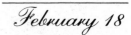

February 18

Question: How Much More Could I Have Done?

For all they did cast in of their abundance; but she of her want did cast in all that she had, even her living. Mark 12:44

Before the judgment seat of Christ my service will be judged not by how much I have done but by how much I could have done!

In God's sight, my giving is measured not by how much I have given but by how much I had left after I made my gift.

Not by its size is my gift judged, but by how much of me there is in it. No man gives at all until he has given all! No man gives anything acceptable to God until he has first given himself in love and sacrifice.

While Christ was the perfect example of the healthy, normal man, He yet did not live a normal life. He sacrificed many pure enjoyments to give Himself to the holy work of moral rescue. His conduct was determined not by what was legitimate or innocent, but by our human need.

He pleased not Himself but lived for the emergency; and as He was, so are we in this world!

It is in view of this that all our Christian service must be evaluated.

My old friend Tom Haire, the praying plumber, told me one day that he was going back home for a rest.

"I am preached out," he said, "and I must wait on the Lord. There are some spiritual matters that I want to get straightened out. I want to appear before the judgment seat now while I can do something about it!"

Stricter Discipline for God's Willing Children

No chastening for the present seemeth to be joyous, but grievous: nevertheless afterward it yieldeth the peaceable fruit of righteousness. . . . Hebrews 12:11

If God has singled you out to be a special object of His grace you may expect Him to honor you with stricter discipline and greater suffering than less favored ones are called upon to endure.

If God sets out to make you an unusual Christian He is not likely to be as gentle as He is usually pictured by the popular teachers. A sculptor does not use a manicure set to reduce the rude, unshapely marble to a thing of beauty. The saw, the hammer and the chisel are cruel tools, but without them the rough stone must remain forever formless and unbeautiful.

To do His supreme work of grace within you He will take from your heart everything you love most. Everything you trust in will go from you. Piles of ashes will lie where your most precious treasures used to be.

Thus you will learn what faith is; you will find out the hard way, but the only way open to you, that true faith lies in the will, that the joy unspeakable of which the apostle speaks is not itself faith but a slow-ripening fruit of faith. You will learn, too, that present spiritual joys may come and go as they will without altering your spiritual status or in any way affecting your position as a true child of the heavenly Father.

Then you will also learn, probably to your astonishment, that it is possible to live in all good conscience before God and men and still feel nothing of the "peace and joy" you hear talked about so much by immature Christians!

February 20

"Create in Me a Clean Heart, O God"

Jesus answered and said unto him, Verily, verily, I say unto thee, Except a man be born again, he cannot see the kingdom of God. John 3:3

The miracle of the new birth was foreshadowed in the Old Testament record: "Create in me a clean heart, O God; and renew a right spirit within me."

There was at least a hint of miracle within the human breast—not the reasoning of yourself into a position, but something happening that could not be explained!

Coming into the New Testament, there is no longer any hinting or suggesting about the miracle of the new birth—it is boldly and openly declared. Our Saviour said that if we come to Him and are not born again, we cannot enter the kingdom of God—that we must be born from above.

Paul told the Corinthians: "If any man be in Christ, he is a new creature: old things are passed away; behold, all things are become new."

You couldn't make it any stronger than that! Something happens in a man's nature that no man can explain!

Just the moment that a man's experience in Christ can be broken down and explained by the psychologists, we have a church member on our hands—and not a Christian! For that which must happen in the new birth can never be explained by psychology or psychiatry. The professional can only stand off respectfully and say, "Behold the works of the Lord." He can never explain it! And in that great and terrible day to come, many will be shocked when they find that they depended upon a mental assent to Christianity instead of upon the miracle of the new birth!

Only Servants of Truth Can Know the Truth

. . .So is every one that is born of the Spirit. John 3:8

Only the servants of truth can ever know truth. You can fill your head full of knowledge but the day that you decide that you are going to obey God, it will get down into your heart. You shall know!

I once read a book about the inner life of a man who was a sharp intellectual. By his own admission, he stood outside and examined spiritual people from the outside but nothing ever reached him. And that's possible!

You cannot argue around this. Read your Bible—any version you want—and if you are honest you will admit that it is either obedience or inward blindness. You can repeat the Book of Romans word for word and still be blind inwardly. You can know the doctrine of justification by faith and take your stand with Luther and the Reformation and still be blind inwardly. For it is not the body of truth that enlightens: it is by the Spirit of truth.

If you are willing to obey the Lord Jesus, He will illuminate your spirit, inwardly enlighten you; and the truth you have known will then be known spiritually, and power will begin to flow up and out and you will find yourself changed—marvelously changed.

It is rewarding to believe in a Christianity that really changes men and women. In that great day of Christ's coming, all that will matter is whether we have been inwardly illuminated, inwardly regenerated, inwardly purified!

The question is: do we really know Jesus in this way?

Keys to Greatness: Submission and Service

. . .Whosoever will be great among you, let him be your minister; And who-soever will be chief among you, let him be your servant. Matthew 20:26, 27

The essence of Christ's teaching concerning greatness was this: true greatness among humans must be found in character, not in ability or position.

While a few philosophers and religionists of pre-Christian times had noted the fallacy in man's ideas of dominion and status, it was Christ who defined and demonstrated true greatness.

"Let him be your minister: let him be your servant." It is that simple and that easy—and that difficult!

We have but to follow Christ in service to the human race, a selfless service that seeks only to serve, and greatness will be ours! That is all, but it is too much, for it runs counter to all that is Adam in us. Adam still feels the instinct for dominion; he hears deep within him the command, "Replenish the earth and subdue it." There-fore he does not take kindly to the command to serve!

Sin must go and Adam must give way to Christ: so says our Lord in effect. By sin men have lost dominion, even their very right to it, until they win it back by humble service.

Though redeemed from death and hell by the vicarious labor of Christ on the cross, still the right to have dominion must be won by each man separately. Each must fulfill a long apprenticeship as a servant before he is fit to rule.

After Christ had served (and His service included death) God highly exalted Him and gave Him a name above every name. As a man He served and won His right to have dominion. He knew where true greatness lay—and we do not.

God Will Not Play along with Adam

Let this mind be in you, which was also in Christ Jesus. Philippians 2:5

There is great need for us to learn the truths of the sovereignty of God and the Lordship of Christ.

God will not play along with Adam; Christ will not be "used" by any of Adam's selfish brood.

We had better learn these things fast if this generation of young Christians is to be spared the supreme tragedy of following a Christ who is merely a Christ of convenience and not the true Lord of glory at all!

I confess to a feeling of uneasiness about this when I observe the questionable things Christ is said to do for people these days. He is often recommended as a wonderfully obliging but not too discriminating Big Brother who delights to help us to accomplish our ends, and who further favors us by forbearing to ask any embarrassing questions about the moral and spiritual qualities of those ends.

In our eagerness to lead men to "accept" Christ we are often tempted to present for acceptance a Christ who is little more than a caricature of "that holy thing" which was conceived by the Holy Ghost, born of the virgin Mary, to be crucified and rise the third day to take His place on the right hand of the Majesty in the heavens.

The whole purpose of God in redemption is to make us holy and to restore us to the image of God! To accomplish this, He disengages us from earthly ambitions and draws us away from the cheap and unworthy prizes that worldly men set their hearts upon.

The Early Disciples Burned with an Inward Fire

. . .In whom, though now ye see him not, yet believing, ye rejoice with joy unspeakable and full of glory. 1 Peter 1:8

If there is any reality within the whole sphere of human experience that is by its very nature worthy to challenge the mind, charm the heart and bring the total life to a burning focus, it is the reality that revolves around the Person of Christ!

If He is who and what the Christian message declares Him to be, then the thought of Him should be the most stimulating to enter the human mind.

God dwells in a state of perpetual enthusiasm. He is delighted with all that is good and lovingly concerned about all that is wrong. No wonder the Spirit came at Pentecost as the sound of a rushing mighty wind and sat in tongues of fire on every forehead. In so doing, He was acting as one of the Persons of the blessed Godhead.

Whatever else happened at Pentecost, one thing that cannot be missed was the sudden upsurging of moral enthusiasm. Those first disciples burned with a steady, inward fire. They were enthusiastic to the point of complete abandon!

But what do we find in our day? We find the contradictory situation of noisy, headlong religious activity carried on without moral energy or spiritual fervor! In the churches it is hard to find a believer whose blood count is normal and whose temperature is up to standard. We look in vain among the professed followers of Christ for the flush and excitement of the soul in love with God.

The low level of moral enthusiasm among us may have a significance far deeper than we are willing to believe!

The Importance of Right Relationship with God

The Spirit itself beareth witness with our Spirit, that we are children of God. Romans 8:16

Many men and women are seeking counsellors to aid them with their confessed feelings of emptiness and inadequacy. Each seems to have a plea about becoming a "whole person."

The importance of coming back into right relationship with God cannot be overestimated as we seriously think and study and pray.

By the mysterious operation of the Spirit of God in the new birth, that which is called by Peter "the divine nature" enters the deep-in core of the believer's heart and establishes residence there. "If any man have not the Spirit of Christ, he is none of his," for "the Spirit itself beareth witness with our spirit, that we are the children of God" (Rom. 8:9, 16).

Such a one is a true Christian, and only such. Baptism, confirmation, the receiving of the sacraments, church membership—these mean nothing unless the supreme act of God in regeneration also takes place!

Religious externals may have a meaning for the God-inhabited soul; for any others they are not only useless but may actually become snares, deceiving them into a false and perilous sense of security.

"Keep thy heart with all diligence" is more than a wise saying; it is a solemn charge laid upon us by the One who cares most about us!

February 26

Test Your Conduct: What Are Your Motives?

But ye denied the Holy One. . .And killed the Prince of life, whom God hath raised from the dead;. . . Acts 3:14, 15

The test by which all conduct must finally be judged is motive.

As water cannot rise higher than its source, so the moral quality in an act can never be higher than the motive that inspires it. For this reason, no act that arises from an evil motive can be good, even though some good may appear to come out of it.

Every deed done out of anger or spite, for instance, will be found at last to have been done for the enemy and against the Kingdom of God!

In this matter of motive, as in so many other things, the Pharisees afford us clear examples.

They remain the world's most dismal religious failures, not because of doctrinal error nor because they were careless or lukewarm, nor because they were outwardly persons of dissolute life.

Their whole trouble lay in the quality of their religious motives. They prayed, but they prayed to be heard of men. They gave generously to the service of the temple, but they sometimes did it to escape their duty toward their parents, and this was an evil. They judged sin and stood against it when found in others, but this they did from self-righteousness and hardness of heart.

That this is not a small matter may be gathered from the fact that those orthodox and proper religionists went on in their blindness until at last they crucified the Lord of glory with no inkling of the gravity of their crime!

February 27

Rationalism: A Danger in Today's Christianity

Did not Moses give you the law, and yet none of you keepeth the law? Why go ye about to kill me? John 7:19

The theological battle line in our day is not necessarily between the fundamentalist and the liberal.

There is a difference between them, of course. The fundamentalist says, "God made the heaven and the earth." The liberal says, "Well, that is a poetic way of stating it—but actually, it came up by evolution."

The warfare, the dividing line today, is between evangelical rationalists and evangelical mystics. I will explain what I mean.

There is today an evangelical rationalism which is the same doctrine held by the Jewish religion in the day of Jesus. They said the truth is in the word, and if you want to know truth, go to the rabbi and learn the word. If you get the word, you have the truth.

That is also the view of evangelical rationalism in our day: "If you learn the text you've got the truth!"

This evangelical rationalism will kill the truth just as quickly as liberalism will, though in a more subtle way. The evangelical rationalist wears our uniform but he insists that the body of truth is all you need. Believe the body of truth and you are on your way to heaven and you cannot backslide and you will get a crown in the last day!

I believe the Bible is a living book, a revelation from God. But there must be illumination before revelation can get to your soul. It is not enough that I hold an inspired book in my hands—I must have an inspired heart. Truth has a soul as well as a body!

February 28

Faith in God Never Adds up to Gullibility

That we henceforth be no more children, tossed to and fro, and carried about with every wind of doctrine. . . . Ephesians 4:14

Let me tell you of the dangerous logic of the gullible Christian who does not realize that it may be fatal to believe everything that happens to come along!

I have met Christians with no more discrimination than the ostrich. Because they must believe certain things, they feel that they must believe everything.

Because they are called upon to accept the invisible they go right on to accept the incredible. God can and does work miracles: *ergo*, everything that passes for a miracle must be of God!

God has spoken to man—therefore they feel that every man who claims to have had a revelation from God must be accepted as a prophet. Whatever is unearthly must be heavenly; whatever cannot be explained must be received as divine. The prophets were rejected, therefore everyone who is rejected is a prophet. The saints were misunderstood, they agree, so everyone who is misunderstood is a saint.

This is the kind of dangerous logic that can be as injurious as unbelief itself!

Faith is at the root of all true worship and without faith it is impossible to please God. But faith never means gullibility. The man who believes everything is as far from God as the man who refuses to believe anything. Faith engages the Person and promises of God and rests upon them with perfect assurance—and of such faith we can never have too much.

Credulity, on the other hand, never honors God, for it shows as great a readiness to believe anybody as to believe God Himself!

February 29

God Expects Gratitude when He Gives Us Gifts

Thanks be unto God for his unspeakable gift. 2 Corinthians 9:15

Because we are so very human there is real danger that we may inadvertently do the human thing and turn our blessings upside down. Unless we watch and pray in dead earnest we may turn our good into evil and make the grace of God a trap instead of a benefit!

Men are notoriously lacking in gratitude. Bible history reveals that Israel often took God's gifts too casually and so turned their blessings into a curse. This human fault appears also in the New Testament, and the activities of Christians through the centuries show that as Christ was followed by Satan in the wilderness so truth is often accompanied by a strong temptation to pride.

Among the purest gifts we have received from God is truth. Another gift, almost as precious, and without which the first would be meaningless, is our ability to grasp truth and appreciate it.

For these priceless treasures we should be profoundly grateful; for them our thanks should rise to the Giver of all good gifts throughout the day and in the night seasons. And because these and all other blessings flow to us by grace without merit or worth on our part, we should be very humble and watch with care lest such undeserved favors, if unappreciated, be taken from us!

The very truth that makes men free may be and often is fashioned into chains to keep them in bondage. Never forget that there is no pride so insidious and yet so powerful as the pride of orthodoxy.

March 1

Jesus Christ Is Every Man's Contemporary

Be still, and know that I am God. . . ." Psalm 46:10

Our fathers had much to say about stillness, and by stillness they meant the absence of motion or the absence of noise, or both. They felt that they must be still for at least a part of the day, or that day would be wasted!

God can be known in the tumult if His providence has for the time placed us there, but He is known best in the silence. So they held, and so the sacred Scriptures declare. Inward assurance comes out of the stillness. We must be still to know!

There has hardly been another time in the history of the world when stillness was needed more than it is today, and there has surely not been another time when there was so little of it or when it was so hard to find.

Christ is every man's contemporary. His presence and His power are offered to us in this time of mad activity and mechanical noises as certainly as to fishermen on the quiet lake of Galilee or to shepherds on the plains of Judea. The only condition is that we get still enough to hear His voice and that we believe and heed what we hear.

As we draw nearer to the ancient Source of our being we find that we are no longer learned or ignorant, modern or old-fashioned, crude or cultured, white or colored: in that awesome Presence we are just men and women. Artificial distinctions fade away. Thousands of years of education disappear in a moment and we stand again where Adam and Eve stood after the Fall, where Cain stood, and Abel, outside the Garden, frightened and undone and fugitive from the terror of the broken law, desperately in need of a Saviour!

March 2

Spiritual Excellence: Freedom in the Spirit

Now the Lord is that Spirit: and where the Spirit of the Lord is, there is liberty. 2 Corinthians 3:17

The essence of true religion is spontaneity, the sovereign movings of the Holy Spirit upon and in the free spirit of redeemed men. This has through the years of human history been the hallmark of spiritual excellency, the evidence of reality in a world of unreality.

When religion loses its sovereign character and becomes mere form this spontaneity is lost also, and in its place come precedent, propriety, system—and the file-card mentality!

Back of the file-card mentality is the belief that spirituality can be organized. Then is introduced into religion those ideas which never belong there—numbers, statistics, the law of averages and other such natural and human things. And creeping death always follows!

Now a file card is a very harmless little tool and a very useful one for some purposes. Its danger comes from the well-known human tendency to depend upon external helps in dealing with internal things.

Here's how the file card works when it gets into the Christian life and begins to create mental habits: it divides the Bible into sections fitted to the days of the year and compels the Christian to read according to rule. No matter what the Holy Spirit may be trying to say to a man, still he goes on reading where the card tells him, dutifully checking if off each day. This can be a deadly snare, and often liable to quench the spontaneous operation of the Spirit!

Sinful Man: Uncomfortable in God's Presence

And the Lord God called unto Adam, and said unto him, Where art thou?
Genesis 3:9

Sin never feels comfortable in the divine presence!

Adam and his wife hid themselves from the presence of the Lord among the trees of the garden. Their fear and chagrin for the moment overcame their conscious need of God. Jonah, in his determined refusal to obey God's command, rose up to flee to Tarshish from the presence of the Lord.

Peter, with a sudden acute consciousness of personal guilt, sought not to flee from the Lord's presence but begged the Lord instead to depart from him!

Men need God above everything else, yet are uncomfortable in His presence. This is the self-contradictory moral situation sin has brought us into.

The notion that there is a God but that He is comfortably far away is not embodied in the doctrinal statement of any Christian church. Anyone who dared admit that he held such a creed would be considered a heretic and avoided by respectable religious people; but our actions, and especially our spontaneous utterances, reveal our true beliefs better than any conventional creed can do.

If we are to judge by these, I think it can hardly be denied that the average Christian thinks of God as being at a safe distance, looking the other way!

Christianity Is What Christ Says It Is

Set your affection on things above, not on things on the earth. Colossians 3:2

No one who knows what the New Testament is about will worry over the charge that Christianity is "otherworldly."

Of course it is—and that is precisely where its power lies!

Christianity, which is faith in Christ, trust in His promises and obedience to His commandments, rests down squarely upon the Person of Christ.

What He is, what He did and what He is doing—these provide a full guarantee that the Christian's hopes are valid.

Christianity is what Christ says it is. His power becomes operative toward us as we accept His words as final and yield our souls to believe and obey.

Christ is not on trial; He needs no character witnesses to establish His trustworthiness!

He came as the Eternal God in time's low tabernacle. He stands before no human tribunal, but all men stand before Him now and shall stand for judgment at the last.

Let any man bring the faith of Christ to the bar of man's opinion, let him try to prove that the teachings of Christ are in harmony with this philosophy or that religion and he is in fact rejecting Christ while seeking to defend Him!

Let no one apologize for the powerful emphasis Christianity lays upon the basic doctrine of the world to come. When Christ arose from death and ascended into heaven He established forever three important facts, namely, that this world has been condemned to ultimate dissolution, that the human spirit persists beyond the grave and that there is indeed a world to come!

March 5

You Will Find Christ Everywhere in the Bible

...To us there is but one God, the Father, of whom are all things, and we in him; and one Lord Jesus Christ, by whom are all things.... 1 Corinthians 8:6

I do not mind telling you that I have always found Jesus Christ beckoning to me throughout the Scriptures. I am convinced that it was God's design that we should find the divine Creator, Redeemer and Lord whenever we search the Scriptures.

The Son of God is described by almost every fair and worthy name in the creation. He is called the Sun of Righteousness with healing in His wings. He is called the Star that shone on Jacob. He is described as coming forth with His bride, clear as the moon. His Presence is likened unto the rain coming down upon the earth, bringing beauty and fruitfulness. He is pictured as the great sea and as the towering rock. He is likened to the strong cedars. A figure is used of Him as of a great eagle, going literally over the earth.

Where the person of Jesus Christ does not stand out tall and beautiful and commanding, as a pine tree against the sky, you will find Him behind the lattice, but stretching forth His hand. If He does not appear as the sun shining in his strength, He may be discerned in the reviving by the promised gentle rains.

Our Lord Jesus Christ was that One divinely commissioned to set forth the mystery and the majesty and the wonder and the glory of the Godhead throughout the universe. It is more than an accident that both the Old and New Testaments comb heaven and earth for figures of speech or simile to set forth the wonder and glory of God!

March 6

The Christian Message: Prophetic, Not Diplomatic

For Christ sent me. . .to preach the gospel: not with wisdom of words, lest the cross of Christ should be made of none effect. 1 Corinthians 1:17

We who witness and proclaim the gospel must not think of ourselves as public relations agents sent to establish good will between Christ and the world.

We must not imagine ourselves commissioned to make Christ acceptable to big business, the press, modern education, or the world of sports.

We are not diplomats but prophets, and our message is not a compromise but an ultimatum!

God offers life, but not an improved old life. The life He offers is life out of death. It stands always on the far side of the cross. Whoever would possess it must pass under the rod. He must repudiate himself and concur in God's just sentence against him.

What does this mean to the individual, the condemned man who would find life in Christ Jesus? How can this theology be translated into life?

Simply, he must repent and believe. He must forsake his sins and then go on to forsake himself.

Let him cover nothing, defend nothing, excuse nothing.

Let him not seek to make terms with God, but let him bow his head before the stroke of God's stern displeasure and acknowledge himself worthy to die.

Having done this, let him gaze with simple trust upon the risen Saviour, and from Him will come life and rebirth and cleansing and power. The cross that ended the earthly life of Jesus now puts an end to the sinner; and the power that raised Christ from the dead now raises him to a new life along with Christ!

March 7

A Great Need among Us: More Reverence

. . .Let us have grace, whereby we may serve God acceptably with reverence and godly fear. Hebrews 12:28

The theory held in some churches seems to be that if the service is unplanned the Holy Spirit will work freely.

Now that would be true if all the worshipers were reverent and Spirit-filled. But mostly there is neither order nor Spirit, just a routine prayer that is, except for minor variations, the same week after week, and a few songs that were never much to start with and have long ago lost all significance by meaningless repetition!

We of the nonliturgical churches tend to look with some disdain upon those churches that follow a carefully prescribed form of service, and certainly there must be a good deal in such services that has little or no meaning for the average participant—this not because it is carefully prescribed but because the average participant is what he is.

The liturgical service is at least beautiful, carefully worked out through the centuries to preserve a spirit of reverence among the worshipers. In many of our meetings there is scarcely a trace of reverent thought, no recognition of the unity of the body, little sense of the divine Presence, no moment of stillness, no solemnity, no wonder, no holy fear!

The whole Christian family stands desperately in need of a restoration of penitence, humility and tears. May God send them soon!

March 8

Christ Established True Values for the Human Race

So Christ was once offered to bear the sins of many; and unto them that look for him shall he appear the second time without sin unto salvation. Hebrews 9:28

The Christian faith engages the profoundest problems the human mind can entertain and solves them completely and simply by pointing to the Lamb of God!

The problems of origin and destiny have escaped the philosopher and the scientist, but the humblest follower of Christ knows the answer to both.

"In the beginning" found Christ there at the creation of all things, and "the world to come" will find Him there at their regeneration.

There is about the Christian faith a quiet dogmatism, a cheerful intolerance. It feels no need to appease its enemies or compromise with its detractors. Christ came from God, out of eternity, to report on the things He had seen and heard and to establish true values for the confused human race.

Then, He drew a line between this world and the world to come and said, in effect: "Choose ye this day."

The choice is between an earthly house which we can at best inhabit but a little while and the house of the Lord where we may dwell forevermore.

The church is constantly being tempted to accept this world as her home, but toward the world to come we are all headed.

How unutterably wonderful that we Christians have one of our own kind to go ahead and prepare a place for us!

That place will be in a world divinely ordered, beyond death and parting, where there is nothing that can hurt or make afraid.

March 9

Effective Prayer: Letting All Our Pretenses Go

Even so ye also outwardly appear righteous unto men, but within ye are full of hypocrisy and iniquity. Matthew 23:28

The basic artificiality of civilized human beings is hard to shake off. It gets into our very blood and conditions our thoughts, attitudes and relationships much more seriously than we imagine.

The desire to make a good impression has become one of the most powerful of all the factors determining human conduct. That gracious (and scriptural) social lubricant called courtesy has in our times degenerated into a completely false and phony etiquette that hides the true man under a shimmery surface as thin as the oil slick on a quiet pond. The only times some persons expose their real self is when they get mad.

With this perverted courtesy determining almost everything men and women say and do in human society, it is not surprising that it should be hard to be completely honest in our relations with God. It carries over as a kind of mental reflex and is present without our being aware of it.

Nevertheless, it is an attitude extremely hateful to God. Christ detested it and condemned it without mercy when He found it among the Pharisees. The artless little child is still the divine model for all of us. Prayer will increase in power and reality as we repudiate all pretense and learn to be utterly honest before God as well as before men!

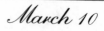

March 10

Anticipation of Heaven: More Than Eschatology

But now they desire a better country, that is, an heavenly: wherefore God is not ashamed to be called their God: for he hath prepared for them a city.
Hebrews 11:16

We have come to a wretched emphasis in the Christian church, so that when we talk about the future we talk about "eschatology" instead of heaven!

We must confess that Christians are living too much in the "present now"—and the anticipation of better things to come has almost died out of the church of Christ.

We find ourselves so well-situated now, that we don't really need any tomorrow's heaven. We don't need to hope—we have everything well enough now!

In this kind of emphasis, the fact remains that the true Christian is one who is kind of sick of this world. When God works a miracle within the human breast, heaven becomes the Christian's home immediately, and he is drawn to it as the bird is drawn in the springtime to fly north.

The Christian does have a homeland, and the fact that we are not anticipating it and looking forward to it with any pleasure is a serious mark of something that is wrong with us.

When I find someone who is settled down too snugly into this world and its system, I am forced to doubt whether he has ever truly been born again.

Actually, it is true that all of the Christians I meet who really amount to something for God are those very much out of key with their age—very, very much out of tune with their generation! Remember, you are on earth and God is in heaven—so don't be afraid to dream high spiritual dreams, believing what your Bible says.

March 11

The Delusive Glory of This World's Kingdoms

Then saith Jesus unto him, Get thee hence, Satan; for it is written, Thou shalt worship the Lord thy God, and him only shalt thou serve. Matthew 4:10

The delusive quality of all human glory is taught throughout the Bible, and with bold emphasis in the New Testament. It has been taught also with great clarity by the saints and faithful brethren since the days of the apostles.

Satan once tried to bring about the downfall of Christ by offering Him all the kingdoms of the world and the glory in them.

In presenting to the Man Jesus the glory of the world he was shrewdly taking advantage of a known weakness in the human race. The trick should have worked, and it would have worked but for one thing: This was no fallen man Satan was attempting to seduce. It was a sinless Man full of the Holy Ghost and wisdom, whose penetrating glance pierced the world's attractive exterior.

Beneath its gaudy allurements He saw the corruption and the decay. He knew its glory was but bait to catch foolish victims. He knew its bright promises were all lies. Our Lord saw what other men could not see. He saw not beauty but death, a garish death that must be purchased at the price of the soul. What He saw revolted Him—He would have no part of it!

All this Jesus knew; and Satan for all his wisdom did not know that He knew it. The devil is familiar with the Bible, but still he did not know or he would not have attempted the impossible, and that to his own confusion and permanent loss of face!

Here is sufficient proof that the devil is wise—but not wise enough!

Christ Died Even for Those Who Hated Him

Neither is there salvation in any other: for there is none other name under heaven given among men, whereby we must be saved. Acts 4:12

Our Lord Jesus Christ came and demonstrated the vast difference between being charitable and being tolerant! He was so charitable that in His great heart He took in all the people in the world and was willing to die even for those who hated Him!

But even with that kind of love and charity crowning His being, Jesus was completely frank and open when He taught: "If you are not on my side, you are against me!" There is no "twilight zone" in the teachings of Jesus—no place in between.

So, charity is one thing, but tolerance is quite another matter.

Suppose we take the position of compromise that many want us to take: "Everyone come, and be saved if you want to. But if you do not want to be saved, maybe there is some other way that we can find for you. We want you to believe in the Lord Jesus Christ if you will, but if you do not want to, there may be a possibility that God will find some other way for you because there are those who say that there are many ways to God."

To take that position would not be a spirit of tolerance on our part—it would be downright cowardice! We would be guilty with so many others of a spirit of compromise that so easily becomes an anti-God attitude. Tolerance easily becomes a matter of cowardice if spiritual principles are involved, if the teachings of God's Word are ignored and forgotten!

March 13

Men Will Not Praise You for Genuine Spirituality

But as we are allowed of God to be put in trust with the gospel, even so we speak; not as pleasing men but God. . . . 1 Thessalonians 2:4

What we do for God must be done in the power of the Holy Spirit and we know and accept the fact that we may have little praise from men.

But what we do accomplish for Him as true spiritual work done with eternity in view will have His praise written across it!

Most of us have never heard, or do not remember, the name of the humble sixteen-year-old girl whose singing ministry brought such spiritual results in the Welsh revivals with Evan Roberts.

This quiet, humble girl would sing the gospel songs and much has been said about her spiritual gift—the Spirit-given ability to glorify Jesus Christ as Saviour when she sang. Not too much has ever been said about her voice, but the record is clear that she was a gifted soul—that the Holy Spirit seemed to be singing and moving through her yielded expression.

Evan Roberts would then rise to preach and there was little left for him to do. He said that he would quote from the Scriptures and add an exhortation and the people were ready to come to Christ. She had melted them with the warmth and the power of the Spirit!

Oh, what we would be tempted to do with her ministry in this day! We would put her on the coast-to-coast network and show off her talent—and spoil her! Thank God that they knew better than to start writing her life story.

She was a beautiful example of the humble use of our spiritual gifts for the glory of Jesus Christ—a simple Welsh girl willingly controlled by the Holy Spirit of God!

March 14

God's Voice Still Entreats Lost Mankind

For the earnest expectation of the creature waiteth for the manifestation of the sons of God. For we know that the whole creation groaneth and travaileth in pain together until now. Romans 8:19, 22

Why is it that the shining world of which men have dreamed, and that every man secretly believes is somewhere before him, is nevertheless lost to men?

It can only be because we are out of the way.

The world we inhabit is a lost world. It is a sick, fallen planet upon which we ride. The sacred revelation declares plainly that the inhabitants of the world are also lost, by a mighty, calamitous visitation of woe which is still upon them.

But with this, it also tells us a glorious fact—that this lost race has not been given up!

Thankfully, there is a voice that calls, a voice that entreats! If we were not lost, there would be no voice behind us saying, "This is the way, walk ye in it."

I say again that we have not been given up. That is plain from the Book of Genesis. Recall that the sound of God's gentle voice was heard saying, "Adam, where art thou?"—and that voice has never died out!

All of His entreating calls blend into one, whether it be the voice of God's love, or the voice of Jesus' blood, or the voice of conscience, or the voice of the dead or of the living, or of the lost or of the saved!

So, the holy writer says the lost planet is full of vanity and has lost its meaning, crying like a woman in travail—but waiting, as it were, to be born again into the liberty of the sons of God, and saved from decay and corruption!

March 15

Truth Addresses Itself to the Total Man

Sanctify them through thy truth: thy word is truth. John 17:17

The Bible is, among other things, a book of revealed truth. That is, certain facts are revealed that could not be discovered by the most brilliant mind. These facts are of such a nature as to be past finding out.

These are facts that were hidden behind a veil, and until certain men who spoke as they were moved by the Holy Ghost took away that veil no mortal man could know them.

The lifting of the veil of unknowing from undiscoverable things we call divine revelation.

What is generally overlooked among humankind is that truth as set forth in the Christian Scriptures is a moral thing; it is not addressed to the intellect only, but to the will also. It addresses itself to the total man, and its obligations cannot be discharged by grasping it mentally.

Truth engages the citadel of the human heart and is not satisfied until it has conquered everything there. The will must come forth and surrender its sword. It must stand at attention to receive orders, and those orders it must joyfully obey. Short of this any knowledge of Christian truth is inadequate and unavailing.

Bible exposition without moral application raises no opposition. It is only when the hearer is made to understand that truth is in conflict with his heart that resistance sets in. As long as people can hear orthodox truth divorced from life they will attend and support churches and institutions without objection!

No One for Whom Christ Died Is Worthless

Every one that is proud in heart is an abomination to the Lord; though hand join in hand, he shall not be unpunished. Proverbs 16:5

Contempt for another human being is an affront to God almost as grave as idolatry, for while idolatry is disrespect for God Himself, contempt is disrespect for the being He made in His own image.

Contempt says of a man, "Raca! Fool! This fellow is of no worth. I attach to his person no value whatsoever!" The person guilty of thus appraising a human being is thoroughly bad. The gravity of the situation lies not in the fact that a man can cry "Fool!" but that he can entertain in his heart the contempt which the word expresses.

Contempt is an emotion possible only where there is great pride. The error in moral judgment that undervalues another always springs out of the error that overvalues one's self. The contemptuous man esteems himself too highly, and for reasons that are invalid. His high opinion of himself is not based upon his position as a being made in God's image; he esteems himself for fancied virtues which he does not possess. The error in his judgment is moral, not intellectual.

Here is our warning: the Christian believer's disapprobation of the evil ways of men and women must not betray him into contempt for them as human beings! He must reverence the humanity of every man—for no one for whom Christ died can be common or worthless. To esteem anyone worthless who wears the form of a man is to be guilty of an affront to the Son of Man! We are to hate sin in ourselves and in all men, but never undervalue the man in whom the sin is found.

March 17

A Bible Fact: A Regenerated Man Knows God

Wherefore, sirs, be of good cheer: for I believe God, that it shall be even as it was told me. Acts 27:25

The Bible assumes as a self-evident fact that men can know God with at least the same degree of immediacy as they know any other person or thing that comes within the field of their experience.

The same terms are used to express the knowledge of God as are used to express knowledge of physical things:

"O TASTE and see that the Lord is good."

"All thy garments SMELL of myrrh, and aloes, and cassia."

"My sheep HEAR my voice."

"Blessed are the pure in heart, for they shall SEE God."

These are but four of countless such passages from the Word of God. And more important than any proof text is the fact that the whole import of the Scripture is toward this belief.

We apprehend the physical world by exercising the faculties given us for the purpose, and we possess spiritual faculties by means of which we can know God and the spiritual world if we will obey the Spirit's urge and begin to use them.

That a saving work must first be done in the heart is taken for granted here. The spiritual faculties of the unregenerate man lie asleep in his nature; they may be quickened to active life again by the operation of the Holy Spirit in regeneration!

A Selfish Lust: Man's Desire for First Place

And when the centurion. . .saw that he so cried out, and gave up the ghost, he said, Truly this man was the Son of God. Mark 15:39

The current mania of men and women to succeed in the world is a good thing perverted. The desire to fulfill the purpose for which we were created is of course a gift from God, but sin has twisted this impulse about and turned it into a selfish lust for first place and top honors. By this lust the whole world of mankind is driven as by a demon, and there is no escape.

When we come to Christ we enter a different world. The New Testament introduces us to a spiritual philosophy infinitely higher than and altogether contrary to that which motivates the world. According to the teaching of Christ the poor in spirit are blessed; the meek inherit the earth; the first are last and the last first; the greatest man is the one that best serves others and the one who loses everything is the only one that will have everything at last. The successful man of the world will see his hoarded treasures swept away by the tempest of judgment; the righteous beggar goes to Abraham's bosom and the rich man burns in the fires of hell.

Our Lord died an apparent failure, discredited by the leaders of established religion, rejected by society and forsaken by His friends. The man who ordered Him to the cross was the successful statesman whose hand the ambitious hack politician kissed. It took the resurrection to demonstrate how gloriously Christ had triumphed and how tragically the governor had failed. The resurrection and the judgment will demonstrate before all worlds who won and who lost. We can wait!

March 19

Jesus Christ: Our Chief Joy and Delight

Be glad in the Lord, and rejoice, ye righteous; and shout for joy, all ye that are upright in heart. Psalm 32:11

I must agree with the psalmist, even in our modern day, that the joy of the Lord is still the strength of His people. I do believe that the sad world around us is attracted to spiritual sunshine—the genuine thing, that is!

Some churches train their greeters and ushers to smile, showing as many teeth as possible. But I can sense that kind of display—and when I am greeted by a man who is smiling because he has been trained to smile, I know I am shaking the flipper of a trained seal!

But when the warmth and delight and joy of the Holy Spirit are in a congregation and the folks are just spontaneously joyful and unable to hide the happy grin, the result is a wonderful influence upon others. Conversely, the reason we have to search for so many things to cheer us up is the fact that we are not really joyful and contentedly happy within!

I admit that we live in a gloomy world and that international affairs, nuclear rumors and threats, earthquakes and riots cause people to shake their heads in despair and say, "What's the use?"

But we are Christians and Christians have every right to be the happiest people in the world! We do not have to look to other sources—for we look to the Word of God and discover how we can know the faithful God above and draw from His resources.

Why should the children of the King hang their heads and tote their own burdens, missing the mark about Christian victory? All this time the Holy Spirit has been wanting to make Jesus Christ our chief joy and delight!

God Blesses His Children for Holy Intentions

Jesus answered, If I honour myself, my honour is nothing: it is my Father that honoureth me. . . . John 8:54

"Them that honour me I will honour," said God once to a priest of Israel, and that ancient law of the kingdom stands today unchanged by the passing of time or the changes of dispensation. The whole Bible and every page of history proclaim the perpetuation of that law.

"If any man serve me, him will my Father honour," said our Lord Jesus, tying in the old with the new and revealing the essential unity of His ways with men.

It seems plain that almost any Bible character who honestly tried to glorify God in his earthly walk was so honored. See how God overlooked weaknesses and failures as He poured upon His servants grace and blessing untold. Let it be Abraham, Jacob, David, Daniel, Elijah or whom you will; honor followed honor as harvest the seed. The man of God set his heart to exalt God above all; God accepted his intention as fact and acted accordingly. Not perfection, but holy intention made the difference!

In our Lord Jesus Christ this law was seen in simple perfection. He sought not His own honor, but the honor of the God who sent Him.

"If I honour myself," He said on one occasion, "my honour is nothing; it is my Father that honoureth me." So far had the proud Pharisees departed from this law that they could not understand one who honored God at his own expense.

God Is Glorified in Our Moral Victories

For to be carnally minded is death; but to be spiritually minded is life and peace. Romans 8:6

In the Pauline epistles, the gravitational pull of the heart in one direction or another is called "the mind." In the eighth chapter of Romans, for instance, when Paul refers to the "mind" he is referring to the sum of our dominant desires.

The mere intellect, then, is not the mind: the mind is intellect plus an emotional tug strong enough to determine action!

As Christians, our only safety lies in complete honesty. We must surrender our hearts to God so that we have no unholy desires, then let the Scriptures pronounce their judgment on a contemplated course. If the Scriptures condemn an object, we must accept that judgment and conform to it, no matter how we may for the moment feel about it.

To want a thing, or feel that we want it, and then to turn from it because we see that it is contrary to the will of God is to win a great battle on the way to spiritual mindedness.

To bring our desires to the cross and allow them to be nailed there with Christ is a good and a beautiful thing.

To be tempted and yet to glorify God in the midst of it is to honor Him where it counts. This is more pleasing to God than any amount of sheltered and untempted piety could ever be!

God is always glorified when He wins a moral victory over us, and we are always benefited, immeasurably and gloriously benefited!

The blood of Christ will cleanse not only actual sins but the very inward desires so that we will not want to sin. A blessed state indeed, and blessed are they that reach it!

The True Minister: Man of God Speaking to Men

But watch thou in all things, endure afflictions, do the work of an evangelist, make full proof of thy ministry. 2 Timothy 4:5

The Christian minister, as someone has pointed out, is a descendant not of the Greek orator but of the Hebrew prophet!

The differences between the orator and the prophet are many and radical, the chief being that the orator speaks for himself while the prophet speaks for God.

The orator originates his message and is responsible to himself for its content. The prophet originates nothing but delivers the message he has received from God who alone is responsible for it, the prophet being responsible to God for its delivery only. The prophet must hear the message clearly and deliver it faithfully, and that is indeed a grave responsibility; but it is to God alone, not to men!

It is a dubious compliment to a preacher to say that he is original. The very effort to be original has become a snare to many a young man fresh out of seminary, who rejects the pure wheat of the Word and tries to nourish his congregation on chaff of his own manufacture. It may even be golden chaff, but chaff nevertheless that can never feed the soul.

The true preacher is a man of God speaking to men; he is a man of heaven giving God's witness on earth. Because he is a man of God he can decode the message he receives from heaven and deliver it in the language of earth!

God Is Not Dependent on Our Human Success

Humble yourselves therefore under the mighty hand of God, that he may exalt you in due time. 1 Peter 5:6

Why is it that the professed Christian church seems to have learned so little from our Lord's plain teaching and example concerning human failure and success?

We are still seeing as men see and judging after the manner of man's judgment. How much eager beaver religious work is done out of a carnal desire to make good? How many hours of prayer are wasted beseeching God to bless projects that are geared to the glorification of little men? How much sacred money is poured out upon men who, in spite of their tear-in-the-voice appeals, nevertheless seek only to make a fair show in the flesh?

The true Christian should turn away from all this. No man is worthy to succeed until he is willing to fail. No man is morally worthy of success in religious activities until he is willing that the honor of succeeding should go to another if God so wills.

God may allow His servant to succeed when He has disciplined him to a point where he does not need to succeed to be happy. The man who is elated by success and cast down by failure is still a carnal man.

God will allow His servant to succeed when he has learned that success does not make him dearer to God or more valuable in the total scheme of things.

Our great honor lies in being just what Jesus was and is. To be accepted by those who accept Him, rejected by all who reject Him, loved by those who love Him. What greater glory could come to any man?

Concept of the Trinity: Infinite Love Poured Out

Elect according to the foreknowledge of God the Father, through sanctification of the Spirit, unto obedience and sprinkling of the blood of Jesus Christ. . . . 1 Peter 1:2

We are surely aware that as human beings we can never know all of the Godhead. If we were capable of knowing all of the Godhead perfectly, we would be equal to the Godhead.

The early fathers in the church, in illustrating the trinity, pointed out that God the eternal Father is an infinite God, and that He is love. The very nature of love is to give itself but the Father could not give His love fully to anyone not fully equal to Himself. Thus we have the revelation of the Son Who is equal to the Father and of the eternal Father pouring out His love into the Son, Who could contain it, because the Son is equal with the Father!

Further, those ancient wise men reasoned, if the Father were to pour out His love on the Son, a medium of communication equal both to the Father and to the Son would be required, and this was the Holy Ghost!

So we have their concept of the Trinity—the ancient Father in the fullness of His love pouring Himself through the Holy Ghost, Who is in being equal to Him, into the Son Who is in being equal to the Spirit and to the Father!

Thus, all that man can know of God and His love in this life is revealed in Jesus Christ.

Jesus Knows All about You—and Still Loves You

And Jesus came and spake unto them, saying, All power is given unto me in heaven and in earth. Matthew 28:18

Have you ever heard one of our modern, Christian activists say, "I don't know when I will find a doctrine of the deeper life that is satisfactory to me!"

There is really only one answer to this kind of a quest—turn your eyes upon Jesus and commit yourself fully to Him because He is God and Christ, Redeemer and Lord, "the same yesterday, today and forever!"

In these matters of spiritual blessing and victory, we are not dealing with doctrines—we are dealing with the Lord of all doctrine! We are dealing with a Person who is the Resurrection and the Source from whom flows all doctrine and all truth.

How can we be so ignorant and so dull that we try to find our spiritual answers and the abounding life by looking beyond the only One who has promised that He would never change? How can we so readily slight the Christ of God who has limitless authority throughout the universe?

How long should it take us to yield completely and without reservation to this One who has been made both Lord and Christ—and yet continues to be the very same Jesus who still loves us with an everlasting love?

The very same Jesus—who knows all your troubles and weaknesses and sins, and loves you in spite of everything!

The New Man in Christ Is a Perpetual Miracle

For as many as are led by the Spirit of God, they are the sons of God.
Romans 8:14

The man of God, the true Spirit-filled man of God, is a perpetual miracle!

He has come to his knowledge of God by the wonder of the new birth and the illumination of the Spirit. Therefore his life is completely different from the world around him.

Consider with me the words of 1 John 2:27: "But the anointing which ye have received of him abideth in you, and ye need not that any man teach you: but as the same anointing teacheth you of all things, and is truth, and is no lie, and even as it hath taught you, ye shall abide in him."

John was a teacher and he says that your knowledge of God is not taught you from without—it is received by an inner anointing!

What are we going to do with this truth? Are we going to open the door of our personality—fling it wide?

Let us not be afraid of the Holy Spirit—He is an illuminator. He is light to the inner heart. He will show us more of God in a moment than we can learn in a lifetime without Him. He will not throw out what we have learned if it is the truth—He will set it on fire, that's all! He will add fire to the altar.

The blessed Holy Spirit waits to be honored. He will honor Christ as we honor Christ. He waits—and if we will throw open our hearts to Him, a new sun will rise on us! I know this by personal experience in my own life and ministry.

It Is Modern Man Himself Who Is the Dreamer

Ye are all the children of light, and the children of the day: we are not of the night, nor of darkness. . .let us watch and be sober. 1 Thessalonians 5:5, 6

We of the Christian faith need not go on the defensive, for it is the modern man of the world who is the dreamer, not the Christian believer!

The sinner can never be quite himself. All his life he must pretend. He must act as if he were never going to die, and yet he knows too well that he is. He must act as if he had not sinned, when in his deep heart he knows very well that he has. He must act unconcerned about God and judgment and the future life, and all the time his heart is deeply disturbed about his precarious condition. He must keep up a front of nonchalance while shrinking from facts and wincing under the lash of conscience. All his adult life he must dodge and hide and conceal. When he finally drops the act he either loses his mind or tries suicide.

If realism is the recognition of things as they actually are, the Christian is of all persons the most realistic. He of all intelligent thinkers is the one most concerned with reality. He pares things down to their stark essentials and squeezes out of his mind everything that inflates his thinking. He demands to know the whole truth about God, sin, life, death, moral accountability and the world to come. He wants to know the worst about himself in order that he may do something about it. He takes into account the undeniable fact that he has sinned. He recognizes the shortness of time and the certainty of death. These he does not try to avoid or alter to his own liking. They are facts and he faces them full on.

The believer is a realist—his expectations are valid and his faith well grounded!

March 28

True Wisdom: Listening to the Words Jesus Spoke

Many therefore of his disciples, when they had heard this, said; This is an hard saying, who can hear it? John 6:60

In the world of men we find nothing approaching the virtues of which Jesus spoke in the opening words of the famous Sermon on the Mount. Instead of poverty of spirit we find the rankest kind of pride; instead of meekness, arrogance; instead of mourners we find pleasure seekers; instead of hunger after righteousness we hear men saying, "I am rich and increased with goods and have need of nothing"; instead of mercy we find cruelty; instead of purity of heart, corrupt imaginings; instead of peacemakers we find men quarrelsome and resentful; instead of rejoicing in mistreatment we find them fighting back with every weapon at their command!

Into a world like this the sound of Jesus' words comes wonderful and strange, a visitation from above. It is well that He spoke, for no one else could have done it as well; and it is good that we listen, for His words are the essence of truth.

Jesus does not offer an opinion for He never uttered opinions. He never guessed; He knew, and He knows! His words are not as Solomon's were, the sum of sound wisdom or the results of keen observation. He spoke out of the fullness of His Godhead, and His words are very Truth itself. He is the only one who could say "blessed" with complete authority for He is the Blessed One come from the world above to confer blessedness upon mankind!

Best of all, His words were supported by deeds mightier than any performed on this earth by another man.

It is wisdom for us to listen!

March 29

Believing: Directing the Heart's Attention to Jesus

And looking upon Jesus as he walked, he saith, Behold the Lamb of God!
John 1:36

The Hebrew epistle instructs us to run life's race "looking unto Jesus the author and finisher of our faith," for faith is not a once-done act, but a continuous gaze of the heart at the Triune God!

Believing, actually, is directing the heart's attention to Jesus. It is lifting the mind to "behold the Lamb of God," and never ceasing that beholding for the rest of our lives. Distractions may hinder, but once the heart is committed to Him, after each brief excursion away from Him the attention will return again and rest upon Him like a wandering bird coming back to its window.

I would emphasize this one committal, this one great volitional act which establishes the heart's intention to gaze forever upon Jesus. God takes this intention for our choice and makes what allowances He must for the thousand distractions which beset us in this evil world.

Faith is a redirecting of our sight, a getting out of the focus of our own vision and getting God into focus.

When we lift our inward eyes to gaze upon God we are sure to meet friendly eyes gazing back at us, for it is written that the eyes of the Lord run to and fro throughout all the earth. The sweet language of experience is, "Thou God seest me." When the eyes of the soul looking out meet the eyes of God looking in, heaven has begun right here on earth!

Salvation: A Right Relation between God and Man

But now in Christ Jesus ye who sometimes were far off are made nigh by the blood of Christ. Ephesians 2:13

The cause of all our human miseries is a radical moral dislocation, an upset in our relation to God and to each other.

For whatever else the Fall of man may have been, it was most certainly a sharp change in man's relation to his Creator. He adopted toward God an altered attitude, and by so doing destroyed the proper Creator-creature relation in which, unknown to him, his true happiness lay.

Essentially salvation is the restoration of a right relation between man and his Creator, a bringing back to normal of the Creator-creature relation.

A satisfactory spiritual life will begin with a complete change in relation between God and the sinner; not a judicial change merely, but a conscious and experienced change affecting the sinner's whole nature.

The atonement in Jesus' blood makes such a change judicially possible and the working of the Holy Spirit makes it emotionally satisfying. The story of the prodigal son perfectly illustrates this later phase.

He had brought a world of trouble upon himself by forsaking the position which he had properly held as son of his father. At bottom his restoration was nothing more than a reestablishing of the father-son relation which had existed from his birth and had been altered temporarily by his act of sinful rebellion. This story overlooks the legal aspects of redemption, but it makes beautifully clear the experiential aspects of salvation.

No Burial in Sight for the Faith of Our Fathers

To the general assembly and church of the firstborn, which are written in heaven, and to God the Judge of all, and to the spirits of just men made perfect. Hebrews 12:23

There is a notion abroad that Christianity is on its last legs, or possibly already dead and just too weak to lie down. In the minds of many who do not understand Christianity, the chief proof of her death is said to be her failure to provide leadership for the world just when she needs it most.

Let me say that those who would come forward to bury the faith of our fathers have reckoned without the host. Just as Jesus Christ was once buried away with the full expectation that He had been gotten rid of, so His church has been laid to rest times without number; and as He disconcerted His enemies by rising from the dead so the church has confounded hers by springing again to vigorous life after all the obsequies had been performed over her coffin and the crocodile tears had been shed at her grave!

Christianity is going the way her Founder and His apostles said it would go. Its development and direction were predicted almost two thousand years ago, and this itself is a miracle!

Had Christ been less than God and His apostles less than inspired they could not have foretold with such precision the state of the church so far removed from them in time and circumstance. The true church is the repository of the life of God among men, and if in one place the frail vessels fail, that life will break out somewhere else! Of this we may be sure.

By Creation, We Have the Capacity to Know God

All things that the Father hath are mine: therefore said I, that he shall take of mine, and shall shew it unto you. John 16:15

God wants to comunicate with us through the avenues of our minds, our wills and our emotions. The continuous and unembarrassed interchange of love and thought between God and the soul of the redeemed man is the throbbing heart of New Testament religion!

The intercourse between God and the soul is known to us in conscious personal awareness. It is personal: that is, it does not come through the body of believers, as such, but is known to the individual, and to the body through the individuals which compose it. And it is conscious: that is, it does not stay below the threshold of consciousness and work there unknown to the soul.

You and I are in little (our sins excepted) what God is in large. Being made in His image we have within us the capacity to know Him. The moment the Spirit has quickened us to life in regeneration our whole being senses its kinship to God and leaps up in joyous recognition. That is the heavenly birth without which we cannot see the kingdom of God!

It is, however, not an end but an inception. That is where we begin, but where we stop no man has yet discovered, for there is in the awful and mysterious depths of the Triune God neither limit nor end!

April 2

Plan of Redemption: God Has Not Abandoned Man

. . .God was manifest in the flesh, justified in the Spirit, seen of angels, preached unto the Gentiles, believed on in the world, received up into glory.
1 Timothy 3:16

For mankind, the earth has become the symbol of death and mortality, but in the very face of this, the Christian still knows for certain that God has not forgotten him. Man who was made in the image of God has not been forsaken—God promised a plan to restore that which had been made in His image.

Only that creature whom He called "man" did God make in His own image and likeness. So, when man failed and sinned and fell, God said, "I will go down now."

God came down to visit us in the form of a man, for in Christ Jesus we have the incarnation, "God manifest in the flesh." God Himself came down to this earthly island of man's grief and assumed our loss and took upon Himself our demerits, and in so doing, redeemed us back unto Himself. Jesus Christ, the King of glory, the everlasting Son of the Father, in His victory over sin and death opened the kingdom of heaven to all believers!

Beyond His death and resurrection and ascension, the present work of Jesus Christ is twofold. It is to be an advocate above—a risen Saviour with high priestly office at the throne of God; and the ministry of preparing a place for His people in the house of His Father and our Father, as well.

That is what the Bible teaches. That is what the Christian church believes. It is the essence of the doctrines of the Christian church relating to atonement and salvation!

April 3

Worth of a Soul: God Gave His Only Son

. . .Or what shall a man give in exchange for his soul? Matthew 16:26

In the world's markets, something which has no value for a disinterested person may be considered of great value to another who desires it and purchases it. In this sense, we may learn how dear and precious we are to Christ by what He was willing to give for us!

Many Christians are tempted to downgrade themselves too much. I am not arguing against true humility and my word to you is this: Think as little of yourself as you want to, but always remember that our Lord Jesus Christ thought very highly of you—enough to give Himself for you in death and sacrifice!

If the devil comes to you and whispers that you are no good, don't argue with him. In fact, you may as well admit it, but then remind the devil: "Regardless of what you say about me, I must tell you how the Lord feels about me. He tells me that I am so valuable to Him that He gave Himself for me on the cross!"

So the value is set by the price paid—and in our case, the price paid was our Lord Himself, and the end that the Saviour had in view was that He might redeem us from all iniquity, that is, from the power and consequences of iniquity.

One of Wesley's hymns speaks of "the double cure" for sin. The wrath of God against sin and the power of sin in the human life—both of these were dealt with when Christ gave Himself for us. He redeemed us with a double cure!

April 4

God Shares His Good Pleasure with His Own

Whom have I in heaven but thee? and there is none upon earth that I desire beside thee. Psalm 73:25

It is the nature of God to share. His mighty acts of creation and redemption were done for His good pleasure, but His pleasure extends to all created things.

One has only to look at a healthy child at play or listen to the song of a bird at sundown and he will know that God meant His universe to be a joyful one.

Those who have been spiritually enabled to love God for Himself will find a thousand fountains springing up from the rainbow-circled throne and bringing countless treasures which are to be received with reverent thanksgiving as being the overflow of God's love for His children. Each gift is a bonus of grace which because it was not sought for itself may be enjoyed without injury to the soul. These include the simple blessings of life, such as health, a home, a family, congenial friends, food, shelter, the pure joys of nature or the more artificial pleasures of music and art.

The effort to find these treasures by direct search apart from God has been the major activity of mankind throughout the centuries; and this has been man's burden and man's woe!

God wills that we should love Him for Himself alone with no hidden reasons, trusting Him to be to us all our natures require. Our Lord said all this much better: "Seek ye first the kingdom of God, and his righteousness; and all these things shall be added unto you."

April 5

All Had a Share in Putting Jesus on the Cross

For Christ also hath once suffered for sins, the just for the unjust, that he might bring us to God, being put to death in the flesh, but quickened by the Spirit. 1 Peter 3:18

There is a strange conspiracy of silence in the world today—even in religious circles—about man's responsibility for sin, the reality of judgment, and about an outraged God and the necessity for a crucified Saviour.

But still there lies a great shadow upon every man and every woman—the fact that our Lord was bruised and wounded and crucified for the entire human race! This is the basic human responsibility that men are trying to push off and evade.

Let us not eloquently blame Judas nor Pilate. Let us not curl our lips at Judas and accuse: "He sold Him for money!"

Oh, they were guilty, certainly! But they were our accomplices in crime. They and we put Him on the cross, not they alone. That rising malice and anger that burns so hotly in your breast today put Him there! The evil, the hatred, the suspicion, the jealousy, the lying tongue, the cheating, the carnality, the fleshly love of pleasure— all of these in natural man joined in putting Him on the cross!

There is a powerful movement swirling throughout the world designed to give people peace of mind in relieving them of any historical responsibility for the trial and crucifixion of Jesus Christ. But we may as well admit it. Every one of us in Adam's race had a share in putting Him on the cross!

April 6

Our Lord Jesus Was Bruised for Our Iniquities

. . .He was wounded for our transgressions, he was bruised for our iniquities. . . . Isaiah 53:5

The word "iniquity" is not a good word—and God knows how we hate it! But the consequences of iniquity cannot be escaped.

The prophet reminds us clearly that the Saviour was bruised for our iniquities.

We deny it, and say "No!" but the fingerprints of all mankind are plain evidence against us—the fingerprints of man found in every dark cellar and in every alley and in every dimly lighted evil place throughout the world. God knows man from man, and it is impossible to escape our guilt and place our moral responsibility upon someone else.

For our iniquities and our transgressions He was bruised and wounded—and Israel's great burden and amazing blunder was her judgment that this wounded one on the hillside beyond Jerusalem was being punished for His own sin!

The prophet foresaw this historic error in judgment, and he himself was a Jew, saying: "We thought He was smitten of God. We thought that God was punishing Him for His own iniquity for we did not know then that God was punishing Him for our transgressions and our iniquities."

For our sakes, He was profaned by ignorant and unworthy men!

We Are Amazed That God Has Forgiven Us

For I am the least of the apostles. . .But by the grace of God I am what I am. . . . 1 Corinthians 15:9, 10

Every humble and devoted believer in Jesus Christ must have his own periods of wonder and amazement at this mystery of godliness—the willingness of the Son of Man to take our place in judgment so that the people of God could be a cleansed and spiritual people!

If the amazement has all gone out of it, something is wrong, and you need to have the stony ground broken up again!

The Apostle Paul, one of the holiest men who ever lived, was not ashamed of his times of remembrance and wonder over the grace and kindness of God. He knew that God did not hold his old sins against him forever!

Knowing the old account was all settled, Paul's happy heart assured him again and again that all was well.

He could only shake his head in amazement and confess: "I am unworthy to be called, but by His grace, I am a new creation in Jesus Christ!"

I make this point about the faith and assurance and rejoicing of Paul in order to say that if that humble sense of perpetual penance ever leaves our justified being, we are on the way to backsliding!

April 8

The Christian: Citizen of Heaven Living on Earth

And they that be wise shall shine as the brightness of the firmament; and they that turn many to righteousness as the stars for ever and ever. Daniel 12:3

Let a man become enamored of Eternal Wisdom and set his heart to win her and he takes on himself a full-time, all-engaging pursuit! Thereafter his whole life will be filled with seekings and findings, self-repudiations, tough disciplines and daily dyings as he is being crucified unto the world and the world unto him.

The regenerated man has been inwardly separated from society as Israel was separated from Egypt at the crossing of the Red Sea. The Christian is a man of heaven temporarily living on earth. Though in spirit divided from the race of fallen men he must yet in the flesh live among them. In many things he is like them but in others he differs so radically from them that they cannot but see and resent it.

From the days of Cain and Abel the man of earth has punished the man of heaven for being different. The long history of persecution and martyrdom confirms this.

But, we must not get the impression that the Christian life is one of continuous conflict, one unbroken irritating struggle against the world, the flesh and the devil.

A thousand times no!

The heart that learns to die with Christ soon knows the blessed experience of rising with Him, and all the world's persecutions cannot still the high note of holy joy that springs up in the soul that has become the dwelling place of the Holy Spirit!

April 9

A Beautiful Reality: We Do Love Christ, Never Having Seen Him

That the trial of your faith. . .might be found unto praise and honour and glory at the appearing of Jesus Christ: Whom having not seen, ye love. . . . 1 Peter 1:7, 8

The Apostle Peter, who had seen Jesus Christ in the flesh with his own eyes, passed along to every believing Christian the assurance that it is possible for us to love the Saviour and to live a life that will glorify Him even though we have not yet seen Him!

It is as though Peter is urging: "Love Him and work for Him and live for Him. I give you my testimony that it will be worth it all when you look upon His face—for I have seen Him with my own eyes, and I know!"

In his epistle, Peter, who had known Jesus in the flesh, was moved to write to the strangers scattered abroad— the Christians of the dispersion—to remind them that they should love Jesus Christ even though they had not seen Him in the flesh.

The Lord Jesus Himself had set His own stamp of approval and blessing upon all Christians who would believe, never having seen Him in the time of His own flesh. He told Thomas after the resurrection, "Because thou hast seen me, thou hast believed: blessed are they that have not seen, and yet have believed."

God has seen fit to give us wonderful and mysterious faculties, and I truly believe that God has ordained that we may actually know Jesus now, and love Him better never having seen Him, than Peter did when he saw Him!

April 10

On Earth, Only Man Has Capacity for Worship

And God said, Let us make man in our own image, after our likeness. . .So God created man in his own image. . . . Genesis 1:26, 27

The one mark which forever distinguishes man from all other forms of life on earth is that he is a worshiper: he has a bent toward and a capacity for worship.

Apart from his position as a worshiper of God, man has no sure key to his own being; he is but a higher animal, being born much as any other animal, going through the cycle of his life here on earth and dying at last without knowing what the whole thing is about.

If that is all for him, if he has no more reason than the beast for living, then it is an odd thing indeed that he is the only one of the animals that worries about himself, that wonders, that asks questions of the universe.

The very fact that he does these things tells the wise man that somewhere there is One to whom he owes allegiance, One before whom he should kneel and do homage.

The Christian revelation tells us that that One is God the Father Almighty, maker of heaven and earth, who is to be worshiped in the Spirit in the name of Jesus Christ our Lord.

That is enough for us. Without trying to reason it out we may proceed from there. All our doubts we meet with faith's wondering affirmation: "O Lord God, thou knowest," an utterance which Samuel Taylor Coleridge declared to be the profoundest in human speech.

Bible Christianity needs to recapture the spirit of worship, with a fresh revelation of the greatness of God and the beauty of Jesus!

April 11

Believe What God Says He Will Do for Us

Repent ye therefore, and be converted, that your sins may be blotted out, when the times of refreshing shall come from the presence of the Lord. Acts 3:19

True faith requires that we believe everything that God has said about Himself, but also that we believe everything He has said about us!

Until we believe that we are as bad as God says we are, we can never believe that He will do for us what He says He will do. Right here is where popular religion breaks down. It never quite accepts the severity of God or the depravity of man. It stresses the goodness of God and man's misfortune. It makes sin a pardonable frailty and God is not too much concerned about it—He merely wants us to trust in His goodness.

To believe thus is to ground faith upon falsehood and build our eternal hope upon sand. God has spoken. We are all under solemn obligation to hear the affirmations of the Holy Ghost.

To manipulate the Scriptures so as to make them excuse us, compliment us and console us is to do despite to the written Word and to reject the Living Word. To believe savingly in Jesus Christ is to believe all He has said about Himself and all that the prophets and apostles have said about Him.

A dreamy, sentimental faith which ignores the judgments of God against us and listens to the affirmations of the soul is as deadly as cyanide. A faith which passively accepts all of the pleasant texts of the Bible while it overlooks or rejects the stern warnings and commandments of those same Scriptures is not the faith of which Christ and His apostles spoke!

April 12

Christ's Call: Leave the Old, Begin the New

Then Peter began to say unto him, Lo, we have left all, and have followed thee. Mark 10:28

Jesus Christ is a Man come to save men. In Him the divine nature is married to our human nature, and wherever human nature exists there is the raw material out of which He makes followers and saints!

Our Lord recognizes no classes, high or low, rich or poor, old or young, man or woman: all are human and all are alike to Him. His invitation is to all mankind.

In New Testament times persons from many and varied social levels heard His call and responded: Peter the fisherman; Levi the publican; Luke the physician; Paul the scholar; Mary the demon possessed; Lydia the businesswoman; Paulus the statesman. A few great and many common persons came. They all came and our Lord received them all in the same way and on the same terms.

In those early Galilean days Christ's followers heard His call, forsook the old life, attached themselves to Him, began to obey His teachings and joined themselves to His band of disciples. This total commitment was their confirmation of faith. Nothing less would do!

And it is not different today. From any and every profession or occupation men and women may come to Him if they will. He calls us to leave the old life and to begin the new. There must never be any vacuum, never any place of neutrality where the world cannot identify us as truly belonging to Him!

April 13

Generally, We Pray Only as Well as We Live

If I regard iniquity in my heart, the Lord will not hear me. Psalm 66:18

Prayer at its best is the expression of the total life, for all things else being equal, our prayers are only as powerful as our lives.

In the long pull, we pray only as well as we live!

Some prayers are like a fire escape, used only in times of critical emergency—never very enjoyable, but used as a way of terrified escape from disaster. They do not represent the regular life of the one who offers them; rather, they are the unusual and uncommon acts of the spiritual amateur.

Most of us in moments of stress have wished that we had lived so that prayer would not be so unnatural to us and have regretted that we had not cultivated prayer to the point where it would be as easy and as natural as breathing.

No Christian wants to live his whole life on an emergency level. As we go on into God we shall see excellency of the life of constant communion where all thoughts and acts are prayers, and the entire life becomes one holy sacrifice of prayer and worship!

To pray effectively it is required of us that there be no unblessed areas in our lives, no parts of the mind or soul that are not inhabited by the Spirit, no impure desires allowed to live within us, no disparity between our prayers and our conduct.

Undoubtedly the redemption in Christ Jesus has sufficient moral power to enable us to live in a state of purity and love, where our whole life will be a prayer!

April 14

Christianity Is No Longer Producing Saintliness

But grow in grace, and in the knowledge of our Lord and Saviour Jesus Christ. . . . 2 Peter 3:18

It is possible for a whole generation of professing Christians to be victims of poor teaching, low moral standards and unscriptural or extrascriptural doctrines, resulting in stunted growth and retarded development.

It is little less than stark tragedy that an individual Christian may pass from youth to old age in a state of suspended growth and all his life be unaware of it!

Those who would question the truth of this have only to read the First Epistle to the Corinthians and the Epistle to the Hebrews; and church history adds all the further proof that is needed.

In today's Christianity, we have measured ourselves by ourselves until the incentive to seek higher plateaus in the things of the Spirit is all but gone!

The fact is that we are no longer producing saints. We are making converts to an effete type of Christianity that bears little resemblance to that of the New Testament. The average so-called Bible Christian in our times is but a wretched parody on true sainthood!

Clearly, we must begin to produce better Christians!

We must insist on New Testament sainthood for our converts, nothing less; and we must lead them into a state of heart purity, fiery love, separation from the world and poured-out devotion to the Person of Christ.

Only in this way can the low level of spirituality be raised again to where it should be in the light of the Scriptures and of eternal values!

April 15

There Is a Finality in the Biblical Revelation

Therefore we ought to give the more earnest heed to the things which we have heard, lest at any time we should let them slip. Hebrews 2:1

There are men in our day who have studied the Bible and come to the conclusion that since God is vocal in His universe, there is no such thing as an inspired canon of Scripture containing a full body of revealed truth that can serve as the one final source of doctrine and practice.

These teachers reason that if God is still speaking, then we must keep our minds open to further revelation given, it may be, through poets, philosophers, scientists and religionists of various kinds. They would insist that wherever new truth is discovered or new and advanced ideas are brought forth, there God is speaking again as He once spoke by the prophet and seer in olden times.

While we grant such men the right to believe what they will, this one thing is settled: whoever, for whatever reason, denies the finality of the biblical revelation and insists upon a continuing revelation having the same authority as the sacred Scriptures has shut himself out from the name of Christian! He is simply not a Christian in the scriptural and historic meaning of the word.

Between the ideas of a fixed biblical canon and a constantly speaking God there is no contradiction! The point I make is that if the living voice of God were not speaking in the world and in the hearts of men the written Word could have no real meaning for us.

April 16

View God's Wrath in the Light of His Holiness

. . .He that believeth not the Son shall not see life; but the wrath of God abideth on him. John 3:36

The earnest and instructed Christian knows that the wrath of God is a reality, that His anger is as holy as His love, and that between His love and His wrath there is no incompatibility. He further knows (as far as fallen man can know such matters) what the wrath of God is and what it is not.

To understand God's wrath we must view it in the light of His holiness. God is holy and has made holiness to be the moral condition necessary to the health of His universe. Sin's temporary presence in the world only accents this. Whatever is holy is healthy; evil is a moral sickness that must end ultimately in death. The formation of the language itself suggests this, the English word holy deriving from the Anglo-Saxon 'halig,' 'hal' meaning well, whole.

Since God's first concern for His universe is its moral health, that is, its holiness, whatever is contrary to this is necessarily under His eternal displeasure. Wherever the holiness of God confronts unholiness there is conflict.

To preserve His creation God must destroy whatever would destroy it. When He arises to put down destruction and save the world from irreparable moral collapse He is said to be very angry. Every wrathful judgment of God in the history of the world has been a holy act of preservation.

God's wrath is His utter intolerance of whatever degrades and destroys!

April 17

The Cross You Bear Is Yours—Not Christ's

And they that are Christ's have crucified the flesh with the affections and lusts. Galatians 5:24

To go along with Christ step by step and point by point in identical suffering of Roman crucifixion is not possible for any of us, and certainly is not intended by our Lord.

An earnest Christian woman long ago sought help from Henry Suso concerning her spiritual life. She had been imposing austerities upon herself in an effort to feel the sufferings that Christ had felt on the cross. Things were not going so well with her and Suso knew why.

The old saint wrote his spiritual daughter and reminded her that our Lord had not said, "If any man will come after me let him deny himself, and take up MY cross." He had said, "Let him. . .take up his cross." There is a difference of only one small pronoun; but that difference is vast and important.

Crosses are all alike, but no two are identical. Never before nor since has there been a cross experience just like that endured by the Saviour. The whole dreadful work of dying which Christ suffered was something unique in the experience of mankind. It had to be so if the cross was to mean life for the world. The sin-bearing, the darkness, the rejection by the Father were agonies peculiar to the Person of the holy sacrifice. For anyone to claim that experience of Christ would be sacrilege.

Every cross was and is an instrument of death, but no man could die on the cross of another; hence Jesus said, "Let him. . .take up his cross, and follow me!"

A Fallacy: To Think That Time Is a Great Healer

And he trembling and astonished said, Lord, what wilt thou have me to do?. . .Acts 9:6

The most harmful mistake we make concerning time is to think that it has somehow a mysterious power to perfect human nature and change the human personality.

We say of a foolish young man, "Time will make him wiser," or we see a new Christian acting like anything but a Christian and hope that time will someday turn him into a saint.

The truth is that time has no more power to sanctify a man than space has. Indeed, time is only a fiction by which we account for change. It is a transformation, not time, that turns fools into wise men and sinners into saints, Christ bringing it about by means of the changes He works in the heart!

Saul the persecutor became Paul the servant of God, but time did not make the change. Christ wrought the miracle, the same Christ who once changed water into wine. One spiritual experience followed another in fairly rapid succession until the violent Saul became a gentle, God-enamored soul, ready to lay down his life for the faith he once hated. It should be obvious that time had no part in the making of the man of God!

Human nature is not fixed and for this we should thank God day and night! We are still capable of change. We can become something other than what we are. By the power of the gospel the covetous man may become generous, the egotist lowly in his own eyes. The thief may learn to steal no more, the blasphemer to fill his mouth with praises unto God.

April 19

A High Privilege: God Counts Us His Friends

And the scripture was fulfilled which saith, Abraham believed God. . .and he was called the Friend of God. James 2:23

The image of God in man cannot extend to every part of man's being, for God has attributes which He cannot impart to any of His creatures, however favored.

God is uncreated, self-existent, infinite, sovereign, eternal; these attributes are His alone and by their very definition cannot be shared with another. But there are other attributes which He can impart to His creatures and in some measure share with His redeemed children.

Intellect, self-consciousness, love, goodness, holiness, pity, faithfulness—these and certain other attributes are the points where likeness between God and man may be achieved. It is here that the divine-human friendship is experienced!

God, being perfect, has capacity for perfect friendship. Man, being imperfect, can never quite know perfection in anything, least of all in his relationship to the incomprehensible Godhead.

The more perfect our friendship with God becomes the simpler will our lives be. Those formalities that are so necessary to keep a casual friendship alive may be dispensed with when true friends sit in each other's presence. True friends trust each other.

Unquestionably the highest privilege granted to man on earth is to be admitted into the circle of the friends of God. Nothing is important enough to be allowed to stand in the way of our relation to God. We should see to it that nothing on earth shall separate us from God's friendship!

April 20

We Do Not Despise God-given Emotions

But when he saw the multitudes, he was moved with compassion on them, because they fainted, and were scattered abroad. . . . Matthew 9:36

Our emotions are neither to be feared nor despised, for they are a normal part of us as God made us in the first place. Indeed, the full human life would be impossible without them!

A feeling of pity would never arise in the human breast unless aroused by a mental picture of others' distress, and without the emotional bump to set off the will there would be no act of mercy. That is the way we are constituted and what I am saying here is nothing new. Every mother, every statesmen, every leader of men, every preacher of the Word of God knows that a mental picture must be presented to the listener before he can be moved to act, even though it be for his own advantage!

God intended that truth should move us to moral action. The mind receives ideas, mental pictures of things as they are. These excite the feelings and these in turn move the will to act in accordance with the truth. That is the way it should be, and would be had not sin entered and wrought injury to our inner life. Because of sin, the simple sequence of truth—feeling—action may break down in any of its three parts.

The Christian who gazes too long on the carnal pleasures of this world cannot escape a certain feeling of sympathy with them, and that feeling will inevitably lead to behavior that is worldly. To expose our hearts to truth and consistently refuse or neglect to obey the impulses it arouses is to stymie the motions of life within us, and if persisted in, to grieve the Holy Spirit into silence.

April 21

A Blessing: The Unchanging Faithfulness of God

Jesus Christ the same yesterday, and to day, and for ever. Hebrews 13:8

It is a gracious thing in our relationship with the heavenly Father to find that He loves us for ourselves and values our love more than galaxies of new created worlds.

The added blessing is to discover His faithfulness—for what He is today we shall find Him tomorrow, the next day and the next year!

Actually, the fellowship of God with His redeemed family is beyond all telling. He communes with His redeemed ones in an easy, uninhibited fellowship that is restful and healing to the soul.

He is not sensitive nor selfish nor temperamental. He is not hard to please, though He may be hard to satisfy. He expects of us only what He has Himself first supplied.

He is quick to mark every simple effort to please Him, and just as quick to overlook imperfections when He knows we meant to do His will. Surely He loves us for ourselves!

Unfortunately, many Christians cannot get free from their perverted notions of God, and these notions poison their hearts and destroy their inward freedom. These friends serve God grimly, as the elder brother did, doing what is right without enthusiasm and without joy, and seem altogether unable to understand the buoyant, spirited celebration when the prodigal comes home. Their idea of God rules out the possibility of His being happy in His people!

How good it would be if we could learn that God is easy to live with, the sum of all patience, the essence of kindly good will!

April 22

The Word of God: Shortest Route to Spiritual Peace

Till we all come in the unity of the faith, and of the knowledge of the Son of God, unto a perfect man, unto the measure of the stature of the fulness of Christ. Ephesians 4:13

The work of God is not finished in the heart and life of the new believer when the first act of inward adjustment has given him a sense of cleansing and forgiveness, peace and rest for the first time in his life!

The Spirit would go on from there to bring the total life into harmony with that blissful "center." This is wrought in the believer by the Word and by prayer and discipline and suffering.

It could be done by a short course in things spiritual if we were more pliable, less self-willed and stubborn; but it usually takes some time before we learn the hard lessons of faith and obedience sufficiently well to permit the work to be done within us with anything near to perfection.

In bringing many sons unto glory God works with whatever He has in whatever way He can and by whatever means He can, respecting always His own gift to us, the freedom of our wills. But of all means He uses, the Bible is the best.

The Word of God well understood and religiously obeyed is the shortest route to spiritual perfection, and we must not select a few favorite passages to the exclusion of others. Any tinkering with the truth, any liberties taken with the Scriptures, and we throw ourselves out of symmetry and invite stiff discipline and severe chastisement from that loving Father who wills for us nothing less than full restoration to the image of God in Christ!

Letting the Will Be the Master of the Heart

If ye then be risen with Christ, seek those things which are above, where Christ sitteth on the right hand of God. Colossians 3:1

Because the will is master of the heart, it is important to realize that the root of all evil in human nature is the corruption of the will!

The thoughts and intents of the heart are wrong and as a consequence the whole life is wrong. Repentance is primarily a change of moral purpose, a sudden and often violent reversal of the soul's direction.

The prodigal son took his first step upward from the pigsty when he said, "I will arise and go to my father." As he had once willed to leave his father's house, now he willed to return.

To love God with all our heart we must first of all will to do so. We should repent our lack of love and determine from this moment on to make God the object of our devotion. We should read the Scriptures devotionally and set our affections on things above and aim our hearts toward Christ and heavenly things!

If we do these things we may be sure that we shall experience a wonderful change in our whole inward life. Our emotions will become disciplined and directed. We shall begin to taste the "piercing sweetness" of the love of Christ. The whole life, like a delicate instrument, will be tuned to sing the praises of Him who loved us and washed us from our sins in His own blood!

The Preacher: Servant of the Lord and the People

Let no man deceive himself. If any man among you seemeth to be wise in this world, let him become a fool, that he may be wise. For the wisdom of this world is foolishness with God. . . . 1 Corinthians 3:18, 19

Men who are called to be servants of God in the ministry must constantly guard against thinking of themselves as belonging to a "privileged" class.

Our so-called Christian society tends to increase this danger by granting the clergy discounts and other courtesies, and the church itself helps a bad job along by bestowing upon men of God various sonorous honorifics which are either comical or awe-inspiring, depending upon how you look at it.

Seeing whose name he bears, the unconscious acceptance of belonging to a privileged class is particularly incongruous for the minister. Christ came to give, to serve, to sacrifice and to die, and said to His disciples, "As my Father hath sent me, even so send I you." The preacher is a servant of the Lord and of the people. He is in great moral peril when he forgets this.

Remember, the clergyman meets religious people almost excusively. People are on their guard when they are with him. They tend to talk over their own heads and to be for the time the kind of persons they think he wants them to be rather than the kind of persons they are in fact!

This creates a world of unreality where no one is quite himself, but the preacher has lived in it so long that he accepts it as real—and never knows the difference!

Today, Ask God to Remove Every False Trust

The heart is deceitful above all things, and desperately wicked: who can know it? Jeremiah 17:9

Many of us have become extremely skillful in arranging our lives so as to admit the truth of Christianity without being embarrassed by its implications.

We arrange things so that we can get on well enough without divine aid, while at the same time ostensibly seeking it!

We boast in the Lord but watch carefully that we never get caught depending on Him!

To many, Christ is little more than an idea, or at best an ideal: He is not a fact! They talk as if He were real and act as if He were not.

We can prove our faith by our commital to it—and in no other way!

Any belief that does not command the one who holds it is not a real belief: it is a pseudo belief only. And it might shock some of us profoundly if we were brought suddenly face to face with our beliefs and forced to test them in the fires of practical living!

What we need very badly these days is a company of Christians who are prepared to trust God as completely now as they must do at the last day. For each of us the time is surely coming when we shall have nothing but God!

Today is the best time to invite God to remove every false trust, to disengage our hearts from all secret hiding places, and to bring us out into the open where we can discover for ourselves whether we actually trust Him. This is a harsh cure, but it is a sure one!

April 26

Christian Couples: Heirs Together of the Grace of Life

. . .Giving honour unto the wife, as unto the weaker vessel, and as being heirs together of the grace of life. . . . 1 Peter 3:7

The Scriptures teach that the Christian husband and wife are heirs together of the grace of life—that they are one in Jesus Christ, their Saviour!

I suppose there are many Christian husbands whose prayers are not being answered and they can think up a lot of reasons. But the fact is that thoughtless husbands are simply big, overbearing clods when it comes to consideration of their wives.

If the husband would get himself straightened out in his own mind and spirit and live with his wife according to knowledge, and treat her with the chivalry that belongs to her as the weaker vessel, remembering that she is actually his sister in Christ, his prayers would be answered in spite of the devil and all of the other reasons that he gives.

A husband's spiritual problems do not lie in the Kremlin nor in the Vatican but in the heart of the man himself—in his attitude and inability to resist the temptation to grumble and growl and dominate!

There is no place for that kind of male rulership in any Christian home. What the Bible calls for is proper and kindly recognition of the true relationships of understanding and love, and the acceptance of a spirit of cooperation between the husband and wife.

April 27

Happiness: Your Whole Ambition to Be Like Jesus

And be not conformed to this world: but be ye transformed by the renewing of your mind, that ye may prove what is that good, and acceptable, and perfect will of God. Romans 12:2

The assumption that human beings are born "to be happy" is scarcely questioned by anyone in today's society and the effect of this modern hedonism is felt also among the people of God.

The Christian gospel is too often presented as a means toward happiness, to peace of mind or security. There are even those who use the Bible to "relax" them, as if it were a drug.

How far wrong all this is will be discovered easily by the simple act of reading the New Testament through once, with meditation. There the emphasis is not upon happiness but upon holiness. God is more concerned with the state of people's hearts than with the state of their feelings.

Undoubtedly the will of God brings final happiness to those who obey, but the most important matter is not how happy we are but how holy!

The childish clamor after happiness can become a real snare. One may easily deceive himself by cultivating a religious joy without a correspondingly righteous life.

For those who take this whole thing seriously I have a suggestion: Go to God and have an understanding. Tell Him that it is your desire to be holy at any cost and then ask Him never to give you more happiness than holiness! Be assured that in the end you will be as happy as you are holy; but for the time being let your whole ambition be to serve God and be Christlike!

April 28

Sensitive to Religion—but Living like the Devil

. . .Nevertheless when the Son of man cometh, shall he find faith on the earth? Luke 18:8

In our day you can find plenty of men and women in all walks of life who live like the devil while insisting that they are "sensitive" to religion!

If an evangelist sweeps through and the excitement gets big enough, they will go to the meeting and swell the crowd and contribute to the offering—and it will look big.

But here's the catch: after it is all over, the moral standards of the community are right where they were before. I contend that whatever does not raise the moral standard and consciousness of the church or community has not been a revival from God.

The "god" that men believe in now, and to whom they are "sensitive," is a kind of divine Pan with a pipe who plays lovely music while they dance, but he is not a God that makes any moral demands on them.

I still say that any revival that will come to a nation and leave people as much in love with money as they were before and as engrossed in human pleasures is a snare and a delusion!

True faith in God—not in any god, not in religion, but faith in the sovereign God who made heaven and earth and who will require men's deeds—that is the God we must believe in, my friends. Believing in Him, we will seek to crucify our flesh and put on the new man which is renewed in holiness.

That kind of faith in God is all but gone. When the Son of Man cometh, will He find faith on the earth?

_____

Revival Blessings Flow from God's Promises

Rejoice in the Lord alway: and again I say, Rejoice. Philippians 4:4

One characteristic that is largely lacking in the average church today is that of spiritual anticipation.

When Christians meet, they do not expect anything unusual to happen: consequently, only the usual happens, and that usual is as predictable as the setting of the sun.

A psychology of nonexpectation pervades the assembly, a mood of quiet ennui which the minister by various means tries to dispel, the means depending upon the cultural level of the congregation and particularly of the minister.

Christian expectation in the average church follows the program, not the promises. The activities of the saints are laid out for them by those who are supposed to know what they need better than they do. Prevailing spiritual conditions, however low, are accepted as inevitable—what will be is what has been!

The weary slaves of the dull routine find it impossible to hope for anything better.

Today we need a fresh spirit of anticipation that springs out of the promises of God! We must declare war on the mood of nonexpectation, and come together with childlike faith. Only then can we know again the beauty and wonder of the Lord's presence among us.

God Spoke—and It Was Done

In the beginning was the Word, and the Word was with God, and the Word was God. John 1:1

The whole Bible supports the idea that it is the nature of God to speak, to communicate His thoughts to others.

"In the beginning was the Word"—a word is a medium by which thoughts are expressed, and the application of the term to the Eternal Son leads us to believe that self-expression is inherent in the Godhead, and that God is forever seeking to speak Himself out to His creation.

It is not just that God spoke: but God is speaking! He is by His nature continuously articulate. He fills the world with His speaking voice.

One of the great realities with which we have to deal is the Voice of God in His world. The briefest and only satisfying cosmogony is this: "He spake, and it was done!" The "why" of natural law is the living Voice of God in His creation.

This word of God which brought all worlds into being cannot be understood to mean the Bible, for it is the expression of the will of God spoken into the structure of all things. This word of God is the breath of God filling the world with living potentiality. The Voice of God is the most powerful force in nature, for all energy is here only because the power-filled Word is being spoken!

Holy, Holy, Holy: Kneel at Jesus' Feet

My brethren, have not the faith of our Lord Jesus Christ, the Lord of glory, with respect of persons. James 2:1

A system of literature has grown up around the notion that Christianity may be proven by the fact that "great men" believe in Christ!

A magazine article carries the caption that "Senator So-and-So Believes in Christ." The implication is that if the senator believes in Christ, then Christ must be all right.

When did Jesus Christ have to ride in on the coattail of a senator, or a governor, or some other well known man?

No, no, my brother! Jesus Christ stands alone, unique and supreme, self-validating, and the Holy Ghost declares Him to be God's eternal Son. Let all the presidents and all the kings and queens, the senators, and the lords and ladies of the world, along with the great athletes and great actors—let them kneel at His feet and cry, "Holy, holy, holy is the Lord God Almighty!"

Only the Holy Ghost can do this, my brethren. For that reason, I don't bow down to great men. I bow down to the Great Man, and if you have learned to worship the Son of Man, you will not worship other men.

The Holy Spirit is God's imperative of life. If Christ is to be the Christ of God rather than the Christ of intellect, then we must enter in beyond the veil, until the illumination of the Holy Spirit fills our hearts and we are learning at the feet of Jesus—not at the feet of men!

Christs Does in Us What We Cannot Do

When Christ, who is our life, shall appear, then shall ye also appear with him in glory. Colossians 3:4

Writing to the Corinthian believers, Paul promised full spiritual deliverance and stability in the knowledge that Jesus Christ "is made unto us wisdom, righteousness, sanctification and redemption." He also assured the Colossian believers: "You are complete in Him!"

Our great need, then, is simply Jesus Christ. He is what we need. He has what we need. He knows what we need to know. He has the ability to do in us what we cannot do—working in us that which is well-pleasing in God's sight.

This is a difficult point in spiritual doctrine and life for many people who may have been prominent and ambitious, and used to doing their own thing in their own way!

But no matter who we are, we must acknowledge that it is a gracious plan and provision for men and women in the kindness and wisdom of God. Brothers and sisters , we get Christ and glory and fruitfulness, a future and the world to come and the spirits of just men made perfect; we get Jesus, mediator of a new covenant, and the blood of the everlasting covenant; an innumerable company of angels and the church of the firstborn and the New Jerusalem, the city of the living God!

And before we get all that, we have the privilege and the prospect of loving and joyful service for Christ and for mankind on this earth!

May 3

Let Nothing Keep Us from Communion with God

Heaven and earth shall pass away, but my words shall not pass away.
Matthew 24:35

We being what we are and all things else being what they are, the most important and profitable study any of us can engage in is without question the study of theology.

That theology probably receives less attention than any other subject tells us nothing about its importance or lack of it. It indicates, rather, that men are still hiding from the presence of God among the trees of the garden and feel acutely uncomfortable when the matter of their relation to God is brought up!

They sense their deep alienation from God and only manage to live at peace with themselves by forgetting that they are not at peace with God.

It is precisely because God IS, and because man is made in His image and is accountable to Him, that theology is so critically important. Christian revelation alone has the answer to life's unanswered questions about God and human destiny.

To let these authoritative answers lie neglected while we search everywhere else for answers and find none is, it seems to me, nothing less than folly!

Whatever keeps me from the Bible is my enemy, however harmless it may appear to me. Whatever engages my attention when I should be meditating on God and things eternal does injury to my soul. Let the cares of life crowd out the Scriptures from my mind and I have suffered loss where I can least afford it. The secret of life is theological and the key to heaven, as well!

May 4

Man Though Guilty, Is Offered God's Mercy

For when we were yet without strength, in due time Christ died for the ungodly. Romans 5:6

It is vital to any understanding of ourselves and our fellowmen that we believe what is written in the Scriptures about human society—that it is fallen, alienated from God and in rebellion against His laws!

There is plenty of good news in the Bible, but there is never any flattery or back scratching, and what God has spoken is never complimentary to men.

Seen one way, the Bible is a book of doom. It condemns all men as sinners and declares that the soul that sinneth shall die. Always it pronounces sentence against society before it offers mercy; and if we will not own the validity of the sentence we cannot admit the need for mercy!

The coming of Jesus Christ to the world has been so sentimentalized that it means now something utterly alien to the Bible teaching concerning it. Soft human pity has been substituted for God's mercy in the minds of millions, a pity that has long ago degenerated into self-pity. The blame for man's condition has somehow been shifted to God, and Christ's dying for the world has been twisted into an act of penance on God's part. In the drama of redemption, man is viewed as Miss Cinderella who has long been oppressed and mistreated, but now through the heroic deeds of earth's noblest Son is about to don her radiant apparel and step forth a queen. This is humanism—romantically tinted with Christianity!

Lean Back on the Keeping Power of God

. . .Kept by the power of God through faith unto salvation ready to be revealed in the last time. 1 Peter 1:5

Christian believers need always to be leaning back very strongly on the keeping power of God!

The Apostle Peter says plainly that those who are elect, begotten, obedient and believing have this power of God reflected in their daily lives.

Elect: that is God's business and it was His business before we knew anything about it!

Begotten: that is God's business as we believe in His Son!

Obedient and believing: we who are kept by the power of God through faith unto an inheritance!

So there we are—and as Christians, we are not only rich but nobly rich! Rich with riches which need no apology. Riches which have no taint of having come to us through defiled hands.

I wonder when we will begin to behave and to live on the level of our spiritual riches instead of acting like poverty-stricken creatures trying to crawl under a leaf so we will not be seen?

Let's let the world know how rich we really are! Let's tell it—we are being kept by the power of God unto an inheritance reserved in heaven for us!

That is the full-time business of the child of God!

May 6

Prayerful Thoughts of God Are Never a Burden

. . .The effectual, fervent prayer of a righteous man availeth much. James 5:16

It is hardly possible to overstress the importance of unceasing inward prayer on the part of the one who would live the God-conscious life. Prayer at stated times is good and right; we will never outgrow our need of it while we remain on earth. But this kind of prayer must be supported and perfected by the habit of constant, unspoken prayer!

But someone may question whether in a world like this it is possible to think of God constantly. Would it not be too great a burden to try to keep God constantly in the focus of our minds while carrying on our normal activities in this noisy and highly complex civilization?

Malaval had the answer to this: "The wings of the dove do not weigh it down," he said; "they carry and support it. And so the thought of God is never a burden; it is a gentle breeze which bears us up, a hand which supports us and raises us, a light which guides us, and a spirit which vivifies us though we do not feel its working."

We all know how the presence of someone we deeply love lifts our spirits and suffuses us with a radiant sense of peace and well-being. So the one who loves God supremely is lifted into rapture by His conscious Presence!

"Then were the disciples glad, when they saw the Lord."

Most Important: Your Names Written in Heaven

. . .Be ye steadfast, unmoveable, always abounding in the work of the Lord, forasmuch as ye know that your labour is not in vain in the Lord. 1 Corinthians 15:58

Those who are active in Christian service must beware of two opposite pitfalls: the elation that comes with success on the one hand, or the discouragement that comes with failure, on the other.

These may be considered by some as trivial, but the history of the Christian ministry will not support this conclusion. They are critically dangerous and should be guarded against with great care.

The disciples returned to Christ with brimming enthusiasm, saying, "Lord, even the devils are subject unto us through thy name," and He quickly reminded them of another being who had allowed success to go to his head.

"I beheld Satan as lightning fall from heaven," He said. "In this rejoice not, that the spirits are subject unto you; but rather rejoice, because your names are written in heaven."

The second of these twin dangers need not be labored. Every minister of the gospel knows how hard it is to stay spiritual when his work appears to be fruitless. Yet he is required to rejoice in God as certainly when he is having a bad year as when he is seeing great success, and to lean heavily upon Paul's assurance that "your labour is not in vain in the Lord."

Place the Greatest Value on Godliness

He that spared not his own Son, but delivered him up for us all, how shall he not with him freely give us all things? Romans 8:32

Were the church a pure and Spirit-filled body, wholly led and directed by spiritual considerations, certainly the purest and the saintliest men and women would be the ones most appreciated and most honored, but the opposite is true!

Godliness is no longer valued, except for the very old or the very dead!

The saintly souls are forgotten in the whirl of religious activity. The noisy, the self-assertive, the entertaining are sought after and rewarded in every way, with gifts, crowds, offerings and publicity. The Christlike, the self-forgetting, the otherworldly are jostled aside to make room for the latest converted playboy who is usually not too well converted and still very much a playboy.

The whole shortsighted philosophy that ignores eternal qualities and majors in trivialities is a form of unbelief. These Christians who embody such a philosophy are clamoring after present reward; they are too impatient to wait for the Lord's time! The true saint sees farther than this; he cares little for passing values; he looks forward eagerly to the day when eternal things shall come into their own, and godliness will be found to be all that matters.

The wise Christian will be content to wait for that day, and in the meantime, he will serve his generation in the will of God!

It Is Not Fanatical to Love God Supremely

While ye have light, believe in the light, that ye may be the children of light. . . . John 12:36

One of the marks of our modern time is the fact that many are guilty of merely "nibbling" at the truth of the Christian gospel.

If the cross of Jesus Christ means what it should to us and we know that we must carry it and die on it and then rise and live above it, we will have a constant desire to advance and gain spiritual ground!

The nervous people who want to put on the brakes, who feel the necessity for restraint in matters of spiritual desire and yearning for perfection, often use the expression, "Let's not get fanatical about this."

I can only ask: Is it fanaticism to want to go on until you can perfectly love God and perfectly praise Him?

Is it fanatical to find divine joy leaping up within your heart? Is it fanatical to find the willingness within your heart to say, "Yes, Lord! Yes, Lord!" and thus live daily in the will of God so that you are living in heaven while you are living on the earth?

If this is fanaticism, then it is the fanaticism of the Old Testament patriarchs and the Law; it is the fanaticism of the psalmist and of the prophets and the New Testament writers, as well!

Human Suffering: Learn What God Says about It

For in that he himself hath suffered being tempted, he is able to succour them that are tempted. Hebrews 2:18

Anything that gets as much space as the doctrine of human suffering gets in the Scriptures should certainly receive careful, reverent attention from children of the new creation.

We cannot afford to neglect it, for whether we understand it or not we are going to experience some suffering.

From the first cold shock that brings a howl of protest from the newborn infant, down to the last anguished gasp of the aged man, pain and suffering dog our footsteps as we journey here below. It will pay us to learn what God says about it so that we may know how to act and what to expect when it comes.

Because suffering is a real part of human life, Christ Himself took part in the same and learned obedience by the things which He suffered.

It should be said that there is a kind of suffering which profits no one: it is the bitter and defiant suffering of the lost. The man out of Christ may endure any degree of affliction without being any the wiser or the better for it.

There is a common suffering which we must share with all the sons of men—loss, bereavement, heartaches, disappointments, partings, betrayals and griefs of a thousand sorts.

But there is such a thing as consecrated griefs, sorrows that may be common to everyone but which take on a special character when accepted intelligently and offered to God in loving submission.

May 11

Many Christians Still Taking the Broad Road

For many deceivers are entered into the world, who confess not that Jesus Christ is come in the flesh. . . . 2 John 1:7

Deception has always been an effective weapon and is deadliest when used in the field of religion.

Our Lord warned against this when He said, "Beware of false prophets, which come to you in sheep's clothing, but inwardly they are ravening wolves." These words have been turned into a proverb known around the world, and still we continue to be taken in by the wolves.

There was a time, even in the twentieth century, when a Christian knew, or at least could know, where he stood. The words of Christ were taken seriously. A man either was or was not a believer in New Testament doctrine. Clear, sharp categories existed. Black stood in sharp contrast to white; light was separated from darkness; it was possible to distinguish right from wrong, truth from error, a true believer from an unbeliever. Christians knew that they must forsake the world, and there was for the most part remarkable agreement about what was meant by the world. It was that simple.

The whole religious picture has changed. Without denying a single doctrine of the faith, multitudes of Christians have nevertheless forsaken the faith. Anyone who makes a claim to having "accepted Christ" is admitted at once into the goodly fellowship of the prophets and the glorious company of the apostles regardless of the worldliness of his life or the vagueness of his doctrinal beliefs. We can only insist that the way of the cross is still a narrow way!

May 12

The Erotic Is Rapidly Displacing the Spiritual

Teaching us that, denying ungodliness and worldly lusts, we should live soberly, righteously, and godly, in this present world. Titus 2:12

The period in which we now live may well go down in history as the Erotic Age. Sex love has been elevated into a cult. Eros has more worshipers among civilized men today than any other god. For millions, the erotic has completely displaced the spiritual!

Contributing factors are the phonograph and radio, which can spread a love song from coast to coast within a matter of days; the motion picture and television, which enable a whole population to feast their eyes on sensuous women and amorous young men locked in passionate embrace (and this in the living rooms of "Christian" homes and before the eyes of innocent children!). Add to these the myriad of shrewdly contrived advertising campaigns which make sex the not too slyly concealed bait to attract buyers for almost every imaginable product; and degraded columnists who have consecrated their lives to the task of the publicizing of soft, slinky nobodies with the faces of angels and the morals of alley cats.

Now if this god Eros would let us Christians alone I for one would let his cult alone for the whole spongy, fetid mess will sink some day under its own weight and become excellent fuel for the fires of hell. But the cult of Eros is seriously affecting the Christian church.

When God's sheep are in danger the shepherd is morally obliged to grab his weapon and run to their defense. For much of this century timidity disguised as humility has crouched in her corner while the spiritual quality of evangelical Christianity has become progressively worse year by year. How long, O Lord, how long?

May 13

Our Thoughts Reveal What We Are Becoming

. . .If there be any virtue, and if there be any praise, think on these things.
Philippians 4:8

The Bible has a great deal to say about our thoughts; current evangelicalism has practically nothing to say about them. The reason the Bible says so much is that our thoughts are so vitally important to us. The reason evangelicalism says so little is that we are overreacting from the "thought" cults, which would make our thoughts to be very nearly everything and we counter by making them nothing. Both positions are wrong.

Our voluntary thoughts not only reveal what we are—they predict what we will become. The will can become the servant of the thoughts, and to a large degree even our emotions follow our thinking. Thinking stirs feeling and feeling triggers action. That is the way we are made and we may as well accept it.

Thinking about God and holy things creates a moral climate favorable to the growth of faith and love and humility and reverence. We cannot by our thinking regenerate our hearts, nor take our sins away nor change the leopard's spots. But we can by Spirit-inspired thinking help to make our minds pure sanctuaries in which God will be pleased to dwell.

The best way to control our thoughts is to offer the mind to God in complete surrender. The Holy Spirit will accept it and take control of it immediately. Then it will be relatively easy to think on spiritual things, especially if we train our thought by long periods of daily prayer, even talking to God inwardly as we work or travel.

The Characteristic of the Prophet Is Always Love

. . .We were willing to have imparted unto you, not the gospel of God only, but also our own souls, because ye were dear unto us. 1 Thessalonians 2:8

If evangelical Christianity is to stay alive she must repudiate the weaklings who dare not speak out, and she must seek in prayer and much humility the coming again of men of the stuff prophets and martyrs are made of!

God will hear the cries of His people as He heard the cries of Israel in Egypt. And He will send deliverance by sending deliverers. It is His way among men.

A characteristic of the true prophet has always been love. The free man who has learned to hear God's voice and dared to obey it has felt the moral burden that broke the hearts of the Old Testament prophets, crushed the soul of our Lord Jesus Christ and wrung streams of tears from the eyes of the apostles.

The free man has never been a religious tyrant, nor has he sought to lord it over God's heritage. It is fear and lack of self-assurance that has led men to try to crush others under their feet. These have had some interest to protect, some position to secure, so they have demanded subjection from their followers as a guarantee of their own safety.

But the free man—never; he has nothing to protect, no ambition to pursue and no enemy to fear. For that reason he is completely careless of his standing among men. Whether accepted or rejected he will go on loving his people with sincere devotion, and only death can silence his tender intercession for them!

May 15

Polite Society: "Religion Must Not Get Personal"

And their words seemed to them as idle tales, and they believed them not.
Luke 24:11

I remind you that it is characteristic of the natural man to keep himself so busy with unimportant trifles that he is able to avoid settling the most important matters relating to life and existence.

Men and women will gather anywhere and everywhere to talk about every subject from the latest fashions on up to Plato and philosophy—up and down the scale! They talk about the necessity for peace. They may talk about the church and how it can be a bulwark against communism. None of these things are embarrassing subjects.

But the conversation all stops and the taboo of silence becomes effective when anyone dares to suggest that there are spiritual subjects of vital importance to our souls that ought to be discussed and considered. There seems to be an unwritten rule in polite society that if any religious subjects are to be discussed, it must be within the framework of theory—"never let it get personal!"

All the while, there is really only one thing that is of vital and lasting importance—the fact that our Lord Jesus Christ "was wounded for our transgressions; he was bruised for our iniquities; the chastisement of our peace was upon him; and with his stripes we are healed."

May 16

A Silent Christian: Is That Possible?

. . .and with the mouth confession is made unto salvation. Romans 10:10

The Bible links faith to expression—and faith that never gets expression is not a Bible faith. We are told to believe in our hearts and confess with our lips that Jesus Christ is Lord, and we shall be saved.

It is my opinion, brethren, that the silent Christian has something wrong with him!

Psychologists try to deal with abnormal human behavior, linked to deep depression, where people just go into silence. They will not talk—they will not respond. They just shut up, and that's all.

There is something wrong with the mind that does not want to talk and communicate. God gave each of us a mouth and He meant for us to use it to express some of the wonders that generate within our beings.

Someone describing the Quakers said they did not talk about their religion—they lived it. That is a foolish simplification—for the things that are closest to our hearts are the things we talk about and if God is close to our hearts, we will talk about Him!

This quiet religion that apologizes: "I haven't anything to say" does not square with the vision of the heavenly beings who say with their voices, "Holy, holy, holy!"

You may say: "Well, I worship God in my heart."

I wonder if you do. I wonder if you are simply excusing the fact that you have not generated enough spiritual heat to get your mouth open!

God Does Not Have Power: God Is Power

God hath spoken once; twice have I heard this; that power belongeth unto God. Psalm 62:11

It is hard for us sons of the machine age to remember that there is no power apart from God! Whether physical, intellectual, moral or spiritual, power is contained in God, flows out from Him and returns to Him again. The power that works throughout His creation remains in Him even while it operates in an atom or a galaxy!

The notion that power is something God separates from Himself and tosses out to work apart from Him is erroneous. The power of nature is the Presence of God in the universe. This idea is woven into the Book of Job, the Psalms and the Prophets.

The writings of John and Paul in the New Testament harmonize with this Old Testament doctrine, and in the Book of Hebrews it is said that Christ upholds all things by the word of His power.

We must not think of the power of God as wild, irrational energy coursing haphazardly through the world like a lightning stroke or a tornado. This is the impression sometimes created by Bible teachers who keep reminding us that *dunamis,* the Greek word for power, is the root from which comes our word "dynamite." Little wonder that sensitive Christians shrink from contact with such a destructive and unpredictable force.

The power of God is not something God has: it is something God is! Power is something that is true of God as wisdom and love are true of Him. It is, if we might so state it, a fact of His being, one with and indivisible from everything else that He is. The power of God is one with God's will and works only as He wills that it should. It is His holy Being in action!

May 18

The Great Unseen Reality Is God Himself

Let not your heart be troubled: ye believe in God, believe also in me. John 14:1

At the root of the Christian life lies belief in the invisible. The object of the Christian's faith is unseen reality.

In the world of sense around us, the visible becomes the enemy of the invisible; the temporal, of the eternal. That is the curse inherited by every member of Adam's race.

Our uncorrected thinking, influenced by the blindness of our natural hearts and the intrusive ubiquity of visible things, tends to draw a contrast between the spiritual and the real; but actually no such contrast exists. The antithesis lies elsewhere: between the real and the imaginary, between the spiritual and the material, between the temporal and the eternal; but between the spiritual and the real, never! The spiritual is real.

If we would rise into that region of light and power plainly beckoning us through the Scriptures of truth we must break the evil habit of ignoring the spiritual. We must shift our interest from the seen to the unseen.

For the great unseen Reality is God! "He that cometh to God must believe that he is, and that he is a rewarder of them that diligently seek him." This is basic in the life of faith. From there we can rise to unlimited heights.

"Ye believe in God," said our Lord Jesus Christ, "believe also in me." Without the first, there can be no second.

God and the spiritual world are real. We can reckon upon them with as much assurance as we reckon upon the familiar world around us!

May 19

God Would Impart Himself with His Gifts

And God is able to make all grace abound toward you; that ye, always having all sufficiency in all things, may abound to every good work. 2 Corinthians 9:8

Have you had any part in the modern cheapening of the Christian gospel by making God your servant? Have you allowed leanness to come to your soul because you have been expecting that God would come around with a basket, giving away presents?

I feel that we must repudiate this great modern wave of seeking God for His benefits. Anyone can write a best-selling book now—just give it a title like "Seventeen Ways to Get Things from God!"

I would say there are millions who do not seem to know or understand that God wants to give Himself! He wants to impart Himself with His gifts. Any gift that He would give us would be incomplete if it were separated from the knowledge of God Himself.

If I should pray for all of the spiritual gifts listed in Paul's epistles and the Spirit of God should see fit to give them, it would be extremely dangerous for me if, in the giving, God did not give Himself as well.

It is a fact that God has created an environment for all of His creatures. Because God made man in His image and redeemed him, the heart of God Himself is the true environment for the Christian. If there is grief in heaven, I think it must come because we want God's gifts but we do not want God Himself as our environment!

No Task Is Too Big If God Is in It

But Jesus beheld them, and said. . .With men this is impossible; but with God all things are possible. Matthew 19:26.

Young people are concerned and some people are worried, they say, about whether we have the infallible Word of God.

As far as I am concerned, grant me God Himself, and I am not worried about His writing a book. Grant me the Being and Presence of God, and that settles it!

Whenever I find men running to science to find support for the Bible, I know they are rationalists and not true believers!

If God said that Jonah was swallowed by a whale, then the whale swallowed Jonah, and we do not need a scientist to measure the gullet of the whale.

Why are we fussing around finding out the collar size of a whale, or how big his neck is? Grant me God and miracles take care of themselves!

"Is healing for us today?" someone asks.

My reply to that: "Is God still alive?"

And the answer is, "Yes, God is still alive!"

All right, then, healing is for us today. Whatever God did and was able to do and willing to do at any time, God is able and willing to do again, within the framework of His will.

It is not whether we can understand it or not, it is whether God said it or not. If God said "I AM," I respectfully bow and say, "O God, Thou art!"

Letting God prove Himself through the channels of our lives is the answer. Grant me God, and the task will not be too big!

Hope in Ethics: Utterly Unrealistic and Naive

Then shall the King say unto them on his right hand, Come, ye blessed of my Father, inherit the kingdom prepared for you from the foundation of the world. Matthew 25:34

The hope being voiced by many that the nations will "accept the ethics of Jesus, disarm and live like brothers," is utterly unrealistic and naive.

In the first place, the teachings of Jesus were never intended for the nations of the world. Our Lord sent His followers into all the world to make and baptize disciples. These disciples were to be taught to observe the commandments of Christ.

They would thus become a minority group, a peculiar people, in the world but not of it, sometimes tolerated but more often despised and persecuted. And history demonstrates that this is exactly what happened wherever groups of people took the gospel seriously.

To expect of once-born nations conduct possible only to the regenerated, purified, Spirit-led followers of Christ is to confuse the truth of Christianity and hope for the impossible. In the Scriptures, the nations of the earth are symbolized by the lion, the bear and the leopard.

Christians, in sharp contrast, are likened to peaceful sheep in the midst of wolves, who manage to stay alive only by keeping close to the Shepherd. If the sheep will not act like the bear why should we expect the bear to act like the sheep?

It might be well for us Christians to listen less to the news commentators and more to the voice of the Spirit!

May 22

God Stands Ready to Confirm Our Faith in Him

This Jesus hath God raised up, whereof we are all witnesses. Acts 2:32

The difference between faith as it is found in the New Testament and faith as it is found now, is that the faith in the New Testament actually produced something—there was a confirmation of it!

On the day of Pentecost, Peter stood up and then he lifted up his voice. I would remind you that Peter here stands for the whole Church of God. Peter was the first man to get on his feet after the Holy Spirit had come. Peter had believed the Lord's word and he had received confirmation in his own heart.

In our day faith is pretty much a beginning and an end. We have faith in faith—but nothing happens. There is no confirmation. Peter placed his faith in a risen Christ and something did happen. That's the difference!

As in Peter's case, it should be the business of the church to stand up and lift up. Peter became a witness on earth, as the church should be, to things in heaven. The church must be a witness to powers beyond the earthly and the human, and because I know this, it is a source of great grief to me that the church is trying to run on its human powers.

Peter testified to something beyond the earthly which he had experienced. He wanted to influence, urge and exhort those who had not yet experienced it to enter in, for the power from above turns out to be none other than the Spirit of God Himself!

Find Something Better Than Spiritual Curiosity

. . .I am come that they might have life, and that they may have it more abundantly. John 10:10

If the only interest we have in the deeper spiritual life is based on curiosity, it is not enough—regardless of our education or scholarship!

In our day we have seen a great revival of interest in mysticism, and supposedly a great interest in the deeper life. But I find that much of this interest is academic and is based on curiosity. We become interested in aspects of the deeper Christian life much as we become interested in mastering the yo-yo or folk songs or dabbling in Korean architecture or anything else that intrigues us. You can go anywhere now and buy a book about the deeper life because there are curious persons who are swelling the market.

It has been suggested that we should not "waste our time" in trying to help those who are merely curious. But I differ at this point, because it is Jesus' blood that makes the difference and it is because of this hope by the blood of Jesus that any of us may be worthy to listen.

We must leave the sorting out to God! The testing in the matters of spiritual life is by the Spirit of God, not by pastors and preachers. We dare not withhold the open secret of the victorious life because there are those who are merely curious and without true desire.

God's Plain, Good People: Always a Benediction

For he was a good man, and full of the Holy Ghost and of faith: and much people were added unto the Lord. Acts 11:24

We ought to thank God for the examples in the Bible of so many men who were good—even though they were not considered great!

We are grateful not that they failed to achieve greatness but that by the grace of God they managed to acquire plain goodness.

These men move quietly enough across the pages of the Bible, but where they walk there is pleasant weather and good companionship. Such was Isaac, who was the son of a great father and the father of a great son, but who himself never rose above mediocrity. Such were Boaz the ancestor of King David, Joseph the husband of Mary, and Barnabas the son of consolation.

Every pastor knows this kind—the plain people who have nothing to recommend them but their deep devotion to their Lord and the fruit of the Spirit which they all unconsciously display. These are the first to come forward when there is work to be done and the last to go home when there is prayer to be made.

Their presence is a benediction wherever they go. They have no greatness to draw to them the admiring eyes of carnal men but are content to be good men and full of the Holy Ghost!

When they die they leave behind them a fragrance of Christ that lingers long after the cheap celebrities of the day are forgotten.

We extend this tribute to Christian brothers and sisters in spite of the fact that in our world there is not supposed to be anything dramatic in faithfulness or newsworthy in goodness!

May 25

Are You a Settled and Contented Christian?

. . .Let us go on unto perfection. . . . Hebrews 6:1

I wonder why the people of God in our churches are so reluctant to leave the things which are the "first principles" of the doctrine of Christ?

Some of you have heard the gospel many times. You say you have believed and that you have turned away from idols to serve the living God and to wait for His Son from heaven—and yet you do not behave as though you are a settled and contented Christian!

You are not satisfied until you have tried out the latest gospel peddler or the sensationally popular evangelistic services down the street.

If a gospel troupe comes along, you are satisfied for a while because they have cowbells and a musical handsaw and a lot of other gadgets.

In our day we seem to overlook the divine principle of what ought to happen in the life of a truly born-again person. What do we do? We get them into church and then after we get them in, we try to "work" on them.

My reading tells me that in an earlier day believers were better Christians when they were newly converted than many of today's so-called deeper life people—because a miracle had taken place!

They would not accept a pale, ineffective and apologetic "believing." They insisted on a miracle taking place in the human breast. Jesus Christ was their Hope, and they knew full well the guarantee—God had raised Him from the dead!

May 26

Primary Meaning of Pentecost: Christ Is Exalted

Therefore let all the house of Israel know assuredly, that God hath made that same Jesus, whom ye have crucified, both Lord and Christ. Acts 2:36

When you give yourself to prayerful study of the opening chapters of the Book of Acts, you will discover a truth that is often overlooked—the thought that wherever Jesus is glorified, the Holy Spirit comes!

Contrary to what most people unintentionally assume, the important thing was that Jesus had been exalted. The emphasis upon the coming of the Spirit was possible because Christ's work was accomplished and He was glorified at the Father's right hand.

Jesus Himself had said on that last great day of the feast in Jerusalem, recorded in John 7: "He that believeth on me, as the scriptures hath said, out of his belly shall flow rivers of living water. (But this spake he of the Spirit, which they that believe on him should receive: for the Holy Ghost was not yet given; because Jesus was not yet glorified.)"

It is plain that the glorification of Jesus brought the Holy Spirit, and we ought to be able to get hold of that thought instantly. So, we repeat: Where Jesus is glorified, the Holy Spirit comes. He does not have to be begged. When Christ the Saviour is truly honored and exalted, the Spirit comes!

On the day of Pentecost, when the scoffers and scorners said "These men are full of new wine," Peter stood and exalted Jesus of Nazareth and reminded Israel "that God hath made that same Jesus, whom ye crucified, both Lord and Christ." When Christ is truly honored, the Spirit comes!

The Holy Spirit Is to Us All Jesus Would Be

. . .Be filled with the Spirit. Ephesians 5:18

When we think of the Person of the Holy Spirit, we should think of Him as gracious, loving, kind and gentle—just like our Lord Jesus Christ Himself!

When the Scripture says, "Grieve not the Holy Spirit of God," it is telling us that He loves us so much that when we insult Him, He is grieved; when we ignore Him, He is grieved; when we resist Him, He is grieved; and when we doubt Him, He is grieved.

Thankfully, we can please Him by obeying and believing. When we please Him, He responds to us just like a pleased father or loving mother responds. He responds to us because He loves us!

Think of the tragedy and the woe of this hour—that we neglect the most important One who could possibly be in our midst! He is the Holy Spirit of God—yet many are guilty of ignoring and neglecting Him!

Let me assure you that this is the most important thing in the world—that this blessed Holy Spirit is waiting now and can be present with you this minute. Jesus, in His body, is at the right hand of God the Father Almighty, interceding for us. He will be there until He comes again.

But He said He would send another Comforter, the Holy Ghost, His Spirit. We cannot be all that we ought to be for God if we do not believe the Comforter, the Holy Spirit has been sent to be to us all that Jesus would be if He were here now!

May 28

The Holy Spirit: More Than a Poetic Yearning

Howbeit when he, the Spirit of truth is come, he will guide you into all truth. . .and he will show you things to come. John 16:13

The continued neglect of the Holy Spirit by evangelical Christians is too evident to deny or impossible to justify.

Is it not strange that so much is made of the Holy Spirit in the New Testament and so little in Christian writings supposed to be based upon the New Testament? One of the church fathers, in a treatise on the Trinity written in the third century, defended the deity of the Spirit yet said twenty times as much about the Father and the Son as about the Spirit.

It is only fair to admit that there is more in the New Testament about the Son than about the Spirit, but the disproportion is surely not so great as in the writings referred to above, and certainly the all but total neglect of the Spirit in contemporary Christianity cannot be justified by the Scriptures.

In the Scriptures, the Holy Spirit is necessary. There He works powerfully, creatively. In popular Christianity, He is little more than a poetic yearning or at most a benign influence. In the Scriptures He moves in majesty, with all the attributes of the Godhead; here He is a mood, a tender feeling of good will.

Everything that men do in their own abilities is done for time alone: only what is done through the Eternal Spirit will abide eternally!

Spirit Led, We Will Obey the Word of God

And it is the Spirit that beareth witness, because the Spirit is truth. 1 John 5:6

When the Holy Spirit is in full control of our lives, He will expect our obedience to the written Word of God.

But it is part of our human problem that we would like to be full of the Spirit and yet go on and do as we please!

The Holy Spirit who inspired the Scriptures will expect obedience to the Scriptures, and if we do not give that obedience, we will quench Him. This Spirit will have obedience—but people do not want to obey the Lord. Everyone of us is as full as he wants to be. Everyone has as much of God as he desires to have. We do not want to meet the conditions.

Let's use an expensive Cadillac automobile for an illustration. Here is Brother Jones, who would love to drive a Cadillac. But he is not going to buy one, and I will tell you why. He does not want a Cadillac badly enough to be willing to pay the price for it. Certainly he wants it—but he does not want it with that kind of desire—so he is going to continue to drive his old Chevrolet!

Now, it is plain that many people want to be filled with the Spirit, but it is not with that kind of extreme desire that will not be denied. So, we settle for something less!

We do say, "Lord, I would like to be full—it would be wonderful!" but we are not willing to proceed to meet His terms. We do not want to pay the price: the Holy Spirit will expect loving obedience to the Word of God!

Think of the Holy Spirit as a Moral Flame

For to be carnally minded is death; but to be spiritually minded is life and peace:...But ye are not in the flesh, but in the Spirit, if so be that the Spirit of God dwell in you. . . . Romans 8:6, 9

One of the most telling blows which the enemy ever struck at the life of the Church was to create in her a groundless fear of the Holy Spirit! He has been and is so widely misunderstood that the very mention of His Name in some circles is enough to frighten many people into resistance.

Perhaps we may help by examining that fire which is the symbol of the Spirit's Person and Presence.

The Holy Spirit is first of all a moral flame. It is not an accident of language that He is called the HOLY Spirit, for whatever else the word holy may mean it does undoubtedly carry with it the idea of moral purity. And the Spirit, being God, must be absolutely and infinitely pure!

It follows then that whoever would be filled and indwelt by the Spirit should first judge his life for any hidden iniquities; he should courageously expel from his heart everything which is out of accord with the character of God as revealed by the holy Scriptures.

At the base of all true Christian experience must lie a sound and sane morality. No joys are valid, no delights legitimate where sin is allowed to live in life or conduct. No transgression of pure righteousness dare excuse itself on the ground of superior religious experience.

"Be ye holy" is a serious commandment from the Lord of the whole earth. The true Christian ideal is not to be happy but to be holy. The holy heart alone can be the habitation of the Holy Spirit!

God Would Produce Christ's Beauty in Our Lives

And be renewed in the spirit of your mind:. . .put on the new man, which after God is created in righteousness and true holiness. Ephesians 4:23, 24

God is faithful—He is never going to be done with us in shaping us and fashioning us as dear children of God until the day that we will see Him face to face!

Truly, in that gracious day, our rejoicing will not be in the personal knowledge that He saved us from hell, but in the joyful knowledge that He was able to renew us, bringing the old self to an end, and creating within us the new man and the new self in which can be reproduced the beauty of the Son of God!

In the light of that provision, I think it is true that no Christian is where he ought to be spiritually until that beauty of the Lord Jesus Christ is being reproduced in daily Christian life.

I admit that there is necessarily a question of degree in this kind of transformation of life and character.

Certainly there has never been a time in our human existence when we could look into our own being, and say: "Well, thank God, I see it is finished now. The Lord has signed the portrait. I see Jesus in myself!"

Nobody will say that—nobody!

Even though a person has become like Christ, he will not know it, because humility and meekness are also a part of the transformation of true godliness!

June 1

Christ Bridged the Gulf between God and Man

And all things are of God, who hath reconciled us to himself by Jesus Christ. . . . 2 Corinthians 5:18

Paul encouraged the Athenians by reminding them that God was not far from any one of them, that it was He in whom they lived and moved and had their being. Yet men think of Him as farther away than the farthest star. The truth is that He is nearer to us than we are to ourselves!

But how can the conscious sinner bridge the mighty gulf that separates him from God in living experience?

The answer is that he cannot, but the glory of the Christian message is that Christ did! Through the blood of His cross He made peace that He might reconcile all things unto Himself: "And you, that were sometime alienated and enemies in your mind by wicked works, yet now hath he reconciled in the body of his flesh through death, to present you holy and unblameable and unreproveable in his sight" (Col. 1:21, 22).

The new birth makes us partakers of the divine nature. There the work of undoing the dissimilarity between us and God begins. From there it progresses by the sanctifying operation of the Holy Spirit till God is satisfied.

That is the theology of it, but even the regenerated soul may sometimes suffer from the feeling that God is far from him. Put away the evil from you, believe, and the sense of nearness will be restored. God was never away in the first place!

June 2

Our Richest Treasure: Inner Knowledge of God

. . .Ye have dwelt long enough in this mount:. . .Behold, I have set the land before you: go in and possess the land. . . . Deuteronomy 1:6, 8

Large numbers of supposedly sound Christian believers know nothing at all about personal communion with God; and there lies one of the greatest weaknesses of present-day Christianity!

The experiential knowledge of God is eternal life (John 17:3), and increased knowledge results in a correspondingly larger and fuller life. So rich a treasure is this inward knowledge of God that every other treasure is as nothing compared with it!

We may count all things of no value and sacrifice them freely if we may thereby gain a more perfect knowledge of God through Jesus Christ our Lord. This was Paul's testimony (Phil. 3:7-14) and it has been the testimony of all great Christian souls who have followed Christ from Paul's day to ours.

To know God it is necessary that we be like God to some degree, for things wholly dissimilar cannot agree and beings wholly unlike can never have communion with each other. It is necessary therefore that we use every means of grace to bring our souls into harmony with the character of God.

As we move farther up into the knowledge of Christ we open new areas of our beings to attack, but what of it? Remember that spiritual complacency is more deadly than anything the devil can bring against us in our upward struggle. If we sit still to escape temptation, then we are being tempted worse than before and gaining nothing by it.

June 3

Attitude of Worship: Everywhere, All the Time

And whatsoever ye do in word or deed, do all in the name of the Lord Jesus Christ, giving thanks to God and the Father by him. Colossians 3:17

I have to be faithful to what I know to be true, so I must tell you that if you will not worship God seven days a week, you do not worship Him on one day a week!

There is no such thing in heaven as Sunday worship—unless it is accompanied by Monday worship and Tuesday worship and right on through the rest of the week.

Too many of us try to discharge our obligations to God Almighty in one day—usually one trip to church. Sometimes, nobly, we make it two trips to church, but it is all on the same day when we have nothing else to do—and that is supposed to be worship!

I do not say that you must be at church all of the time—how could you be? I am saying that you can worship God at your desk, on an elevated train, or driving in traffic. You can worship God in school, on the basketball court. You can worship God in whatever is legitimate and right and good.

Surely, we can go to church and worship on one day, but it is not true worship unless it is followed by continuing worship in the days that follow. We cannot pray toward the east and walk toward the west and hope for harmony in our beings! You can name the name of Jesus a thousand times, but if you will not follow the nature of Jesus, the name of Jesus will not mean anything to you!

See to it that there is not an hour or a place or an act or a location that is not consecrated and given over to God. You will be worshipping Him—and He will accept it!

June 4

Believe That God Is Infinitely Generous

Whoso is wise, and will observe these things, even they shall understand the lovingkindness of the Lord. Psalm 107:43

To think rightly of God we must conceive of Him as being altogether boundless in His goodness, mercy, love, grace, and in whatever else we may properly attribute to the Deity.

Since God is infinite, whatever He is must be infinite, also; that is, it must be without any actual or conceivable limits. The moment we allow ourselves to think of God as having limits, the one of whom we are thinking is not God but someone or something less than and different from Him.

It is not enough that we acknowledge God's infinite resources; we must believe also that He is infinitely generous to bestow them!

The first is not too great a strain on our faith. Even the deist will admit that the Most High God, possessor of heaven and earth, must be rich beyond the power of man to conceive. But to believe that God is a giver as well as a possessor takes an advanced faith and presupposes that there has been a divine revelation to that effect which gives validity to our expectations. Which indeed there has been—we call this revelation the Bible!

Believing all this, why are we Christians so poverty-stricken? I think it is because we have not learned that God's gifts are meted out according to the taker, not according to the giver!

Though almighty and all-wise, God yet cannot pour a great gift into a small receptacle!

June 5

God's Spirit Is a Gentle, Loving Spirit

To him that overcometh will I grant to sit with me in my throne, even as I also overcame. . . . Revelation 3:21

Genuine holiness of life and spirit can be put into the place of testing without fear! Whenever there is a breakdown of holiness, that is proof there never was any real degree of holiness in the first place.

Whenever Satan has reason to fear a truth very gravely, he produces a counterfeit. He will try to put that truth in such a bad light that the very persons who are most eager to obey it are frightened away from it. Satan is very sly and very experienced in the forming of parodies of truth which he fears the most, and then pawns off his parody as the real thing and soon frightens away the serious-minded saints.

I regret to say that some who have called themselves by a kind of copyrighted name of holiness have allowed the doctrine to harden into a formula which has become a hindrance to repentance, for this doctrine has been invoked to cover up frivolity and covetousness, pride and worldliness.

I have seen the results. Serious, honest persons have turned away from the whole idea of holiness because of those who have claimed it and then lived selfish and conceited lives.

But, brethren, men of God have reminded us in the Word that God does ask and expect us to be holy men and women of God, because we are the children of God! The provision of God by His pure and gentle and loving Spirit is still the positive answer for those who hunger and thirst for the life well pleasing to God!

June 6

True Faith Must Influence Our Daily Living

I am crucified with Christ: nevertheless I live; yet not I, but Christ liveth in me. . . . Galatians 2:20

"Things have come to a pretty pass," said a famous Englishman testily, "when religion is permitted to interfere with our private lives."

To which we may reply that things have come to a worse pass when an intelligent man living in a Protestant country could make such a remark. Had this man never read the New Testament? Had he never heard of Stephen? or Paul? or Peter? Had he never thought about the millions who followed Christ cheerfully to violent death, sudden or lingering, because they did allow their religion to interfere with their private lives?

But we must leave this man to his conscience and his Judge and look into our own hearts. Maybe he but expressed openly what some of us feel secretly. Just how radically has our religion interfered with the neat pattern of our own lives? Perhaps we had better answer that question first.

One picture of a Christian is a man carrying a cross: "If any man will come after me, let him deny himself, and take up his cross, and follow me."

The man with the cross no longer controls his destiny; he lost control when he picked up his cross. That cross immediately became to him an all-absorbing interest, an overwhelming interference. There is but one thing he can do; that is, move on toward the place of crucifixion!

June 7

A Spiritual Rule: Hot Furnace, Cool Chimney

Now we have received. . .the Spirit which is of God; that we might know the things that are freely given to us of God. 1 Corinthians 2:12

In our Christian fellowship two opposite dangers are to be recognized and avoided: they are the cold heart and the hot head!

For downright harmful effects the hot head is often the worst of the two.

The human heart is heretical by nature. Unless well instructed in the Scriptures and fully enlightened by the indwelling Spirit, it may confuse the fervor of the Spirit with the heat of the flesh, and mistake the scintillations of the overheated imagination for the glow of the true Shekinah.

It may be said without qualification that there can never be too much fire if it is the true fire of God, and it can be said as certainly that there cannot be too much cool judgment in religious matters if that judgment is sanctified by the Spirit.

Among the gifts of the Spirit scarcely any one is of greater practical usefulness in these critical times than the gift of discernment. This spiritual gift should be highly valued and frankly sought.

Human sweat can add nothing to the work of the Spirit, especially when it is nerve sweat. The hottest fire of God is cool when it touches the redeemed intellect. It makes the heart glow but leaves the judgment completely calm.

Let love burn on with increasing fervor but bring every act to the test of quiet wisdom. Keep the fire in the furnace where it belongs. An overheated chimney will create more excitement but it is likely to burn the house down. Let the rule be: a hot furnace but a cool chimney!

June 8

We All Stand Daily in the Mercy of God

Let us therefore come boldly unto the throne of grace, that we may obtain mercy, and find grace to help in time of need. Hebrews 4:16

Although God wants His people to be holy as He is holy, He does not deal with us according to the degree of our holiness but according to the abundance of His mercy.

Honesty requires us to admit this!

We do believe in justice and we do believe in judgment. We believe the only reason mercy triumphs over judgment is that God, by a divine, omniscient act of redemption, fixed it so man could escape justice and live in the sea of mercy! The justified man, the man who believes in Jesus Christ, born anew and now a redeemed child of God, lives in that mercy always!

The unjust man, however—the unrepentant sinner—lives in it now in a lesser degree, but the time will come when he will face the judgment of God. Though he had been kept by the mercy of God from death, from insanity, from disease, he can violate that mercy, turn his back on it and walk into judgment. Then it is too late!

Let us pray with humility and repentance for we stand in the mercy of God. What an example we have set for us by the life and faith and spirit of the old Puritan saint, Thomas Hooker, as his death approached.

Those around his bedside said, "Brother Hooker, you are going to receive your reward."

"No, no!" he breathed. "I go to receive mercy!"

June 9

Spiritual Authority: The Word and the Testimony

But there were false prophets also among the people, even as there shall be false teachers among you, who privily shall bring in damnable heresies. . . .
2 Peter 2:1

Whatever it may be in our Christian experience that originates outside the Scriptures should, for that very reason, be suspect until it can be shown to be in accord with them.

If it should be found to be contrary to the Word of revealed truth no true Christian will accept it as being from God. However high the emotional content, no experience can be proved to be genuine unless we can find chapter and verse authority for it in the Scriptures. "To the word and to the testimony" must always be the last and final proof.

Whatever is new or singular should also be viewed with caution until it can furnish scriptural proof of its validity. Throughout the twentieth century quite a number of unscriptural notions have gained acceptance among Christians by claiming that they were among truths that were to be revealed in the last days.

The truth is that the Bible does not teach that there will be new light and advanced spiritual experiences in the latter days; it teaches the exact opposite! Nothing in Daniel or the New Testament epistles can be tortured into advocating the idea that we of the end of the Christian era shall enjoy light that was not known at its beginning.

Beware of any man who claims to be wiser than the apostles or holier than the martyrs of the Early Church. The best way to deal with him is to rise and leave his presence!

June 10

The Wickedness of Unbelief: Making God a Liar

. . .He that believeth not God hath made Him a liar, because he believeth not the record that God gave of his Son. 1 John 5:10

True faith must always rest upon what God is, so it is of utmost importance that, to the limit of our comprehension, we know what He is.

The psalmist said: "They that know thy name will put their trust in Thee," the name of God being the verbal expression of His character, and confidence always rises or falls with known character.

What the psalmist said was simply that they who know God to be the kind of God He is will put their confidence in Him! This is not a special virtue, but the normal direction any mind takes when confronted with the fact. We are so made that we trust good character and distrust its opposite, and that is why unbelief is so intensely wicked!

The character of God, then, is the Christian's final ground of assurance and the solution of many, if not most, of his practical religious problems.

Though God dwells in the center of eternal mystery, there need be no uncertainty about how He will act in any situation covered by His promises. These promises are infallible predictions. God will always do what He has promised to do when His conditions are met. And His warnings are no less predictive: "The ungodly shall not stand in the judgment, nor sinners in the congregation of the righteous" (Ps. 1:5).

We cultivate our knowledge of God and at the same time cultivate our faith. Yet while so doing we look not at our faith but at Christ, its author and finisher!

June 11

Faith Understands: God Framed the Worlds

Through faith we understand that the worlds were framed by the word of God, so that things which are seen were not made of things which do appear. Hebrews 11:3

The human mind requires an answer to the question concerning the origin and nature of all things. The world as we find it must be accounted for in some way. Philosophers and scientists have sought to account for it, the one by speculation, the other by observation, but they have not found the final Truth. Here TRUTH should be spelled indeed with a capital T, for it is nothing less than the Son of God, the Second Person of the blessed Godhead!

Those who believe the Christian revelation know that the universe is a creation. It is not eternal, since it had a beginning, and it is not the result of a succession of happy coincidences whereby an all but infinite number of matching parts accidentally found each other, fell into place and began to hum!

So to believe would require a degree of credulity few persons possess.

Those who have faith are not thrown back upon speculation for the secret of the universe. Faith is an organ of knowledge, and "through faith we understand that the worlds were framed by the word of God, so that things which are seen were not made of things which do appear."

All things came out of the Word, which in the New Testament means the thought and will of God in active expression and is identified with our Lord Jesus Christ!

God's Right: To Ask Obedience of His Creatures

Blessed are they that do his commandments, that they. . .may enter in through the gates into the city. Revelation 22:14

The command to love God with our whole being has seemed to many persons to be impossible of fulfillment, and it may be properly argued that we cannot love by fiat.

Love is too gentle, too frail a creature to spring up at the command of another. It would be like commanding the barren tree to bring forth fruit or the winter forest to be green.

What then can it mean?

The answer is found in the nature of God and of man.

God being who He is must have obedience from His creatures. Man being who he is must render that obedience, and he owes God complete obedience whether or not he feels for Him the faintest trace of love in his heart.

It is a question of the sovereign right of God to require His creatures to obey Him.

Man's first and basic sin was disobedience. When he disobeyed God he violated the claims of divine love with the result that love for God died within him.

Now, what can he do to restore that love to his heart again?

The heart that mourns its coldness toward God needs only to repent its sins, and a new, warm and satisfying love will flood into it. For the act of repentance will bring a corresponding act of God in self-revelation and intimate communion.

Once the seeking heart finds God in personal experience there will be no further problem about loving Him.

June 13

Life's Greatest Honor: Following Christ's Call

Wherefore God also hath highly exalted him, and given him a name which is above every name. Philippians 2:9

The humblest man who heeds the call to follow Christ has an honor far above that given to any king or potentate, for the nations of the earth can bestow only such honor as they possess, while the honor of Christ is supreme over all. God has given Him a name that is above every name!

This being true and being known to the heavenly intelligences, the methods we use to persuade men to follow Christ must seem to them extremely illogical if not downright wrong.

Evangelical Christians commonly offer Christ to mankind as a nostrum to cure their ills, a way out of their troubles, a quick and easy means to the achievement of their personal ends. The message is often so presented as to leave the hearer with the impression that he is being asked to give up much to gain more. And that is not good, however well intentioned it may be!

We are not called to be salesmen, pointing out the good things that will accrue if the right choice is made. No one can come to Christ with the idea of selfish gain in the transaction.

Salvation comes not by "accepting the finished work" or "deciding for Christ." It comes by believing on the Lord Jesus Christ, the whole, living, victorious Lord who, as God and man, fought our fight and won it, accepted our debt as His own and paid it, took our sins and died under them and rose again to set us free. This is the true Christ, and nothing less will do!

Everything God Does Is Worthy of Our Praise

God is a spirit; and they that worship him must worship him in spirit and in truth. John 4:24

It is characteristic of the unregenerate man that he sees God only in nature, and of the immature Christian that he can see God only in grace!

Because sin has injured us so deeply and because the whole transaction of repentance and deliverance from the guilt and power of iniquity makes such a mighty impression upon us emotionally, we naturally tend to appreciate the work of God in redemption more than in nature.

But everything God does is praiseworthy and deserves our deepest admiration. Whether He is making or redeeming a world, He is perfect in all His doings and glorious in all His goings forth.

Yet the long, long ages, however far they may carry us into the mysteries of God, will still find us singing the praises of the Lamb that was slain. For it is hardly conceivable that we sinners can ever forget the wormwood and the gall.

We human sinners above all other creatures have benefited by His grace, so it is altogether natural that we above all others should magnify the blood that bought us and the mercy that pardoned our sins.

Yet we glorify God's redeeming grace no less when we glorify His creating and sustaining power. If we miss seeing God in His works we deprive ourselves of the sight of a royal display of wisdom and power so elevating, so ennobling, so awe-inspiring as to make all attempts at description futile. Such a sight the angels behold day and night forever and ask nothing more to make them perpetually satisfied!

June 15

Scriptural Guidance: Believers May Test Themselves

Beloved, believe not every spirit, but try the spirits whether they are of God: because many false prophets are gone out into the world. 1 John 4:1

The seeker after God's best things is always eager to hear from anyone who offers a way by which he can obtain them. He longs for some new experience, some elevated view of truth, some operation of the Spirit that will raise him above the dead level of religious mediocrity he sees all around him.

These are the times that try men's souls. Our Lord has made it plain not only that there shall be false spirits abroad, endangering our Christian lives, but that they may be identified and known for what they are! I have met Christians who have been led into emotional experiences that were beyond their power to comprehend, and they have inquired eagerly whether or not their experience was of God.

The first test must be: "What has this done to my relationship with and my attitude toward the Lord Jesus Christ?" Do I love God more? Is Jesus Christ still to me the center of all true doctrine? Do I still agree that anything that makes Him less than God has declared Him to be must be rejected?

Again: "How does it affect my attitude toward the Holy Scriptures?" Did this new view of truth spring out of the Word of God itself or was it the result of some stimulus that lay outside the Bible?

Be assured that anything that comes to us from the God of the Word will deepen our love for the Word of God!

June 16

A Possibility: To Mean Right and Still Go Wrong

For this is thankworthy, if a man for conscience toward God endure grief, suffering wrongfully. 1 Peter 2:19

There are areas in our Christian lives where in our effort to be right we may go wrong—so wrong as to lead to spiritual deformity.

To be specific, let me name a few:

When in our determination to be bold we become brazen! Courage and meekness are compatible qualities. Both were found in perfect proportion in Christ, even in conflict with His enemies.

When in our desire to be frank we become rude! Candor without rudeness was always found in the man Christ Jesus. The Christian who boasts that he calls a spade a spade is likely to end by calling everything a spade.

When in our effort to be watchful we become suspicious! Because there are many adversaries the temptation is to see enemies where none exist, or to develop a spirit of hostility to everyone who disagrees with us.

When we seek to be serious and become somber! Gloominess is a defect of character and should never be equated with godliness. Joy is a great therapeutic for the mind.

When we mean to be conscientious and become over-scrupulous! If the devil cannot succeed in destroying the conscience he will settle for making it sick. I know Christians who live in a state of constant distress, fearing that they may displease God. They believe this self-torture to be a proof of godliness, but how wrong they are!

My and Mine: Symptoms of Our Deep Disease

But godliness with contentment is great gain. For we brought nothing into this world, and it is certain we can carry nothing out. 1 Timothy 6:6, 7

There is within the human heart a tough fibrous root of fallen life whose nature is to possess, always to possess!

The pronouns "my" and "mine" look innocent enough in print, but express the real nature of the old Adamic man better than a thousand volumes of theology could do. They are verbal symptoms of our deep disease.

The roots of our hearts have grown down into things, and we dare not pull up one rootlet lest we die. Things have become necessary to us, a development never originally intended. God's gifts now take the place of God, and the whole course of nature is upset by the monstrous substitution!

There can be no doubt that this possessive clinging to things is one of the most harmful habits in the life. Because it is so natural it is rarely recognized for the evil that it is; but its outworkings are tragic.

We are often hindered from giving up our treasures to the Lord out of fear for their safety; this is especially true when those treasures are loved relatives and friends. But we need have no such fears. Our Lord came not to destroy but to save. Everything is safe which we commit to Him, and nothing is really safe which is not so committed.

Our gifts and talents should also be turned over to Him. They should be recognized for what they are, God's loan to us, and should never be considered in any sense our own, for we have no more right to claim credit for special abilities than for blue eyes or strong muscles!

June 18

The True Christian: Still an Enigma to the World

But speaking the truth in love, may grow up into him in all things, which is the head, even Christ. Ephesians 4:15

Today, as in all the centuries, true Christians are an enigma to the world, a thorn in the flesh of Adam, a puzzle to angels, the delight of God and a habitation of the Holy Spirit!

Our fellowship ought to take in all of the true children of God, regardless of who and where and what, if they are washed in the blood, born of the Spirit, walking with God the Father, begotten unto a living hope through the resurrection of Jesus Christ and rejoicing in the salvation to be revealed!

The true Christian fears God with a trembling reverence and yet he is not afraid of God at all. He draws nigh to Him with full assurance of faith and victory, and yet at the same time is trembling with holy awe and fear.

The world will never understand that the Christian, though born on earth, still knows by faith that he is a citizen of heaven!

Some of our critics say: "You Christians talk about yourself and your relation to God as if you were God's very best!"

I have a good answer to that. The very Christian who believes that he is the apple of God's eye is the same unselfish Christian who is giving sacrificially of his money, sending his sons and daughters or going himself to preach the gospel to the least and the last of the peoples of the earth!

The Whole Universe Is Alive with God's Life

Wherefore thou art no more a servant, but a son: and if a son, then an heir of God through Christ. Galatians 4:7

What God in His sovereignty may yet do on a world-scale I do not claim to know; but what He will do for the plain man or woman who seeks His face I believe I do know and can tell others.

Let any person turn to God in earnest, let him begin to exercise himself unto godliness, let him seek to develop his powers of spiritual receptivity by trust and obedience and humility, and the results will exceed anything he may have hoped in his leaner and weaker days!

Any man who by repentance and a sincere return to God will break himself out of the mold in which he has been held, and is willing to go to the Bible itself for his spiritual standards, will be delighted with what he finds there.

Let us say it again: The universal Presence is a fact. God is here!

The whole universe is alive with God's life, and He is no strange or foreign God, but the familiar Father of our Lord Jesus Christ, whose love has for these thousands of years enfolded the sinful race of men.

Always He is trying to get our attention, to reveal Himself to us, to communicate with us! We have within us the ability to know Him in increasing degree as our receptivity becomes more perfect by faith and love and practice.

June 20

Poets Admire Nature: Prophets Look to the Creator

Howbeit then, when ye knew not God, ye did service unto them which by nature are no gods. Galatians 4:8

It is possible to spend a lifetime admiring God's handiwork without acknowledging the presence of the God whose handiwork it is. Nature cannot lift men to God nor serve as a ladder by which he may climb into the divine bosom.

The heavens and the earth were intended to be a semi-transparent veil through which moral intelligences might see the glory of God (Ps. 119:1-6; Rom. 1:19, 20), but for sin-blinded men this veil has become opaque. They see the creation but do not see through it to the Creator; or what glimpses they do have are dim and out of focus.

With what joy the Christian turns from even the purest nature poets to the prophets and psalmists of the Scriptures. These saw God first; they rose by the power of faith to the throne of the Majesty on high and observed the created world from above.

Their love of natural objects was deep and intense, but they loved them not for their own sakes but for the sake of Him who created them. They walked through the world as through the garden of God. Everything reminded them of Him. They saw His power in the stormy wind and tempest; they heard His voice in the thunder; the mountains told them of His strength and the rocks reminded them that He was their hiding place!

The nature poets are enamored of natural objects; the inspired writers are God-enamored men. That is the difference, and it is a vitally important one!

June 21

Christians Drawn by This Present World's Charms

While they promise them liberty, they themselves are the servants of corruption; for of whom a man is overcome, of the same is he brought in bondage. 2 Peter 2:19

With the Bible open before us and a long tradition of truth behind us, there would seem to be no reason for the present tragic failure of Christians to recognize the world's deceptive appeal and to stay clear of it. For there must not be any denial of the facts: the church is being overwhelmed by the kingdoms of the world and the glory of them!

That world which our Saviour once refused to buy at the price of disobedience to God is now wooing His professed followers with every sly, deceptive artifice. The glory which our Lord once rejected with cold scorn is now being admired and sought after by multitudes who make a loud profession of accepting the gospel. The old trick which our Lord saw through so easily is charming His present-day followers into smiling acquiescence.

The devil did not know Christ—but apparently he knows Christians! The lust of the flesh, the lust of the eyes and the pride of life have all been "Christianized" (not by the liberal, mind you, but by the evangelicals) and are now offered along with Christ to everyone who will "believe." Blind leaders of blind souls now insist that Christians should not cut themselves off from the pleasures of the world, so the very values that Christ scorned are now being used to attract people to the gospel.

We stand in need of warning: in spite of prophetic voices that are raised here and there among us, present-day believers are being drawn to the world with irresistible force!

The Profane Man: He Rules out God Completely

And I will say to my soul, Soul, thou hast much goods laid up for many years; take thine ease, eat, drink, and be merry. Luke 12:19

The profane man in today's profane generation has come to the conclusion that he alone is important in this universe—thus he becomes his own god!

He dotes on things—secular things—until he mistakenly assumes that there is nothing in the universe but material and physical values.

It is sad but true that a great and eternal woe awaits the profane and completely secular man whose only religion is in the thought that he probably is not as bad as some other man. I think that there is an Old Testament portion in the Book of Job that fits modern, profane man very well: "Woe is me, that I was ever born, that my mother ever conceived me. Let the stars of the twilight of that night be as darkness. Oh, that I might have been carried from my mother's knees to the grave, where the wicked cease from troubling and the toil-worn are dressed."

Only the darkness of judgment remains for the "self-sufficient" and completely secularized man who has ruled God out of his life and out of his business and out of his home.

I am thinking particularly of those who give lip service to the church and some mental assent to religion, but who have forgotten that they were created, that they have a responsibility to God, and they have ignored Jesus Christ—His Presence, His Voice, His Light!

Do Not Laugh at Something God Takes Seriously

. . .Their conscience also bearing witness, and their thoughts the mean while accusing or else excusing one another. Romans 2:15

One way the devil has of getting rid of things is to make jokes about them—and one of the sick jokes you hear is that the conscience is that part of you which makes you sorry when you get caught!

There are some things that are not the proper objects of humor, and one of them is conscience.

That power of conscience that God has set in the human breast can suddenly isolate a soul, and hang it between heaven and hell, as lonely as if God had never created but one soul—that's not a joking matter.

Remember the conscience is always on God's side—always on God's side! It judges conduct in the light of the moral law, and as the Scripture says, excuses or accuses.

The Light that lighted every man that comes into the world is not a joking matter. The eternal, universal Presence of the luminous Christ is not a joking matter.

Joke about politics if you must joke—they are usually funny, anyway. But don't joke about God and don't joke about conscience, nor death, nor life, nor love, nor the cross, nor prayer.

There is legitimate humor in our lives, and I think it is in us by the gift of God. Your sense of humor does not have to dry up and die. There's plenty to laugh at in the world—but be sure you don't laugh at something that God takes seriously. Conscience is one of those things!

June 24

Right Thinking Spiritually Will Bring Right Living

Holding fast the faithful word as he hath been taught, that he may be able by sound doctrine both to exhort and to convince the gainsayers. Titus 1:9

It would be impossible to overemphasize the importance of sound doctrine in the life of a Christian. Right thinking about all spiritual matters is imperative if we would have right living. As men do not gather grapes of thorns nor figs of thistles, so sound character does not grow out of unsound teaching!

The word 'doctrine' means simply religious beliefs held and taught. It is the sacred task of all Christians, first as believers and then as teachers of religious beliefs, to be certain that these beliefs correspond exactly to truth.

A precise agreement between belief and fact constitutes soundness in doctrine. We cannot afford to have less.

Each generation of Christians must look to its beliefs. While truth itself is unchanging, the minds of men are porous vessels out of which truth can leak and into which error may seep to dilute the truth they contain.

When men deal with things earthly and temporal, they demand the truth; only in religious thought is faithfulness to truth looked upon as a fault!

Increasing numbers of evangelical Christians are becoming ashamed to be found unequivocally on the side of truth, but moral power has always accompanied definitive beliefs. We need right now a return to a gentle dogmatism that smiles while it stands stubborn and firm on the Word of God that liveth and abideth forever!

God Does Not Have to Be Persuaded to Bless Us

Blessed are they which do hunger and thirst after righteousness: for they shall be filled. Matthew 5:6

The problem of the spiritual life is not to persuade God to fill us, but to want God sufficiently to permit Him to do so!

Jesus Himself spoke of our hungering and thirsting after righteousness. Hunger and thirst are physical sensations which in their acute stages may become real pain. It has been the experience of countless seekers after God that when their desires became a pain they were suddenly and wonderfully filled.

Occasionally there appears on the religious scene a person whose unsatisfied spiritual longings become so big and important in the life that they crowd out every other interest. Such a man or woman refuses to be content with the safe and conventional prayers of the frost-bound brethren called upon to "lead in prayer" week after week in the local assemblies. His yearnings carry him away and often make something of a nuisance out of him. His puzzled fellow Christians shake their heads and look knowingly at each other, but like the blind man who cried out after his sight and was rebuked by the disciples, he "cries the more a great deal."

And if he has not yet met the conditions or there is something hindering the answer to his prayer, he may pray on into the late hours. Not the hour of night but the state of his heart decides the time of his visitation!

It is easy to learn the doctrine of personal revival and victorious living; it is quite another thing to take our cross and plod on to the dark and bitter hill of self-renunciation.

Here many are called and few are chosen!

June 26

Be Completely Honest with God When You Pray

But, O Lord of hosts, that triest the righteous, and seest the reins and the heart, let me see thy vengeance on them: for unto thee have I opened my cause.
Jeremiah 20:12

There is a vital element of true prayer which is likely to be overlooked in our artificial age.

That vital element is just plain honesty!

The saintly David M'Intyre once wrote: "Honest dealing becomes us when we kneel in His pure presence."

Then M'Intyre continued: "On one occasion Jeremiah failed to interpret God aright. He cried as if in anger, 'O Lord, thou hast deceived me, and I was deceived.'

"These are terrible words to utter before Him who is changeless truth. But the prophet spoke as he felt, and the Lord not only pardoned him, but met him and blessed him there."

I recall another spiritual writer of unusual penetration has advised frankness in prayer even to a degree that might appear to be downright rudeness. When you come to prayer, he says, and find that you have no taste for it, tell God so without mincing words. If God and spiritual things bore you, admit it frankly.

This advice will shock some squeamish saints, but it is altogether sound nevertheless. God loves the guileless soul even when in his ignorance he is actually guilty of rashness in prayer. The Lord can soon cure his ignorance, but for insincerity no cure is known.

We can learn something at this point if we will!

Christian Responsibility Is a Day-by-Day Reality

Therefore judge nothing before the time, until the Lord come, who both will bring to light the hidden things of darkness, and will make manifest the counsels of the hearts. . . . 1 Corinthians 4:5

When we believe that Christ died for the unjust, making it possible for the unjust to live with the Just in complete moral congruity, do we mean that redeemed and forgiven men and women have no further responsibility to God for their conduct?

Does this mean that now that they are clothed with the righteousness of Christ they will never be called to account for their deeds?

God forbid! How could the moral Governor of the universe release a segment of that universe from the moral law of deeds and consequences and hope to uphold the order of the world?

Within the household of God among the redeemed and justified there is law as well as grace; not the law of Moses that knew no mercy, but the kindly law of the Father's heart that requires and expects of His children lives lived in conformity to the commandments of God.

The Lord told us plainly, as have the apostles, that we must all give account of the deeds done in the body. And He has warned us faithfully of the danger that we shall have for our reward only wood, hay, and stubble in the day of Christ (Rom. 14:7-12; 1 Cor. 3:9-15).

The judgment unto death and hell lies behind the Christian, but the judgment seat of Christ lies ahead. There the question will not be the law of Moses, but how we have lived within the Father's household. We have the Bible before us and the Holy Spirit within. I believe we may anticipate and prepare ourselves for the judgment seat of Christ by honest self-judgment in this life.

June 28

Sad But True: Many Know God Only by Hearsay

In this the children of God are manifest, and the children of the devil: who-soever doeth not righteousness is not of God. . . . 1 John 3:10

Do you realize that there are many, many in the churches of our day who talk some of the Christian language but who know God only by hearsay?

Most of them have read some book about God. They have seen some reflection of the light of God. They may have heard some faint echo of the voice of God, but their own personal knowledge of God is very slight.

Many Christians are staking their reputations on church attendance, religious activity, social fellowship, sessions of singing—because in all of these things they are able to lean upon one another. They spend a lot of time serving as religious props for one another in Christian circles!

Let us look at the example of Jesus. When He was here upon earth, the record shows that He had work to do and He also knew the necessity for activity as He preached and healed, taught and answered questions and blessed the people. He also knew the fellowship of His brethren, those who followed Him and loved Him.

But those were the incidental things in Jesus' life compared to His fellowship with and personal knowledge of the Father. When Jesus went into the mountain to pray and to wait on God all night, He was not alone, for He knew the conscious presence of the Father with Him!

June 29

Do We Really Long for Our Lord to Come?

For the Son of man shall come in the glory of his Father with his angels. . . .
Matthew 16:27

The joyful and personal element in what we call the "blessed hope," the return of Christ to earth, seems to be altogether missing in our day.

If the tender yearning is gone from the advent hope there must be reasons for it, and I think I know what they are.

One is simply that popular fundamentalist theology has emphasized the utility of the cross rather than the beauty of the One who died on it. The saved man's relation to Christ has been made contractual instead of personal. The "work" of Christ has been stressed until it has eclipsed the person of Christ, and what He did for me seems to be more important than what He is to me!

Redemption is seen as an across-the-counter transaction which we "accept," and the whole thing lacks emotional content. We must love someone very much to stay awake and long for his coming, and that may explain the absence of power in the advent hope even among those who still believe in it.

History reveals that times of suffering for the Church have also been times of looking upward. Tribulation has always sobered God's people and encouraged them to look for and yearn after the return of their Lord. God will wean us from the earth some way—the easy way if possible, the hard way if necessary!

God Is Always at the Controls of the Universe

And God saw everything that he had made, and behold, it was very good. . . . Genesis 1:31

I do not know why God does some things, but I am convinced that nothing is accidental in His universe. In the creation chapters of Genesis there is a beautiful exercise in utility—God making an orderly world for a purpose, with everything having a reason for existence.

If I am allowed to go into a hospital operating room, I am completely ignorant about the uses for most of the strange and complex facilities. But the surgeon knows each one and none of those instruments is there by accident.

If I could step into the cab of one of the great, powerful diesel locomotives, I would be perplexed by the many buttons and handles and bars. I could wreck the whole thing in a few minutes. But the engineer knows—and he gets the proper results when he pushes the proper switches and the right buttons.

So, when God Almighty stepped into the cab of His locomotive, which we call the cosmos, He was at the controls and He has always pushed the right buttons.

Just because there are things in the universe beyond my human explanation does not allow me to accuse God of making a lot of unnecessary truck to clutter up the universe. God made everything for some purpose!

July 1

Unchanging: The Love and Compassion of Christ

But made himself of no reputation, and took upon him the form of a servant, and was made in the likeness of men. Philippians 2:7

Because change is everywhere around us at all times on this earth and among human beings, it is difficult for us to grasp the eternal and unchanging nature and person of Jesus Christ.

Nothing about our Lord Jesus Christ has changed down to this very hour. His love has not changed. His compassionate understanding of us has not changed. His interest in us and His purposes for us have not changed.

He is Jesus Christ, our Lord. He is the very same Jesus. Even though He has been raised from the dead and seated at the right hand of the Majesty in the heavens, and made Head over all things to the Church, His love for us remains unchanged.

It is hard for us to accept the majestic simplicity of this constant, wonder-working Jesus. We are used to getting things changed so that they are always bigger and better!

He is Jesus, easier to approach than the humblest friend you ever had! He is the sun that shines upon us, He is the star of our night. He is the giver of our life and the rock of our hope. He is our safety and our future. He is our righteousness, our sanctification, our inheritance.

You will find that He is all of this in that instant that you move your heart towards Him in faith! This is the journey to Jesus that must be made in the depths of the heart and being. This is a journey where feet do not count!

The Nature of True Worship: Wholly Spiritual

Behold, I stand at the door and knock: if any man hear my voice and open the door, I will come in to him. . . . Revelation 3:20

One of the most liberating declarations in the New Testament is this: "The true worshippers shall worship the Father in spirit and in truth: for the Father seeketh such to worship him. God is a Spirit: and they that worship him must worship him in spirit and in truth" (John 4:23, 24). Here the nature of worship is shown to be wholly spiritual. True religion is removed from diet and days, from garments and ceremonies, and placed where it belongs—in the union of the spirit of man with the Spirit of God!

From man's standpoint, the most tragic loss suffered in the Fall was the vacating of his innermost being by the Spirit of God. At the far-in hidden center of man's being is a bush fitted to be the dwelling place of the Triune God. There God planned to rest and glow with moral and spiritual fire. Man by his sin forfeited this indescribably wonderful privilege and must now dwell there alone.

For so intimately private is that place that no creature can intrude; no one can enter but Christ, and He will enter only by the invitation of faith! "Behold, I stand at the door, and knock: if any man hear my voice and open the door, I will come in to him, and will sup with him, and he with me" (Rev. 3:20).

Wrong Choices May Imperil Our Freedom

Thou therefore, my son, be strong in the grace that is in Christ Jesus. 2 Timothy 2:1

There is always danger that a free nation may imperil its freedom by a series of small choices destructive of that freedom.

In the realm of religion right choices are even more critically important!

The casual indifference with which millions of Protestants view their God-blessed religious liberty is ominous. Being let go, they go on weekends to the lakes and mountains and beaches to play shuffleboard, fish and sunbathe. They go where their heart is and come back to the praying company only when the bad weather drives them in. Let this continue long enough and evangelical Protestantism will be ripe for a takeover by Rome!

The Christian gospel is a message of freedom through grace and we must stand fast in the liberty wherewith Christ has made us free. But what shall we do with our freedom?

I think it might be well for us to check our spiritual condition occasionally by the simple test of compatibility. When we are free to go, where do we go? In what company do we feel most at home? Where do our thoughts turn when they are free to turn where they will? When the pressure of work or business or school has temporarily lifted and we are able to think of what we will instead of what we must, what do we think of then?

Are we willing to face up to the answers to these questions, which may tell us more than we can comfortably accept?

July 4

God Never Violates Our Freedom of Choice

. . .And whosoever will, let him take the water of life freely. Revelation 22:17

It is inherent in the nature of man that his will must be free. Made in the image of God who is completely free, man must enjoy a measure of freedom. This enables him to select his companions for this world and the next; it enables him to yield his soul to whom he will, to give allegiance to God or the devil, to remain a sinner or become a saint.

And God respects this freedom. God once saw everything that He had made, and behold, it was very good. To find fault with the smallest thing God has made is to find fault with its Maker. It is a false humility that would lament that God wrought but imperfectly when He made man in His own image. Sin excepted, there is nothing in human nature to apologize for. This was confirmed forever when the Eternal Son became permanently incarnated in human flesh!

So highly does God regard His handiwork that He will not for any reason violate it. He will take nine steps toward us but He will not take the tenth. He will incline us to repent, but He cannot do our repenting for us. It is of the essence of repentance that it can only be done by the one who committed the act to be repented of. God can wait on the sinning man, He can withhold judgment, He can exercise long-suffering to the point where He appears lax in His judicial administration—but He cannot force a man to repent. To do this would be to violate the man's freedom and void the gift of God originally bestowed upon him. The believer knows he is free to choose—and with that knowledge he chooses forever the blessed will of God!

Great Bible Saints: Enraptured Lovers of God

But let all those that put their trust in thee rejoice. . .let them also that love thy name be joyful in thee. Psalm 5:11

Perhaps the most serious charge that can be brought against modern Christians is that we are not sufficiently in love with Christ—love that may rise to a degree of adoration almost beyond the power of the heart to endure!

Neither the word 'adoration' nor any of its forms is found in our familiar King James Bible, but the idea is there in full bloom. The great Bible saints were, above all, enraptured lovers of God. The psalms celebrate the love which David (and a few others) felt for the person of God. Paul confessed that love for Christ carried him beyond himself and made him do extravagant things which to a mind untouched with the delights of such love might seem irrational.

In our Christian circles today it is rare when we find anyone aglow with personal love for Christ. I trust it is not uncharitable to say that a great deal of praise in conservative circles is perfunctory and forced, where it is not downright insincere!

There can be nothing more terrible or more wonderful than to be stricken with love for Christ so deeply that the whole being goes out in a pained adoration of His person, an adoration that disturbs and disconcerts while it purges and satisfies and relaxes the deep inner heart.

This love as a kind of moral fragrance is ever detected upon the garments of the saints—and the list of fragrant saints is long. This radiant love for Christ is to my mind the one sure proof of membership in the church universal!

July 6

The Cross We Bear Must Be Assumed Voluntarily

For unto you it is given in the behalf of Christ, not only to believe on him, but also to suffer for his sake. Philippians 1:29

In the Christian faith there is a real sense in which the cross of Christ embraces all crosses and the death of Christ encompasses all deaths: "If one died for all, then were all dead. . . ."

This is in the judicial working of God in redemption. The Christian as a member of the body of Christ is crucified along with his divine Head. Before God every true believer is reckoned to have died when Christ died. All subsequent experience of personal crucifixion is based upon this identification with Christ on the cross.

But in the practical, everyday outworking of the believer's crucifixion his own cross is brought into play. "Let him. . .take up his cross." That is obviously not the cross of Christ. Rather, it is the believer's own personal cross by means of which the cross of Christ is made effective in slaying his evil nature and setting him free from its power.

The believer's own cross is one he has assumed voluntarily. Therein lies the difference between his cross and the cross on which Roman convicts died. They went to the cross against their will; he, because he chooses to do so. No Roman officer ever pointed to a cross and said, "If any man will, let him!" Only Christ said that, and by so saying He placed the whole matter in the hands of the Christian believer. Each of us, then, should count himself dead indeed with Christ and accept willingly whatever of self-denial, repentance, humility and humble sacrifice that may be found in the path of obedient daily living.

We Reduce the Truth to a Code—and Die Spiritually

Then cried Jesus in the temple. . .I am not come of myself, but he that sent me is true, whom ye know not. John 7:28

Too many people believe that truth is something that can be received and held by the intellect and that truth can be reduced to a code—just as we know and accept that two times two is four.

Two thousand years ago, the theological leaders marveled at Jesus. They said to one another, "How does this man know letters, having never learned?" and "How does He get His wonderful doctrine? He has never been to the schools of the rabbis."

This tells us that those Jewish leaders held "the truth"—and you can spell it with capital letters if you please—to be intellectual merely, capable of being reduced to a code.

To them, there was no mysterious depth in divine Truth, nothing beneath and nothing beyond—two times two made four!

It was exactly here that they parted company with our Saviour, for the Lord Jesus constantly taught the "beyond" and the "beneath." He showed them that He was simply a transparent medium through which God spoke.

He said, "My doctrine is not mine—I am not a rabbi just teaching doctrine that you can memorize and repeat. I say nothing for myself—what the Father speaks, that I speak!"

In His day or in our day, the rationalist sees no beyond and no mystic depths, no mysterious heights, nothing supernatural or divine. He holds the text and the code and the creed and passes it on to others. The result is we are dying spiritually!

July 8

Spirit Taught: The Result Is Spiritual Illumination

Having the understanding darkened. . .because of the blindness of their heart. Ephesians 4:18

It may shock some readers to suggest that there is a difference between being "Bible taught" and "Spirit taught."

Nevertheless, it is so!

It is altogether possible to be instructed in the rudiments of the faith and still have no real understanding of the whole thing. And it is possible to go on to become expert in Bible doctrine and not have spiritual illumination, with the result that a veil remains over the mind, preventing it from apprehending the truth in its spiritual essence.

Most of us are acquainted with churches that teach the Bible to their children, reenforce it with catechism classes, and still never produce in them a living Christianity nor a virile godliness.

Their members show no evidence of having passed from death unto life. None of the earmarks of salvation so plainly indicated in the Scriptures are found among them. Their religious lives are correct and reasonably moral, but wholly mechanical and altogether lacking in radiance.

Many of them are pathetically serious about it all, but they are spiritually blind, getting along with the outward shell of faith while all the time their deep hearts are starving for spiritual reality.

It has been said that "The Scriptures, to be understood, must be read with the same Spirit that originally inspired them." No one denies this, but even such a statement will go over the heads of those who hear it unless the Holy Spirit inflames the heart!

July 9

Humility: A Blessed Thing If You Can Find It

. . .He that humbleth himself shall be exalted. Luke 14:11

Watch out, Christian brothers and sisters, for the danger of arrogance, in assuming that you are somebody, indeed!

God will never let you high-hat somebody else if you are a Christian. He loves you far too much to let you get away with that.

You may ask: "What will the Lord do, then, if I get arrogant and presumptuous, full of pride over my victories and successes?"

Well, the Lord will remind you of His own example, and will rebuke and chasten you in His own way.

Our Lord Jesus Christ would not allow any success or temporary honor to lead Him astray.

The Lord had no servants. He bossed no one around. He was the Lord, but He never took the tyrannical attitude toward anyone.

I think it is very good spiritual advice that we should never tie ourselves up to public opinion and never consider any honors we may receive as being due us because of our superior gifts.

In that day of the triumphal entry into Jerusalem, the crowd acclaimed Him and cried, "Hosanna!" but on the very next Friday they joined in the shout, "Crucify him!"

Humility is a blessed thing if you can find it. Early church fathers wrote that if a man feels that he is getting somewhere in the kingdom of God, that's pride—and until that dies, he is getting nowhere!

July 10

Self Does Not Die without Our Full Consent

For the flesh lusteth against the Spirit and the Spirit against the flesh: and these are contrary the one to the other: so that ye cannot do the things that ye would. Galatians 5:17

The Holy Spirit and the fallen human self are diametrically opposed to each other, for, as the Apostle Paul wrote to the Roman church, "because the carnal mind is enmity against God; for it is not subject to the law of God, neither indeed can be."

Before the Spirit of God can work creatively in our hearts, He must condemn and slay the "flesh" within us; that is, He must have our full consent to displace our natural self with the Person of Christ! This displacement is carefully explained in Romans 6, 7 and 8. When the seeking Christian has gone through the crucifying experience described in chapters 6 and 7 he enters into the broad, free regions of chapter 8. There self is dethroned and Christ is enthroned forever!

In the light of this it is not hard to see why the Christian's attitude toward self is such an excellent test of the validity of his religious experiences. Most of the great masters of the deeper life, such as Fenelon, Molinos, John of the Cross, Madame Guyon and a host of others, have warned against pseudoreligious experiences that provide much carnal enjoyment but feed the flesh and puff up the heart with self-love.

A good rule is this: Nothing that comes from God will minister to my pride or self-congratulation. If I am tempted to be complacent and to feel superior because of an advanced spiritual experience, I should go at once to my knees and repent of the whole thing. I have fallen a victim to the enemy!

July 11

Our Position: Believing God, Defying the Devil

. . .Resist the devil and he will flee from you. James 4:7

It is a gracious thing to be humbled under the loving, chastening hand of God, but when the devil starts tampering with you, dare to resist him!

Brethren, God never meant for us to be kicked around like a football. I stand for believing in God and defying the devil—and our God loves that kind of courage.

It is for us to trust, to trust wholly in the Lord Jesus! This is the only way in which we can conquer fear and live in blessed victory.

I have had times in my life and ministry when the burdens and the pressures seemed to be too much. At these times it seems that even in prayer it is impossible to rise above the load. More than once, by faith that seemed to have been imparted directly from heaven, the Lord has enabled me to claim all that I needed for body, soul and spirit.

On my knees, I have been given freedom and strength to pray, "Now, Lord, I have had enough of this—I refuse to take any more of this heaviness and oppression! This does not come from God—this comes from my enemy, the devil. Lord, in Jesus' name, I will not take it any longer—through Jesus Christ I am victor!"

Will God answer?

At these times, great burdens have just melted, all at once! As the burden rolls away, He answers: "Child, I have waited long to hear you confess that Jesus is victor and in Him you overcome!"

Many Practice Fraud upon Their Own Souls

If we say that we have no sin, we deceive ourselves, and the truth is not in us.
1 John 1:8

Of all forms of deception self-deception is the most deadly, and of all deceived persons the self-deceived are the least likely to discover the fraud!

The reason for this is simple. When a man is deceived by another he is deceived against his will. He is contending against an adversary and is temporarily the victim of the other's guile. Since he expects his foe to take advantage of him he is watchful and quick to suspect trickery.

With the self-deceived it is quite different. He is his own enemy and is working a fraud upon himself. He wants to believe the lie and is psychologically conditioned to do so. He does not resist the deceit but collaborates with it against himself. There is no struggle, because the victim surrenders before the fight begins. He enjoys being deceived!

It is altogether possible to practice fraud upon our own souls and go deceived to judgment. The farther we push into the sanctuary the greater becomes the danger of self-deception. The deeply religious man is far more vulnerable than the easygoing fellow who takes his religion lightly.

Before a man's heart has been wholly conquered by the Spirit of God, he may be driven to try every dodge to save face and preserve a semblance of his old independence. This is always dangerous and if persisted in may prove calamitous!

The Praying Man: Purity and Honesty Are Essential

Ye ask, and receive not, because ye ask amiss, that ye may consume it upon your lusts. James 4:3

Prayer is usually recommended as the panacea for all ills and the key to open every prison door—and it would indeed be difficult to overstate the advantages and privilege of Spirit-inspired prayer.

But we must not forget that unless we are wise and watchful, prayer itself may become a source of self-deception.

There are as many kinds of prayer as there are problems and some kinds are not acceptable to God. The prophets of the Old Testament denounced Israel for trying to hide their iniquities behind their prayers. Christ flatly rejected the prayers of hypocrites and James declared that some religious persons ask and receive not because they ask amiss!

To escape self-deception, the praying man must come out clean and honest. He cannot hide in the cross while concealing in his bosom the golden wedge and the goodly Babylonish garment. Grace will save a man but it will not save him and his idol! The blood of Christ will shield the penitent sinner alone, but never the sinner and his idol! Faith will justify the sinner, but it will never justify the sinner and his sin!

No amount of pleading will make evil good or wrong right. A man may engage in a great deal of humble talk before God and get no response because unknown to himself he is using prayer to disguise disobedience!

Believe It: Christ, the Just, Died for the Unjust

To declare, I say, at this time his righteousness: that he might be just, and the justifier of him which believeth in Jesus. Romans 3:26

The present state of the human race before God is probationary. The world is on trial. The voice of God sounds over the earth, "Behold I set before you the way of life and the way of death. Choose you this day!"

The whole question of right and wrong, of moral responsibility, of justice and judgment and reward and punishment, is sharply accented for us by the fact that we are members of a fallen race, occupying a position halfway between heaven and hell, with the knowledge of good and evil inherent within our intricate natures, along with ability to turn toward good and an inborn propensity to turn toward evil.

The cross of Christ has altered somewhat the position of certain persons before the judgment of God. Toward those who embrace the provisions of mercy that center around the death and resurrection of Christ one phase of judgment is no longer operative. Our Lord stated this truth in this way: "He that heareth my word, and believeth on him that sent me, hath everlasting life, and shall not come into condemnation; but is passed from death unto life" (John 5:24).

When Christ died in the darkness for us men He made it possible for God to remit the penalty of the broken law, reestablish repentant sinners in His favor exactly as if they had never sinned, and do the whole thing without relaxing the severity of the law or compromising the high demands of justice (Rom. 3:24-26). The Just died for the unjust. Thanks be to God for His unspeakable gift!

July 15

If We Confess: Straight, Plain Bible Teaching

For I delivered unto you first of all that which also I received, how that Christ died for our sins according to the scriptures. 1 Corinthians 15:3

Lack of balance in the Christian life is often the direct consequence of overemphasis on certain favorite texts, with a corresponding underemphasis on other related ones. For it is not denial only that makes a truth void; failure to emphasize it will in the long run be equally damaging.

One example of this is the teaching that crops up now and again having to do with confession of sin. It goes like this: Christ died for our sins, not only for all we have committed but for all we may yet commit for the remainder of our lives. When we accept Christ we receive the benefit of everything He did for us in His dying and rising again. In Christ all our current sins are forgiven beforehand. It is therefore unnecessary for us to confess our sins. In Christ they are already forgiven, we are told.

Now, this is completely wrong, and it is all the more wrong because it is half right.

It is written that Christ died for our sins, and again it is written that "if we confess our sins, he is faithful and just to forgive us our sins" (1 John 1:9). These two texts are written of the same company of persons, namely Christians. We dare not compel the first text to invalidate the second. Both are true and one completes the other. The meaning of the two is that since Christ died for our sins if we confess our sins they will be forgiven. To teach otherwise is to attempt to fly on one wing!

The High Casualty Rate among Christians

When his disciples heard it, they were exceedingly amazed, saying, Who then can be saved? Matthew 19:25

"God hath called you to Christ's side," wrote the saintly Rutherford, "and the wind is now in Christ's face in this land; and seeing ye are with Him, ye cannot expect the lee-side or the sunny side of the brae."

Nowhere in the teachings of Christ do we find anything visionary or overoptimistic. He told His hearers the whole truth and let them make up their minds. He might grieve over the retreating form of an inquirer who could not face up to the truth, but He never ran after him to try to win him with rosy promises.

All this is but to say that Christ is honest. We can trust Him. He knows that He will never be popular among the sons of Adam and He knows that His followers need not expect to be. The wind that blows in His face will be felt by all who travel with Him, and we are not intellectually honest when we try to hide that fact from them.

By offering our hearers a sweetness-and-light gospel and promising every taker a place on the sunny side of the brae, we not only cruelly deceive them, we guarantee also a high casualty rate among the converts on such terms.

We tell them that if they will accept Christ He will give them peace of mind, solve their problems, protect their families and keep them happy all day long. They believe us and come, and the first cold wind sends them shivering to some counselor to find out what has gone wrong; and that is the last we hear of many of them!

July 17

Who Sets the Moral Pace for Us Today?

For even hereunto were ye called: because Christ also suffered for us, leaving us an example, that ye should follow his steps. 1 Peter 2:21

The history of Israel and Judah points up a truth taught clearly enough by all history—that the masses are or soon will be what their leaders are. The kings set the moral pace for the people.

Israel sometimes rebelled against her leaders, it is true, but the rebellions were not spontaneous. The people merely switched to a new leader and followed him. The point is, they always had to have a leader.

Whatever sort of man the king turned out to be the people were soon following his leadership. They followed David in the worship of Jehovah, Solomon in the building of the Temple, Jeroboam in the making of a calf and Hezekiah in the restoration of the temple worship.

It is not complimentary to the masses that they are so easily led, but we are not interested in praising or blaming; we are concerned for truth, and the truth is that for better or for worse, religious people follow leaders. A good man may change the moral complexion of a whole nation; or a corrupt and worldly clergy may lead a nation into bondage. The transposed proverb, "Like priest, like people," sums up in four words a truth taught plainly in the Scriptures and demonstrated again and again in religious history.

The rewards of godly leadership are so great and the responsibilities of the leader so heavy that no one can afford to take the matter lightly.

July 18

God's True Prophets Never Applied for the Job

And Moses said unto God, Who am I, that I should go unto Pharaoh, and that I should bring forth the children of Israel out of Egypt? Exodus 3:11

The true minister of the Gospel is one not by his own choice but by the sovereign commission of God!

From a study of the Scriptures one might conclude that the man God calls seldom or never surrenders to the call without considerable reluctance. The young man who rushes too eagerly into the pulpit at first glance seems to be unusually spiritual, but he may in fact only be revealing his lack of understanding of the sacred nature of the ministry.

The call of God comes with an insistence that will not be denied and can scarcely be resisted. Moses fought his call strenuously and lost to the compulsion of the Spirit within him; and the same may be said of many others in the Bible and since Bible times. Christian biography shows that many who later became great Christian leaders at first tried earnestly to avoid the burden of the ministry; but I cannot offhand recall one single instance of a prophet's having applied for the job!

The call to witness and serve God comes to every Christian; the call to be a Voice to mankind comes only to the man who has the Spirit's gift and special enabling. We need not fewer men to show mercy, but we need more men who can hear the words of God and translate them into human speech!

July 19

Faith Is More Than Believing the Evidence

. . .Yea, let God be true, but every man a liar; as it is written, That thou mightest be justified in thy sayings. . . . Romans 3:4

Faith based upon reason may be faith of a kind, but it is not of the character of Bible faith, for it follows the evidence infallibly and has nothing of a moral or spiritual nature in it.

Neither can the absence of faith based upon reason be held against anyone, for the evidence, not the individual, decides the verdict. To send a man to hell whose only crime was to follow evidence straight to its proper conclusion would be palpable injustice; to justify a sinner on the grounds that he had made up his mind according to the plain facts would be to make salvation the result of the workings of a common law of the mind as applicable to Judas as to Paul.

It would take salvation out of the realm of the volitional and place it in the mental, where, according to the Scriptures, it surely does not belong!

True faith rests upon the character of God and asks no further proof than the moral perfections of the One who cannot lie. It is enough that God said it, and if the statement should contradict every one of the five senses and all the conclusions of logic as well, still the believer continues to believe!

"Let God be true, but every man a liar," is the language of true faith. Heaven approves such faith because it rises above mere proofs and rests in the bosom of God!

Christian Experience: Encounter with God

Moreover he said, I am the God of thy father. . .and Moses hid his face, for he was afraid to look upon God. Exodus 3:6

True Christian experience must always include a genuine encounter with God. Without this, religion is but a shadow, a reflection of reality, a cheap copy of the original once enjoyed by someone else of whom we have heard.

It cannot but be a major tragedy in the life of any man to live in a church from childhood to old age and know nothing more real than some synthetic god compounded of theology and logic, but having no eyes to see, nor ears to hear, and no heart to love.

The spiritual giants of old were men who at some time became acutely conscious of the real Presence of God and maintained that consciousness for the rest of their lives.

The first encounter may have been one of terror, as when a "horror of great darkness" fell upon Abram, or as when Moses at the bush hid his face because he was afraid to look upon God. Usually this fear soon lost its content of terror and changed after a while to delightsome awe, to level off finally into a reverent sense of complete nearness to God. The essential point is this: these were men who experienced God!

How otherwise can the saints and prophets be explained? How otherwise can we account for the amazing power for good they have exercised over countless generations? Is it not that they walked in conscious communion with the real Presence and addressed their prayers to God with the artless conviction that they were addressing Someone actually there?

July 21

By Its Very Nature, Love Must Be Voluntary

If any man will do his will, he shall know of the doctrine, whether it be of God. . . . John 7:17

How can the sincere Christian fulfill the scriptural command to love God with all his heart and his neighbor as himself?

Of all the emotions of which the soul is capable, love is by far the freest, the most unreasoning, the one least likely to spring up at the call of duty or obligation, and surely the one that will not come at the command of another.

No law has ever been passed that can compel one moral being to love another, for by the very nature of it love must be voluntary. No one can be coerced or frightened into loving anyone. Love just does not come that way!

The love the Bible enjoins is not the love of feeling: it is the love of willing, the "willed tendency" of the heart.

God never intended that such a being as man should be the plaything of his feelings. The emotional life is a proper and noble part of the total personality, but it is, by its very nature, of secondary importance. Religion lies in the will, and so does righteousness. The only good that God recognizes is a willed good; the only valid holiness is a willed holiness.

It should be a cheering thought that before God every man is what he wills to be. The first requirement in conversion is a rectified will. To meet the requirements of love toward God the soul need but will to love and the miracle begins to blossom like the budding of Aaron's rod!

July 22

Seek God's Glory and Purity

. . .If a man love me he will keep my words: and my Father will love him, and we will come unto him, and make our abode with him. John 14:23

It is an open question whether or not the evangelical movement has sinned too long and departed too far from God to return again to spiritual sanity.

Personally I do not believe it is too late to repent if the Christians of the day would repudiate evil leadership and seek God again in true penitence and tears.

The 'if' is the big problem! Will they?

Or are they too well satisfied with religious frolic and froth even to recognize their sad departure from the New Testament faith?

Our only hope is that renewed spiritual pressure will be exerted increasingly by self-effacing and courageous men who desire nothing but the glory of God and the purity of the Church. May God send us many of them: they are long overdue!

Until such men as these return again to spiritual leadership we may expect a progressive deterioration in the quality of popular Christianity year after year till we reach the point where the grieved Holy Spirit withdraws like the Shekinah from the temple, and we are left like Jerusalem after the crucifixion, God-deserted and alone. In spite of efforts to torture doctrine to prove that the Spirit will not forsake religious men, the record reveals plainly enough that He sometimes does. He has in the past forsaken groups when they have gone too far to make a recovery!

July 23

The Foolish Man: No Store of Eternal Treasure

But God said unto him, Thou fool, this night thy soul shall be required of thee; then whose shall these things be? Luke 12:20

Many of us are forgetting the caution of the Lord Jesus that we ought not to set our hearts on earthly things. He warned that there is a very real danger involved: the same heart of man that was made to commune with God and hold fellowship with the Divine Trinity, to soar away to worlds unknown and behold God upon His throne, that same heart may be locked up in a bank vault or in a jewelry box or somewhere else here on earth!

Jesus gave us the example of the foolish man who accumulated corn, naively telling his soul to rest because he had many barns, and lots and lots of corn. Jesus reminded him that he had to die, and his store of corn, which had a legitimate and proper value on earth, could do him no further good because he had neglected the higher values. He had no store of eternal treasures laid up above!

If we are wise, we will transmute any unit of goods or wealth upwards to another level of value, and the same for our talents and gifts and abilities, mind and strength and nervous energy.

Our faithful missionaries do this, for the ultimate values they seek are the heathen, headhunters, pagans turning to Jesus Christ, putting away their idols and their sins and believing in Jesus with bright, shining faces—singing the gospel and going to heaven, one by one.

These are the true values—the wealth of human beings, translated and changed and purified by the grace of God!

Many Never Cross over into God's Promised Land

And they that are Christ's have crucified the flesh with the affections and lusts. Galatians 5:24

It is very important for earnest Christian believers to understand that long prayer vigils, along with strong crying and tears, are not in themselves meritorious acts.

We must be settled in our knowledge that every blessing flows out of the goodness of God as from a fountain. Even those rewards for good works about which some Bible teachers talk so fulsomely, and which they always set in sharp contrast to the benefits received by grace alone, are at bottom as certainly of grace as is the forgiveness of sin itself.

The holiest apostle can claim no more than that he is an unprofitable servant. The very angels exist out of the pure goodness of God. No creature can "earn" anything in the usual meaning of the word.

All things are by and of the sovereign goodness of God!

Yet for all God's good will toward us He is unable to grant us our heart's desires until all our desires have been reduced to one. When we have dealt with our carnal ambitions, when we have trodden upon the lion and adder of the flesh, have trampled the dragon of self-love under our feet and have truly reckoned ourselves to have died unto sin, then and only then can God raise us to newness of life and fill us with His blessed Holy Spirit!

For every one that actually crosses over into the Promised Land there are many who stand for a while and look longingly across the river and then turn sadly back to the comparative safety of the sandy wastes of the old life!

July 25

Our First Service for God: Inward Devotion

But one thing is needful; and Mary hath chosen that good part, which shall not be taken away from her. Luke 10:42

Some Christians seem to feel that it is a mark of spirituality to attend banquets and seminars and workshops and conferences and courses, night after night, week after week!

This brings up a lesson from the New Testament concerning the sisters, Martha and Mary. I think it is plain that Martha loved Jesus but her concept of devotion was activity—that because she loved the Lord, she ought to be doing something all the time to show it.

Mary also loved the Lord Jesus but with a different attitude in her devotion. She was fervently occupied in spirit about the love of His Godhead! Our Lord knew the difference then and He knows the difference today.

Jesus commended Mary for knowing the value of the one thing that is necessary—that God should be loved and praised above all other business which may occupy us bodily or spiritually. Mary was fervently occupied in spirit about the love of His Godhead I like that—although I know it sounds strange and almost heretical to our modern activists!

My plea is that we will not be satisfied to continue on as "external" Christians. I believe that our Lord wants us to learn more of Him in worship before we become busy for Him. He wants an inner experience of the heart as our first service, and out of that will grow the profound and divine activities which are necessary!

Absence of Repentance Brings Spiritual Uncertainty

In meekness instructing those that oppose themselves; if God peradventure will give them repentance to the acknowledging of the truth. 2 Timothy 2:25

The man who is seriously convinced that he deserves to go to hell is not likely to go there, while the man who believes that he is worthy of heaven will certainly never enter that blessed place.

I use the word "seriously" to accent true conviction and to distinguish it from mere nominal belief.

It is possible to go through life believing that we believe, while actually having no conviction more vital than a conventional creed inherited from our ancestors or picked up from the general religious notions current in our social circle. If this creed requires that we admit our own depravity, we do so and feel proud of our fidelity to the Christian faith. But from the way we love, praise and pamper ourselves it is plain enough that we do not consider ourselves worthy of damnation!

The poor quality of Christian faith and the uncertainties that mark the lives of a host of church members grow out of our modern evangelistic scene's absence of real repentance. So, too, the absence of repentance is the result of an inadequate view of sin and sinfulness held by those who present themselves in the inquiry room.

"No fears, no grace," said Bunyan. "Though there is not always grace where there is fear of hell, yet, to be sure, there is no grace where there is no fear of God. For the fear of God is the beginning of wisdom, and they that lack the beginning have neither middle nor end."

Faith and Holiness Linked to Christ's Return

. . .But we know that when he shall appear, we shall be like him; for we shall see him as he is. 1 John 3:2

The Bible does not approve of modern curiosity that plays with the Scriptures and which seeks only to impress credulous and gullible audiences!

I cannot think of even one lonely passage in the New Testament which speaks of Christ's revelation, manifestation, appearing or coming that is not directly linked with moral conduct, faith and spiritual holiness.

The appearing of the Lord Jesus on this earth once more is not an event upon which we may curiously speculate—and when we do only that we sin! The prophetic teacher who engages in speculation to excite the curiosity of his hearers without providing them with a moral application is sinning even as he speaks.

There have been enough foolish formulas advanced about the return of Christ by those who were simply curious to cause many believers to give the matter no further thought or concern. But Peter said to expect "the appearing of Jesus Christ."

Paul said there is a crown of righteousness laid up in glory for all those who love His appearing. John spoke of his hope of seeing Jesus and bluntly wrote: "Every man that hath this hope in him purifieth himself, even as he is pure."

Are you ready for the appearing of Jesus Christ? Or are you among those who are merely curious about His coming?

July 28

Wrong Desires Pervert Our Moral Judgments

Blessed are they which do hunger and thirst after righteousness: for they shall be filled. Matthew 5:6

Unsanctified desire will stop the growth of any Christian life and conversely, purified desires will tend towards righteousness by a kind of gentle moral gravitation.

In the moral world, right desires tend toward life and evil ones toward death—that in essence is the scriptural teaching on this subject!

Whatever a man wants badly enough and persistently enough will determine the man's character.

Wrong desire perverts the moral judgment so that we are unable to appraise the desired object at its real value. However we try, still a thing looks morally better because we want it. For that reason, our heart is often our worst counselor, for if it is filled with desire it may give us bad advice, pleading the purity of something that is in itself anything but pure!

When our dominant desires are bad the whole life is bad as a consequence. When the desires are good the life comes up to the level of our desires, provided that we have within us the enabling Spirit.

At the root of all true spiritual growth is a set of right and sanctified desires. The whole Bible teaches that we can have whatever we want badly enough if, it hardly need be said, our desire is according to the will of God!

The desire after God and holiness is back of all real spirituality, and when that desire becomes dominant in the life nothing can prevent us from having what we want. The longing cry of the God-hungry soul can only be, "Oh, to be like Thee!"

Our View of God's Presence Is Not Pantheism

If I were hungry I would not tell thee: for the world is mine, and the fullness thereof. Psalm 50:12

The fact that God dwells in His creation and is everywhere indivisibly present in all His works is boldly taught by prophet and apostle and is accepted by Christian theology generally.

That is, it appears in the books, but for some reason it has not sunk into the average Christian's heart so as to become a part of his believing self. Christian teachers shy away from its full implications, probably for fear of being charged with pantheism, but the doctrine of the divine Presence is definitely not pantheism.

Pantheism's error is too palpable to deceive anyone. It is that God is the sum of all created things. Nature and God are one to the pantheist, so that whoever touches a leaf or a stone touches God. That is of course to degrade the glory of the incorruptible Deity and, in an effort to make all things divine, banish all divinity from the world entirely.

The truth is that while God dwells in His world He is separated from it by a gulf forever impassable. However closely He may be identified with the work of His hands they are and must eternally be other than He, and He is and must be antecedent to and independent of them.

He is transcendent above all His works even while He is immanent within them. He is here and the whole universe is alive with His life!

Christ's Words Are for the Children of God

Thy word have I hid in mine heart, that I might not sin against thee. Psalm 119:11

The gracious words of Christ are for the sons and daughters of grace, not for the Gentile nations whose chosen symbols are the lion, the eagle, the dragon and the bear!

So, the notion that the Bible is addressed to everybody has wrought confusion within and without the church. The effort to apply the teaching of the Sermon on the Mount to the unregenerate nations of the world is one example of this. Courts of law and the military powers of the earth are urged to follow the teachings of Christ, an obviously impossible thing for them to do. To quote the words of Christ as guides for policemen, judges and generals is to misunderstand those words completely and to reveal a total lack of understanding of the purposes of divine revelation.

Not only does God address His words of truth to those who are able to receive them, He actually conceals their meaning from those who are not. The parables of Christ were the exact opposite of the modern "illustration" which is meant to give light: the parables were "dark sayings" and Christ asserted He sometimes used them so that His disciples could understand and His enemies could not.

The natural man must know in order to believe; the spiritual man must believe in order to know!

Contemplating the Sweet Mystery of the Godhead

O the depths of the riches both of the wisdom and knowledge of God! How unsearchable are his judgments, and his ways past finding out! Romans 11:33

Christian theology teaches that God in His essential nature is both inscrutable and ineffable. By simple definition this means that He is incapable of being searched into or understood, and that He cannot tell forth or utter what He is.

This inability lies not in God but in the limitations of our creaturehood: "Why inquirest thou after my name, for it is secret?"

Only God knows God in any final meaning of the word know: "Even so the things of God knoweth no man, but the Spirit of God."

God in His essential Being is unique in the only sense that word will bear. That is, there is nothing like Him in the universe. What He is cannot be conceived by the mind because He is "altogether other" than anything with which we have had experience before. The mind has no material with which to start. No man has ever entertained a thought which can be said to describe God in any but the vaguest and most imperfect sense. Where God is known at all it must be otherwise than by our creature-reason.

In a famed treatise on the Trinity written in the third century, Novatian said: "Every possible statement that can be made about God expresses some possession or virtue of God, rather than God Himself. The conception of God as He is can only be grasped in one way—by thinking of Him as a Being whose attributes and greatness are beyond our powers of understanding, or even of thought."

August 1

Many Spiritual Blessings in Christ Go Unclaimed

Blessed be the God and Father of our Lord Jesus Christ, who hath blessed us with all spiritual blessings in heavenly places in Christ. Ephesians 1:3

Those spiritual blessings in heavenly places which are ours in Christ may be divided into three classes:

The first is those which come to us immediately upon our believing unto salvation, such as forgiveness, justification, regeneration, sonship to God and baptism into the Body of Christ. In Christ we possess these even before we know that they are ours!

The second class is those riches which are ours by inheritance but which we cannot enjoy in actuality until our Lord returns. These include ultimate mental and moral perfection, the glorification of our bodies, the completion of the restoration of the divine image in our redeemed personalities and the admission into the very presence of God to experience forever the Beatific Vision. These treasures are as surely ours as if we possessed them now!

The third class consists of spiritual treasures which are ours by blood atonement but which will not come to us unless we make a determined effort to possess them. These are deliverance from the sins of the flesh, victory over self, the constant flow of the Holy Spirit through our personalities, fruitfulness in Christian service, awareness of the Presence of God, growth in grace, an increasing consciousness of union with God and an unbroken spirit of worship. These are to us what the Promised Land was to Israel, to be entered into as our faith and courage mount.

August 2

Spiritual Radiance Comes from an Inner Witness

. . .And hereby we know that he abideth in us, by the Spirit which he hath given us. 1 John 3:24

One distinguishing mark of the earliest Christians was their radiance, for the sun had come up in their hearts and its warmth and light made unnecessary any secondary sources of assurance.

They had the inner witness!

Great power and great grace marked their lives, enabling them to rejoice to suffer shame for the name of Jesus.

It is obvious in our day that the average evangelical Christian is without this radiance. The efforts of some of our teachers to cheer our drooping spirits are futile because those same teachers reject the very phenomenon that would naturally produce joy, namely, the inner witness. Instead of the inner witness we now substitute logical conclusions drawn from texts. There is no witness, no immediacy of knowledge, no encounter with God, no awareness of inner change.

Where there is a divine act within the soul there will always be a corresponding awareness. This act of God is self-validating. It is its own evidence and addresses itself directly to the religious consciousness.

Charles Wesley in a triumphant hymn wrote: ·
> "His Spirit answers to the blood,
> And tells me I am born of God!"

To the salvation-by-logical-conclusion devotees such language is plain heresy. If it is heresy, I run to join such a glorious heretic, and may God send us many more!

August 3

Faith: Our Minds Brought into Accord with Truth

And the Lord direct your hearts into the love of God, and into the patient waiting for Christ. 2 Thessalonians 3:5

This we must remember: faith is not a noble quality found only in superior men. It is not a virtue attainable by a limited few. It is not the quality to persuade ourselves that black is white or that something we desire will come to pass if we only wish hard enough.

Faith is simply the bringing of our minds into accord with the truth. It is adjusting our expectations to the promises of God in complete assurance that the God of the whole earth cannot lie!

As long as we question the wisdom of any of God's ways our faith is still tentative and uncertain. While we are able to understand, we are not quite believing. Faith enters when there is no supporting evidence to corroborate God's word of promise and we must put our confidence blindly in the character of the One who made the promise.

A man looks at a mountain and affirms, "That is a mountain." There is no particular virtue in the affirmation. It is simply accepting the fact that stands before him and bringing his belief into accord with the fact. The man does not create the mountain by believing, nor could he annihilate it by denying.

And so with the truth of God! The believing man accepts a promise of God as a fact as solid as a mountain and vastly more enduring. His faith changes nothing except his own personal relation to the word of promise. God's Word is true whether we believe it or not. Human unbelief cannot alter the character of God!

August 4

The Devil Never Forgives Those Who Escape Bondage

But Peter said, Ananias, why hath Satan filled thine heart to lie to the Holy Ghost?. . . Acts 5:3

As we move farther on in the Christian life we may expect to encounter increased hostility from the enemy of our souls. Although this is seldom presented to Christians as a fact of life it is a very solid fact indeed as every experienced Christian knows, and one we shall learn how to handle or stumble over to our own undoing.

If Satan opposes the new convert he opposes still more bitterly the Christian who is pressing on toward a higher life in Christ. The Spirit-filled life is not, as many suppose, a life of peace and quiet pleasure. It is likely to be something quite the opposite.

Satan hates the true Christian for several reasons. One is that God loves him, and whatever is loved by God is sure to be hated by the devil. Another is that the Christian, being a child of God, bears a family resemblance to the Father and to the household of faith.

A third reason is that a true Christian is a former slave who has escaped from the galley, and Satan cannot forgive him for this affront. A fourth reason is that a praying Christian is a constant threat to the stability of Satan's government. The Christian is a holy rebel loose in the world with access to the throne of God.

Satan never knows from what direction his danger will come. Who knows when another Elijah will arise, or another Daniel? or a Luther, a Finney or a Booth?

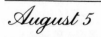

Deliverance: Saved from the World's Nervous Scramble

For we have need of patience, that, after ye have done the will of God, ye might receive the promise. Hebrews 10:36

Christians have often been accused of being reactionary because they cannot show any enthusiasm for the latest scheme that someone thinks up to bring in the millennium.

Well, it is not to be wondered at. A true Christian's firsthand acquaintance with God saves him from the nervous scramble in which the world is engaged and which is popularly touted as progress.

A real Christian is an odd number anyway. He feels supreme love for One whom he has never seen, talks familiarly every day to Someone he cannot see, expects to go to heaven on the virtue of Another, empties himself in order to be full, admits he is wrong so he can be declared right, goes down in order to get up, is strongest when he is weakest, richest when he is poorest, and happiest when he feels worst!

He dies so he can live, gives away so he can keep, sees the invisible, hears the inaudible and knows that which passes knowledge.

The man who has met God is not looking for something—he has found it. He is not searching for light—upon him the Light has already shined!

His religion is not hearsay. He is not a copy, not a facsimile print: he is an original from the hand of the Holy Ghost!

He may hear the tin whistle starting every new parade, but he will be cautious. He is waiting for a trumpet note that will call him away from the hurly-burly and set in motion a series of events that will result at last in a new heaven and a new earth.

He can afford to wait!

August 6

Love Must Leave When Resentment Moves In

Forbearing one another, and forgiving one another, if any man have a quarrel against any: even as Christ forgave you, so also do ye. Colossians 3:13

I do not believe that a spirit of resentment can dwell in a loving heart.

In the course of scores of conferences and hundreds of conversations I have many times heard people say: "I resent that!"

But I have never heard those words used by any man or woman living in conscious Christian victory!

Before resentment can enter, love must take its flight and bitterness take over. The bitter soul will compile a list of slights at which it takes offense and will watch over itself like a mother bear over her cubs.

Few sights are more depressing than that of a professed Christian defending his supposed rights and bitterly resisting any attempt to violate them. Such a Christian has never accepted the way of the cross. The sweet graces of meekness and humility are unknown to him.

The only cure for this sort of thing is to die to self and rise with Christ into newness of life. The man who sets the will of God as his goal will reach that goal, not by self-defense, but by self-abnegation. Then no matter what sort of treatment he receives from his fellow men he will be altogether at peace.

The will of God has been done—whether by curses or compliments he cares not, for he seeks not one or the other but only to do the will of God at any cost!

If there be some who take pleasure in holding him down, he is still content within himself, and will not resent them, for he seeks not advancement but the will of God.

August 7

True Believers Do Not Shy Away from Obedience

But now being made free from sin, and become servants to God, ye have your fruit unto holiness, and the end everlasting life. Romans 6:22

It has been quite overlooked in recent times that the faith of Christ is an absolute arbiter!

It preempts the whole redeemed personality and seizes upon the individual to the exclusion of all other claims. Or more accurately, it makes every legitimate claim on the Christian's life conditional, and without hesitation decides the place each claim shall have in the total scheme.

The act of commital to Christ in salvation releases the believing man from the penalty of sin, but it does not release him from the obligation to obey the words of Christ. Rather it brings him under the joyous necessity to obey!

Look at the epistles of the New Testament and notice how largely they are given over to what is erroneously called "hortatory" matter. By dividing the epistles into "doctrinal" and "hortatory" passages we have relieved ourselves of any necessity to obey. The doctrinal passages require from us nothing except that we believe them. The so-called hortatory passages are harmless enough for the very word by which they are described declares them to be words of advice and encouragement rather than commandments to be obeyed. This is a palpable error.

The exhortations in the epistles are to be understood as apostolic injunctions carrying the weight of mandatory charges from the Head of the Church. They are intended to be obeyed, not accepted or rejected as we will. If we would have God's blessing upon us we must begin to obey!

August 8

Our Final Accountability Will Be to Our Maker

So then every one of us shall give account of himself to God. Romans 14:12

It was the belief in the accountability of man to his Maker that made America great at one time. One of our great leaders was Daniel Webster who confessed: "The most solemn thought that has ever entered my mind is my accountability to my Maker!"

Men are free to decide their own moral choices, but they are also under the necessity to account to God for those choices. That makes them both free and also bound—for they are bound to come to judgment and give an account of the deeds done in the body.

You have probably heard the concept that every man stands only before the bar of his own reason and of his own conscience.

This is the infamous relativity of morals that is taught in many of our universities and colleges. Our young folks are taught that each man is a law unto himself and that good is whatever brings social approval and that evil is whatever brings social disapproval.

If that were true, there would be as many moral codes as there are human beings, and each one of us would be our own witness, prosecutor, judge, jury and jailer!

No, God is not going to make man accountable to himself; neither is He going to make you and me accountable to the law, finally, nor to human society, finally.

We are accountable to the One who gave us being. We are accountable to the One out of whose heart we were loved, and who laid His laws upon us. The idea of man's accountability only to himself is so silly as scarcely to be worthy of consideration!

August 9

Spiritual Receptivity May Be Increased by Exercise

My soul thirsteth for God, for the living God: when shall I come and appear before God? Psalm 42:2

Pick at random a score of great saints whose lives and testimonies are widely known. Let them be Bible characters or well-known Christians of post-biblical times. I venture to suggest that the one vital quality which they had in common was spiritual receptivity. They acquired the lifelong habit of spiritual response. They were not disobedient to the heavenly vision!

Receptivity is not a single thing; it is a compound, rather, a blending of several elements within the soul. It is an affinity for, a bent toward, a sympathetic response to, a desire to have. It may be increased by exercise or destroyed by neglect. It is a gift of God, indeed, but one which must be recognized and cultivated as any other gift if it is to realize the purpose for which it was given.

The idea of spiritual cultivation and exercise, so dear to the saints of old, has now no place in our total religious picture. It is too slow, too common. We now demand glamour and fast flowing dramatic action. We have been trying to apply machine-age methods to our relations with God. We read our chapter, have our short devotions and rush away, hoping to make up for our deep inward bankruptcy by attending another gospel meeting or listening to another thrilling story told by a religious adventurer lately returned from afar.

It will require a determined heart and more than a little courage to wrench ourselves loose from the grip of our times and return to biblical ways!

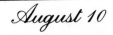

August 10

Bold Men Needed in the Warfare of the Soul

. . .Neither count I my life dear to myself. . .that I might finish my course with joy, and the ministry, which I have received of the Lord Jesus, to testify the gospel of the grace of God. Acts 20:24

The Church at this moment needs men, the right kind of men, bold men. The talk is that we need revival, that we need a new baptism of the Spirit—and God knows we must have both; but God will not revive mice. He will not fill rabbits with the Holy Ghost!

We languish for men who feel themselves expendable in the warfare of the soul, who cannot be frightened by threats of death because they have already died to the allurements of this world. Such men will be free from the compulsions that control and squeeze weaker men.

This kind of freedom is necessary if we are to have prophets in our pulpits again instead of mascots. These free men will serve God and mankind from motives too high to be understood by the rank and file of religious entertainers who today shuttle in and out of the sanctuary.

They will make no decisions out of fear, take no course out of a desire to please, accept no service for financial considerations, perform no religious act out of mere custom; nor will they allow themselves to be influenced by the love of publicity or the desire for reputation.

The true Church has never sounded out public expectations before launching her crusades. Her leaders heard from God, they knew their Lord's will and did it. Their people followed them—sometimes to triumph, oftener to insults and public persecution—and their sufficient reward was the satisfaction of being right in a wrong world!

August 11

Church Must Discern between Popularity and Greatness

If any man serve me, let him follow me; and where I am, there shall also my servant be: if any man serve me, him will my Father honour. John 12:26

Human society generally has fallen into the error of assuming that greatness and fame are synonymous. Americans appear to take for granted that each generation provides a certain number of superior men and the democratic processes unerringly find those men and set them in a place of prominence. How wrong can people get!

We have but to become acquainted with, or even listen to, the big names of our times to discover how wretchedly inferior most of them are! Many appear to have arrived at their present eminence by pull, brass, nerve, gall and lucky accident.

If we would see life steadily and see it whole we must make a stern effort to break away from the power of that false philosophy that equates greatness with fame. The two may be and often are oceans and continents apart!

If the church were a body wholly unaffected by the world we could toss the above problem over to the secular philosophers; but the truth is that the church also suffers from this evil notion!

Christians have fallen into the habit of accepting the noisiest and most notorious among them as the best and the greatest. They too have learned to equate popularity with excellence. In open defiance of the Sermon on the Mount, they have given their approval not to the meek but to the self-assertive; not to the mourner but to the self-assured; not to the pure in heart who see God but to the publicity hunter who seeks headlines!

August 12

The Glory of the Cross: Atonement and Forgiveness

Surely he hath borne our griefs, and carried our sorrows: yet we did esteem him stricken, smitten of God, and afflicted. Isaiah 53:4

Never make any mistake about this—the suffering of Jesus Christ on the cross was not punitive! It was not for Himself and not for punishment of anything that He Himself had done.

The suffering of Jesus was corrective. He was willing to suffer in order that He might correct us and perfect us.

Brethren, that is the glory of the cross! That is the glory of the kind of sacrifice that was for so long in the heart of God! That is the glory of the kind of atonement that allows a repentant sinner to come into peaceful and gracious fellowship with his God and Creator!

It began in His wounds and ended in our purification!

It began in His bruises and ended in our cleansing!

That painful and acute conviction that accompanies repentance may well subside and a sense of peace and cleansing come, but even the holiest of justified men will think back over his part in the wounding and chastisement of the Lamb of God.

A sense of shock will still come over him!

A sense of wonder will remain—wonder that the Lamb that was wounded should turn his wounds into the cleansing and forgiveness of one who wounded Him!

August 13

God Still Speaks through Those Who Can Weep

Be afflicted, and mourn, and weep; let your laughter be turned to mourning. . . . James 4:9

The Bible was written in tears and to tears it will yield its best treasure. God has nothing to say to the frivolous man.

It was to Moses, a trembling man, that God spoke on the mount, and that same man later saved the nation when he threw himself before God with the offer to have himself blotted out of God's book for Israel's sake. Daniel's long season of fasting and prayer brought Gabriel from heaven to tell him the secret of the centuries. When the beloved John wept much because no one could be found worthy to open the seven-sealed book, one of the elders comforted him with the joyous news that the Lion of the tribe of Judah had prevailed.

The psalmists often wrote in tears, the prophets could hardly conceal their heavyheartedness, and the Apostle Paul in his otherwise joyous epistle to the Philippians broke into tears when he thought of the many who were enemies of the cross of Christ and whose end was destruction. Those Christian leaders who shook the world were one and all men of sorrows whose witness to mankind welled out of heavy hearts.

There is no power in tears, per se, but tears and power ever lie close together in the Church of the Firstborn! By the law of just compensation, the heart of the religious trifler will be destroyed by the exceeding brightness of the truth he touches. Tearless eyes are finally blinded by the light at which they gaze!

August 14

Explore God's High Purposes in Salvation

Make you perfect in every good work to do his will, working in you that which is wellpleasing in his sight, through Jesus Christ. . . . Hebrews 13:21

There seems to be a great throng of professing Christians in our churches today whose total and amazing testimony sounds like this: "I am thankful for God's plan in sending Christ to the cross to save me from hell."

I am convinced that it is a cheap, low-grade and misleading kind of Christianity that impels people to rise and state: "Because of sin I was deeply in debt—and God sent His Son, who came and paid all my debts."

Of course believing Christian men and women are saved from the judgment of hell and it is a reality that Christ our Redeemer has paid the whole slate of debt and sin that was against us. But what does God say about His purposes in allowing Jesus to go to the cross and to the grave? What does God say about the meaning of death and resurrection for the Christian believer?

Surely we know the Bible well enough to be able to answer that: God's highest purpose in the redemption of sinful humanity was based in His hope that we would allow Him to reproduce the likeness of Jesus Christ in our once-sinful lives!

So, acknowledging this, we are able to humbly testify with the Apostle Paul: "I have been crucified with Christ—and the life which I now live in the flesh I live by the faith of the Son of God!"

There Are No Shortcuts to a Godly Life

I press toward the mark for the prize of the high calling of God in Christ Jesus. Philippians 3:14

The causes of retarded spiritual progress are many. It would not be accurate to ascribe the trouble to one single fault.

One there is, however, which is so universal that it may easily be the main cause: failure to give time to the cultivation of the knowledge of God!

The temptation to make our relation to God judicial instead of personal is very strong. Believing for salvation has these days been reduced to a once-done act that requires no further attention. The young believer becomes aware of an act performed rather than of a living Saviour to be followed and adored.

The Apostle Paul was anything but an advocate of the once-done, automatic school of Christianity. He devoted his whole life to the art of knowing Christ!

We may as well accept it: there is no shortcut to sanctity. Even the crises that come in the spiritual life are usually the result of long periods of thought and prayerful meditation. As the wonder grows more and more dazzling there is likely to occur a crisis of revolutionizing proportions. But that crisis is related to what has gone before in the preparation of waiting upon God.

It may come as a sudden sweet explosion, an uprushing of a tide that has been increasing its pressure within until we can no longer contain it!

August 16

God's Love: A Quality That Cannot Be Defined

Hereby perceive we the love of God, because he laid down his life for us: and we ought to lay down our lives for the brethren. 1 John 3:16

Can you really define the word "love" for me?

I do not believe you can actually define love—you can describe it but you cannot define it. A person or a race which has never heard of the word "love" can never come to an understanding of what love is even if they could memorize the definitions in all of the world's dictionaries.

But just consider what happens to any simple, freckle-faced boy with his big ears and his red hair awry when he first falls in love and the feeling of it comes into every part of his being. All at once, he knows more about love than all of the dictionaries put together!

That is why I say that love can only be understood by the feeling of it. The same is true with the warmth of the sun. Tell a man who has no feeling that it is a warm day and he will never understand what you mean. But take a normal man who is out in the sun and he will soon know it is warm. You can know more about the sun by feeling than you can by description.

So, there are qualities in God that can never be explained by the intellect and can only be known by the heart, the innermost being. That is why I say that I do believe in feeling. I believe in what the old writers called religious affection—and we have so little of it because we have so little of true repentance, obedience, separation and holy living!

August 17

The True Christian Is a Saint in Embryo

. . .The appearing of our Saviour Jesus Christ, who hath abolished death, and hath brought life and immortality to light through the gospel. 2 Timothy 1:10

Christianity, being in full accord with all the facts of existence, takes into account the acknowledged moral imbalance in human life, and the remedy it offers is not a new philosophy but a new life!

The ideal to which the Christian aspires is not to walk in the perfect way but to be transformed by the renewing of his mind and conformed to the likeness of Christ!

The true Christian is a saint in embryo. The heavenly genes are in him and the Holy Spirit is working to bring him on into a spiritual development that accords with the nature of the Heavenly Father from whom he received the deposit of divine life. Yet he is here in this mortal body subject to weakness and temptation, and his warfare with the flesh sometimes leads him to do extreme things.

The work of the Holy Spirit in the human heart is not an unconscious or automatic thing. Human will and intelligence must yield to and cooperate with the benign intentions of God. I think it is here that we go astray.

Either we try to make ourselves holy and fail miserably, as we certainly must; or we seek to achieve a state of spiritual passivity and wait for God to perfect our natures in holiness as one might wait for a robin egg to hatch or a rose to burst into bloom. The New Testament knows nothing of the working of the Spirit in us apart from our own moral responses. Watchfulness, prayer, self-discipline and acquiescence in the purposes of God are indispensable to any real progress in holiness!

August 18

The Example of Jesus: Hold No Grudges

Then said Jesus, Father, forgive them; for they know not what they do. . . .
Luke 23:34

Jesus Christ left us an example for our daily conduct and from it there can be no appeal. He felt no bitter resentment and he held no grudge against anyone!

Even those who crucified Him were forgiven while they were in the act. Not a word did He utter against them nor against the ones who stirred them up to destroy Him.

How evil they all were He knew better than any other man, but He maintained a charitable attitude toward them. They were only doing their duty, and even those who ordered them to their grisly task were unaware of the meaning of their act.

To Pilate, Jesus said: "Thou couldest have no power at all against me, except it were given thee from above."

So He referred everything back to the will of God and rose above the swampland of personalities.

The person with the resentful heart takes just the opposite course, however. He grows every day harder and more acrimonious as he defends his reputation, his rights, his ministry, against his imagined foes!

The worst feature about this whole thing is that it does no good to call attention to it. The bitter heart is not likely to recognize its own condition. The resentful man in the meantime will grow smaller and smaller trying to get bigger, and he will become more and more obscure trying to become known. As he pushes on toward his selfish goal his very prayers will be surly accusations against the Almighty and his whole relationship toward other Christians will be one of suspicion and distrust!

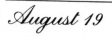

August 19

We Can Sanctify the Ordinary Each Day

And he said unto me, My grace is sufficient for thee: for my strength is made perfect in weakness. . . . 2 Corinthians 12:9

Today more than ever we Christians need to learn how to sanctify the ordinary!

In this cynical generation, people have been overstimulated to the place where their nerves are jaded and their tastes corrupted. Everything is common and almost everything boring. The sacred has been secularized, the holy vulgarized and worship converted into a form of entertainment.

Like it or not, that is the world in which we find ourselves and we are charged with the responsibility to live soberly, righteously and godly right in the middle of it!

The danger is that we allow ourselves to be too much affected by the degenerate tastes and low views of the Hittites and Jebusites among whom we dwell and so learn the ways of the nations, to our own undoing, as Israel did before us.

When the whole moral and psychological atmosphere is secular and common how can we escape its deadly effects? How can we sanctify the ordinary and find true spiritual meaning in the common things of life?

The answer is plainly apparent but to some of us it will seem too tame and ordinary. It is to consecrate the whole of life to Christ and begin to do everything in His name and for His sake. That just means that we begin to do for Christ's sake what we had formerly been doing for our own!

August 20

We Have within Us the Spirit of Optimism

. . .And lo, I am with you alway, even unto the end of the world. . . .
Matthew 28:20

As earnest Christian believers, we must face today as children of tomorrow. We must meet the uncertainties of this world with the certainty of the world to come!

The political, social and economic convulsions of our day only confirm the long-range wisdom of Jesus Christ and prove the authenticity of the prophetic Word. Christians who may live even in the worst of times will still know within themselves a spirit of optimism. They are on the winning side and they cannot lose!

The promise of the Lord Jesus, "Lo, I am with you!" makes ultimate defeat impossible.

To any man or woman, pure in heart, nothing really bad can happen. They may die, but what is death to a Christian?

Not death, but sin, should be our great fear. Without doubt the heavens being on fire shall be dissolved, and the earth and the works that are therein shall be burned up. Sooner or later that will come.

But what of it?

Do not we, according to His promise, look for new heavens and a new earth, wherein dwelleth righteousness?

Let us beware allowing our spiritual comforts to rise and fall with world news or the changing world situations. We who lean upon Jesus and trust in the watchful love of a heavenly Father are not dependent upon these things for our peace.

For children of the new creation, the darker the night the brighter faith shines and the sooner comes the morning!

August 21

The Quality of True Faith Is Moral, Not Mental

I will bring the blind by a way that they knew not; I will lead them in paths that they have not known. . . . Isaiah 42:16

Sometimes we are prone to blame ourselves for unbelief when our trouble is nothing more than inability to visualize. There are some truths set forth in the Scriptures that place a great strain upon our minds. Divine revelation assures us that certain things are true which imagination simply will not grasp.

We believe them but we cannot see them in the mind's eye!

To think right we must distinguish believing from visualizing. The two are not the same. One is moral and the other mental. Unwillingness to believe proves that men love darkness rather than light, while inability to visualize indicates no more than lack of imagination, something that will not be held against us at the judgment seat of Christ.

True faith is not the intellectual ability to visualize unseen things to the satisfaction of our imperfect minds; it is rather the moral power to trust Christ!

To be unafraid when going on a journey with his father the child need not be able to imagine events; he need but know the father! Jesus Christ is our all in all— we need but trust Him and He will take care of the rest.

I have found deep satisfaction in these words of the prophet: "I will bring the blind by a way they knew not; I will lead them in paths they have not known: I will make darkness light before them, and crooked things straight. These things will I do unto them, and not forsake them" (Isa. 42:16).

August 22

Men in Love with Sin Do Not Receive Christ

. . .Men loved darkness rather than light, because their deeds were evil. John 3:19

I do not believe anyone has ever rejected Jesus Christ on philosophical grounds. Israel did not reject the Lord because of philosophical reasons. Israel's rejection was for moral reasons.

The man who continues in his rejection of Christ has a pet sin somewhere—he's in love with iniquity. He rejects Jesus on moral grounds, and then hides behind false philosophy—philosophical grounds.

I believe that every one of those who are having "intellectual difficulties" is hiding because he is morally reprobate. When we fall in love with our sin, we can imagine and manufacture 10,000 syllogisms to keep us away from the cross.

A blind man can argue that there is no sunshine, but when he gets his sight, the sunshine floods in!

How wonderful it is that when a person gives up his sin and puts his pride under his feet and looks at the light, the whole body and mind are flooded with light. I have talked with people who have come out of rationalism and atheism and all the rest—and they smile at you with clear eyes and say, "Oh, it is wonderful now; the light has flooded in."

Jesus said, "For everyone that doeth evil hateth the light, neither cometh to the light lest his deeds should be reproved." This is the condemnation—that light is come into the world, and men love darkness rather than light, because their deeds are evil. The natural man has a perverse antipathy to the light because it interferes with his iniquity!

August 23

We Make Religion Easy for the Moral Rebel

And they departed from the presence of the council, rejoicing that they were counted worthy to suffer shame for his name. Acts 5:41

The story of the earliest Christians is a story of faith under fire. The opposition was real. To continue "steadfastly" as Luke records was to continue against serious opposition. Steadfastness is required only when we are under attack, mental or physical.

Those first believers turned to Christ with the full understanding that they were espousing an unpopular cause that could cost them everything. Shortly after Pentecost some were jailed, many lost all their earthly goods, a few were slain outright and hundreds were "scattered abroad."

They could have escaped all this by the simple expedient of denying their faith and turning back to the world; but this they steadfastly refused to do.

Here again is seen the glaring discrepancy between biblical Christianity and that of present-day evangelicals, particularly in the United States. To make converts we are forced to play down the difficulties and play up the peace of mind and worldly success enjoyed by those who accept Christ!

We will never be completely honest with our hearers until we tell them the blunt truth that as members of a race of moral rebels they are in a serious jam, and one they will not get out of easily. If they refuse to repent and believe on Christ they will most surely perish; if they do turn to Him, the same enemies that crucified Him will try to crucify them.

We Must Surrender: God Must Have His Way

How much better it is to get wisdom than gold! and to get understanding rather to be chosen than silver! Proverbs 16:16

The man who will not brook interference is under no compulsion to follow Christ. "If any man will," said our Lord, and thus freed every man and placed the Christian life in the realm of voluntary choice.

I have long believed that a man who spurns the Christian faith outright is more respected before God and the heavenly powers than the man who pretends to religion but refuses to come under its total domination. The first is an overt enemy, the second a false friend. It is the latter who will be spued out of the mouth of Christ; and the reason is not hard to understand.

Truth is a glorious but hard mistress. She never consults, bargains or compromises. She cries from the top of the high places, "Receive my instruction, and not silver; and knowledge rather than choice gold." After that, every man is on his own. He may accept or refuse, receive or set at naught as he pleases; and there will be no attempt at coercion, though the man's whole destiny is at stake.

Were this an unfallen world the path of truth would be a smooth and easy one. Here the natural man receives not the things of the Spirit of God; the flesh lusts against the Spirit and the Spirit against the flesh, and these are contrary one to another. In that contest there can be only one outcome. We must surrender and God must have His way. His glory and our eternal welfare require that it be so!

August 25

We Settle for Words: Deeds Are Too Costly

My little children, let us not love in word, neither in tongue; but in deed and in truth. 1 John 3:18

The practice of substituting words for deeds is not something new, for the Apostle John saw it in his day and warned against it.

James also had something to say about the vice of words without deeds: "If a brother or sister be naked, and destitute of daily food, and one of you say unto them, Depart in peace, be ye warmed and filled; notwithstanding ye give them not those things which are needful to the body; what doth it profit?"

We settle for words in religion because deeds are too costly. It is easier to pray, "Lord, help me to carry my cross daily" than to pick up the cross and carry it. But since the mere request for help to do something we do not actually intend to do has a certain degree of religious comfort, we are content with repetition of the words.

What then? Shall we take a vow of silence? Shall we cease to pray and sing and write and witness until we catch up on our deeds?

I say no, that would not help. While we have breath we must speak to men about God and to God about men.

To escape this snare of words without deeds, let us say nothing we do not mean. Break the habit of conventional religious chatter. Speak only as we are ready to take the consequences. Believe God's promises and obey God's commandments. Practice the truth so that we may with propriety speak the truth. Deeds give body to words. As we do acts of power our words will take on authority and a new sense of reality will fill our hearts!

August 26

Religious Work Should Be Most Open to Inspection

Let all things be done decently and in order. 1 Corinthians 14:40

A spirit of candor would do much to remove the widespread suspicion that Christian people are preoccupied with unrealities. Complete frankness with God, with our own souls and with our critics would take away many a sword from the hands of our enemies.

We have never gone along with the tender-minded saints who fear to examine religious things lest God be displeased. On the contrary, we believe that God's handiwork is so perfect that it invites inspection. If God performs the work no matter how closely we look into it we may be sure that we will be forced to stand back in wonder and exclaim, "My Lord and my God!"

Of all work done under the sun religious work should be the most open to examination. There is positively no place in the church for sleight of hand or double talk. Everything done by the churches should be completely above suspicion. The true Church will have nothing to hide. Her books will be available to anyone for inspection at any time. Her officers will insist upon an audit by someone from the outside.

Just what quality does a child possess that Christians must have to please our Father who is in heaven? Could it be candor? The little child is so frank that he is often embarrassing to his elders—but maybe he has found the secret!

Caution: Our Ego Will Try to Act Spiritual

Not of works, lest any man should boast. Ephesians 2:9

Boasting is particularly offensive when it is heard among the children of God, the one place above all others where it should never be found. Yet it is quite common among Christians, though often disguised somewhat by the use of the stock expression, "I say this to the glory of God!"

Another habit not quite so odious is belittling ourselves. This might seem to be the exact opposite of boasting, but actually it is the same old sin traveling under a nom de plume. It is simply egoism trying to act spiritual. It is impatient Saul hastily offering an unacceptable sacrifice to the Lord.

Self-derogation is bad for the reason that self must be there to derogate. Self, whether swaggering or groveling, can never be anything but hateful to God!

God is very patient with His children and often tolerates in them carnal traits so gross as to shock their fellow Christians. But that is only for a while. As more light comes to our hearts, and especially as we go on to new and advanced spiritual experiences, God begins to impose disciplines upon us to purge us from the same faults He tolerated before.

After we have learned our lesson the Lord may restore what He has taken away, for He is more concerned with our souls than with our service. But sometimes our boasting or belittling hurts us permanently and excludes us from blessings we might have enjoyed.

August 28

Our Lord Looks for Heavenly Minded Christians

Father, I will that they also, whom thou hast given me, be with me where I am; that they may behold my glory. . . . John 17:24

I am sure that our Lord is looking for heavenly-minded Christians, for His Word encourages us to trust Him with such a singleness of purpose that He is able to deliver us from the fear of death and the uncertainties of tomorrow!

If we had actually reached a place of such spiritual commitment that the wonders of heaven were so close that we longed for the illuminating Presence of our Lord, we would not go into such a fearful and frantic performance every time we find something wrong with our physical frame.

I do not think that a genuine, committed Christian ever ought to be afraid to die. We do not have to fear because Jesus promised that He would prepare a proper place for all of those who shall be born again, raised up out of the agony and stress of this world through the blood of the everlasting covenant into that bright and gracious world above.

Notice that Jesus said, "In my Father's house are many mansions." If it is His Father's house, it is also our Father's house because the Lord Jesus is our elder brother. Jesus also said, "I go to my Father and your Father—my God and your God."

If the Father's house is the house of Jesus, it is also the house of all of His other sons and daughters! And we Christians are much better off than we really know!

The Bible Is Not Addressed to Just Anybody

The grass withereth, the flower fadeth: but the word of our God shall stand forever. Isaiah 40:8

That many people find the Bible hard to understand will not be denied by those acquainted with the facts.

I venture to give a short answer to the question, "Why is the Bible hard to understand?": I believe that we find the Bible difficult because we try to read it as we would read any other book, and it is not the same as any other book!

The Bible is a supernatural book and can be understood only by supernatural aid. It is not addressed to just anybody. Its message is directed to a chosen few. Whether these few are chosen by God in a sovereign act of election or are chosen because they meet certain qualifying conditions I leave to each one to decide as he may.

But whatever may have taken place in eternity, it is obvious what happens in time: some believe and some do not; some are morally receptive and some are not; some have spiritual capacity and some have not. It is to those who do and are and have that the Bible is addressed. Those who do not and are not and have not will read it in vain!

The saving power of the Word is reserved for those for whom it is intended. The secret of the Lord is with them that fear Him. The impenitent heart will find the Bible but a skeleton of facts without flesh or life or breath!

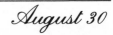

August 30

Simple Rules for the Christian in Discouragement

Behold, God is my salvation; I will trust and not be afraid. . . . Isaiah 12:2

Christian men and women should be aware that there is danger in a defeated spirit within us, for it can plunge us into discouragement.

Discouragement, by the way, is hardly a sin. But it can lead to any number of sins, for to discourage is to dishearten. In such a case, we may still go to church, but we have little appetite for it. Nothing means anything to us. Hymns are dull and tasteless and the sermon is a bore.

I want to give you some rules for the time of discouragement:

First, do not accept the judgment of your own heart about the matter. A discouraged heart will always go astray, so do not think about yourself the way you feel about yourself!

Instead, go to God and Christ. God loves you, and Christ loves you enough to have died for you. He thought you were worth something. Remember that discouraged Gideon was hiding until God sought him out and said, "Get up, thou mighty man of God!"

The second rule is this: make no important decisions while you are discouraged. Don't resign your job. Don't sell your property. Get down before God and ask Him to take the defeat out of your spirit and the reverses out of your heart.

Finally, go to the Bible and read the promises of God. Read and claim the promises until your heart leaps with the joy of His promises. Remember that the living God is everything. Our victory cannot enrich God and our defeat cannot impoverish Him. Live on the side where the promises of God are bright!

August 31

God Is the Most Winsome of All Beings

. . . Truly our fellowship is with the Father, and with his Son, Jesus Christ.
1 John 1:3

Nothing twists and deforms the human soul more than a low or unworthy conception of God and His kindness.

To a Pharisee in the days of Christ, the service of God was a bondage which he did not love but from which he could not escape without a loss too great to bear.

The God of the Pharisees was not a God easy to live with, so his religion became grim and hard and loveless. It had to be so, for our notion of God must always determine the quality of our religion.

Much Christianity since the days of Christ's flesh has also been grim and severe. And the cause has been the same—an unworthy or an inadequate view of God.

Instinctively we try to be like our God, and if He is conceived to be stern and exacting, so will we ourselves be.

From a failure properly to understand God comes a world of unhappiness among good Christians even today. The Christian life is thought to be a glum, unrelieved cross-carrying under the eye of a stern Father who expects much and excuses nothing—a God austere, peevish, highly temperamental and extremely hard to please!

The kind of life which springs out of such libelous notions must of necessity be but a parody on the true life in Christ.

The truth is that God is the most winsome of all beings and His service one of unspeakable pleasure. Those who trust Him have found His mercy always in triumph over justice, through the blood of the everlasting covenant!

September 1

There Is Delight in True Service for God

And to know the love of Christ, which passeth knowledge, that ye might be filled with all the fulness of God. Ephesians 3:19

The Bible instructs the Christian believer that he should be dedicated to the glory of the One whom we have not yet seen, because we love Him. That is the sum of Christianity—to know Him and to love Him!

"This is eternal life, that they might know me," Jesus taught. So, the knowledge of God is eternal life and the knowledge of setting forth the life of God in man is the business of the church.

It is a wonderful facet of love that we always take pleasure and delight in doing those things that are pleasing to the one we love. I find that the believing Christian who really loves his Lord is never irked or irritated in the service he is giving to Jesus Christ. The Lord will give him delight in true service for God—and I say it this way because generally the irksome and boring features of Christian service are some of the things that people and organizations have added on. I refer to things that have no scriptural validity.

It is always pleasant and delightful to set forth the praises of someone you really love. Those who truly love Jesus Christ find it one of the greatest pleasures in life to be able simply to describe how we discovered His great love for us, and how we are trying to return that love and devotion as we serve Him in faith each day!

Do Not Hope to Win the Lost by Being Agreeable

Watch ye, stand fast in the faith, quit you like men, be strong. 1 Corinthians 16:13

In our day, religion may be very precious to some persons, but hardly important enough to cause division or risk hurting anyone's feelings!

In all our discussions there must never be any trace of intolerance, we are reminded; but obviously we forget that the most fervent devotees of tolerance are invariably intolerant of everyone who speaks about God with certainty. And there must be no bigotry—which is the name given to spiritual assurance by those who do not enjoy it!

The desire to please may be commendable enough under certain circumstances, but when pleasing men means displeasing God it is an unqualified evil and should have no place in the Christian's heart. To be right with God has often meant to be in trouble with men. This is such a common truth that one hesitates to mention it, yet it appears to have been overlooked by the majority of Christians today.

There is a notion abroad that to win a man we must agree with him. Actually, the exact opposite is true!

The man who is going in a wrong direction will never be set right by the affable religionist who falls into step beside him and goes the same way. Someone must place himself across the path and insist that the straying man turn around and go in the right direction.

Our Moral Climate Does Not Encourage Faith

And ye shall be hated of all men for my name's sake: but he that endureth to the end shall be saved. Matthew 10:22

There is a plain and evident fact in genuine Christianity that is often overlooked by eager evangelists bent on getting results: that to accept Christ it is necessary that we reject whatever is contrary to Him!

Let us not be shocked by the suggestion that there are disadvantages to the life in Christ. Everyone who has lived for Christ in a Christless world has suffered some losses and endured some pains that he could have avoided by the simple expedient of laying down his cross.

The contemporary moral climate does not favor a faith as tough and fibrous as that taught by our Lord and His apostles. The delicate, brittle saints being produced in our religious hothouses today are hardly to be compared with the committed, expendable believers who once gave their witness among men. And the fault lies with our leaders. They are too timid to tell the people all the truth. They are now asking men to give to God that which costs them nothing!

When will Christians learn that to love righteousness it is necessary to hate sin? that to accept Christ it is necessary to reject self? that to follow the good way we must flee from evil? that a friend of the world is an enemy of God? that God allows no twilight zone between two altogethers where the fearful and the doubting may take refuge at once from hell to come and the rigors of present discipline?

September 4

Capacity to Think: God Wants You to Understand

Thou wilt keep him in perfect peace, whose mind is stayed on thee. . . . Isaiah 26:3

The Book of Proverbs tells us about the man who lies on his bed, turning like a door on its hinges, while the weeds grow up in his garden, choking and killing his crop. Then, when harvest has come, he has nothing and is reduced to begging for help.

Now, staying in bed when he should be cultivating his garden may not be overly sinful—but I think there is no argument but what a willfully lazy man is a sinful man!

It follows, then, in my estimation, that a person who is intellectually lazy is a sinful person. God had a reason for giving us our heads with intellectual capacity for thinking and reasoning and considering. But what a great company of humans there are who refuse to use their heads and many of these are Christians, we must confess.

Many a preacher would like to challenge the intellectual and thinking capacity of his congregation, but he has been warned about preaching over the people's heads.

As a preacher, I deny that any of the truths of God which I teach and expound are over the heads of the people. I deny it!

I say to my Christian brother: "You ought to take that head of yours, oil it and rub the dust off and begin to use it as God has always expected you would. God expects you to understand and have a grasp of His truth because you need it from day to day!"

In God's Plan the Doctrine of Faith Is Central

Therefore being justified by faith, we have peace with God through our Lord Jesus Christ. Romans 5:1

In the divine scheme of salvation, the doctrine of faith is central, so that every benefit flowing from the atonement of Christ comes to the individual through the gateway of faith!

Forgiveness, cleansing, regeneration, the Holy Spirit, all answers to prayer, are given to faith and received by faith. There is no other way! This is common evangelical doctrine and is accepted wherever the cross of Christ is understood.

Faith, as the Bible knows it, is confidence in God and His Son Jesus Christ; it is the response of the soul to the divine character as revealed in the Scriptures; and even this response is impossible apart from the prior inworking of the Holy Spirit.

Faith is a gift of God to a penitent soul and has nothing whatsoever to do with the senses or the data they afford.

Faith is a miracle; it is the ability God gives to trust His Son, and anything that does not result in action in accord with the will of God is not faith, but something else short of it!

Faith and morals are two sides of the same coin. Indeed, the very essence of faith is moral. Any professed faith in Christ as personal Saviour that does not bring the life under plenary obedience to Christ as Lord is inadequate and must betray its victim at the last!

A Minister Must Not Be a Privileged Idler

But I keep under my body, and bring it into subjection: lest that by any means when I have preached to others, I myself should be a castaway. 1 Corinthians 9:27

I know that my writing this will not win me friends, but some men called to the ministry end up doing what comes naturally and just take it easy!

It is easy for the minister to be turned into a privileged idler, a social parasite with an open palm and an expectant look. He has no boss within sight; he is not often required to keep regular hours, so he can work out a comfortable pattern of life that permits him to loaf, putter, play, doze and run about at his pleasure.

To avoid this danger, the minister should voluntarily impose upon himself a life of labor as arduous as that of a farmer, a serious student or a scientist. No man has any right to a way of life less rugged than that of the workers who support him. No preacher has any right to die of old age if hard work will kill him!

On the other hand, it should be said that some men of God have learned to labor in the Holy Spirit and have thus escaped both idleness and death-by-exhaustion, and have lived to a great age. Such men were Moses and Samuel in olden times and men like John Wesley, Bishop Asbury, A. B. Simpson and Pastor Philpott of more recent times.

These wrought mighty deeds without injuring their constitutions, but not every man has been able to find their secret!

Good Literature: Responsibility of Christian Home

The thoughts of the wicked are an abomination to the Lord; but the words of the pure are pleasant words. Proverbs 15:26

It is my belief that we Christians are bound in all conscience to discourage the reading of subversive literature and to promote as fully as possible the circulation of good books and magazines.

Just what part evil literature has played in the present moral breakdown throughout the world will never be known till men are called forth to answer to a holy God for their unholy deeds, but it must be very great indeed!

For thousands of young people the first doubt about God and the Bible came with the reading of some evil book. We must respect the power of ideas, and printed ideas are as powerful as spoken ones. They may have a longer fuse but their explosive power is just as great.

Our Christian faith teaches us to expect to answer for every idle word; how much more severely shall we be held to account for every evil word, whether printed or spoken.

The desire to appear broad-minded is one not easy to overcome, for it is rooted in our ego and is simply a none-too-subtle form of pride. In the name of broadmindedness many a Christian home has been opened to literature that sprang not from a broad mind, but from a mind little and dirty and polluted with evil!

We require our children to wipe their feet before entering the house. Dare we demand less of the literature that comes into our home?

Without Divine Illumination, Theology Is Dead

That your faith should not stand in the wisdom of men, but in the power of God. 1 Corinthians 2:5

Surely God has something to say to the pure in heart which He cannot say to the man of sinful life. But what He has to say is not theological, it is spiritual, and spiritual truths cannot be received in the ordinary way of nature!

"The natural man receiveth not the things of the Spirit of God: for they are foolishness unto him: neither can he know them, because they are spiritually discerned." So wrote the Apostle Paul to the believers at Corinth.

Our Lord referred to this kind of Spirit-enlightened knowledge many times. To Him it was the fruit of a divine illumination, not contrary to but altogether beyond mere intellectual light.

The necessity for spiritual illumination before we can grasp spiritual truths is taught throughout the entire New Testament and it is altogether in accord with the teachings of the Psalms, the Proverbs and the Prophets. The New Testament draws a sharp line between the natural mind and the mind that has been touched by divine fire. When Peter made his good confession, "Thou art the Christ, the Son of the living God," our Lord replied, "Blessed art thou, Simon Bar-jona: for flesh and blood hath not revealed it unto thee, but my Father which is in heaven."

The sum of what I am saying is that there is an illumination, divinely bestowed, without which theological truth is information and nothing more. While this illumination is never given apart from theology, it is entirely possible to have theology without the illumination!

September 9

Unbelief: A Luxury No Man or Woman Can Afford

But when the young man heard that saying, he went away sorrowful; for he had great possessions. Matthew 19:22

Jesus could not have made it any plainer in His teachings that every man during his lifetime must decide for himself whether or not he can afford the terrible luxury of unbelief!

When the rich young ruler learned the cost of discipleship he went away sorrowing. He could not give up the sunny side of the brae. But thanks be to God, there are some in every age who refuse to go back! The Acts of the Apostles is the story of men and women who turned their faces into the stiff wind of persecution and loss and followed the Lamb whithersoever He went. They knew that the world hated Christ without a cause and hated them for His sake; but for the glory that was set before them they continued steadfastly on the way.

What is it that Christ has to offer us that is sound, genuine and desirable?

He offers forgiveness of sins, inward cleansing, peace with God, eternal life, the gift of the Holy Spirit, victory over temptation, resurrection from the dead, a glorified body, immortality and a dwelling place in the house of the Lord forever! These are a few of the benefits that come to us as a result of faith in Christ and total committal to Him.

To accept the call of Christ changes the returning sinner indeed, but it does not change the world. The wind still blows toward hell and the man who is walking in the opposite direction will have the wind in his face. We had better take this into account: If the unsearchable riches of Christ are not worth suffering for, we should know it now and cease to play at religion!

Bible History: Be Careful Whose Advice You Follow

The way of a fool is right in his own eyes; but he that hearkeneth unto counsel is wise. Proverbs 12:15

No man has any right to offer advice who has not first heard God speak. No man has any right to counsel others who is not ready to hear and follow the counsel of the Lord!

This rule of listening only to those who have first listened to God will save us from many a snare, for in any group of ten persons at least nine are sure to believe that they are qualified to offer advice to others.

It seems that in no other field of human interest are people as ready to offer advice as in the field of religion and morals. Yet it is precisely in this field that the average person is least qualified to speak wisely and is capable of the most harm when he does speak.

For this reason, we should select our counselors carefully, and selection inevitably carries with it the idea of rejection.

David warns against the counsel of the ungodly and Bible history gives examples of men who made a failure of their lives because they took wrong advice.

It is especially important that young people learn whose counsel to trust. Having been in the world for such a short time they have not had much experience and must look to others for advice. Those who boast the loudest of their independence, for example, have picked up from someone the idea that independence is a virtue, and their very eagerness to be individualistic is the result of the influence of others. They are what they are because of the counsel they have followed.

Redemption: A Moral Restoration to the Divine Image

Now the Lord of peace himself give you peace always by all means. . . . 2 Thessalonians 3:16

Symmetry is a right proportion of parts in relation to each other and to the whole. By this simple definition symmetry of character is both highly desirable and extremely difficult to attain. Yet it is precisely what Christ had in supreme degree and what every one of us needs if we are to become saints in something beside name!

We can hardly conceive of God's creating us in such a way that we should be forced to sacrifice one good thing to attain another.

If redemption is a moral restoration to the divine image, (and it must be that ultimately), then we may expect one of the first acts of God in the Christian's life to be a kind of moral tuning-up, a bringing into harmony the discordant elements within the personality, an adjustment of the soul to itself and to God. And that He does just this is the testimony of everyone who has been truly converted!

The new believer may state it in other language and the emotional lift he enjoys may be so great as to prevent calm analysis, but the gist of his testimony will be that he has found peace, a peace he can actually feel! The twists and tensions within his heart have corrected themselves as a result of his new orientation to Christ.

He can then sing,

> "Now rest, my long-divided heart;
> Fixed on this blissful center rest."

More Concern Today for Fruit Than for the Root

. . .The root of the righteous shall not be moved. Proverbs 12:3

One marked difference between the faith of our fathers as conceived by the fathers and the same faith as understood and lived by their children is that the fathers were concerned with the root of the matter, while their present-day descendants seem concerned only with the fruit.

Today we write the biographies of the Augustines, the Luthers and the Wesleys and celebrate their fruit, but the tendency is to ignore the root out of which the fruit sprang.

"The root of the righteous yielded fruit," said the wise man in the Proverbs. Our fathers looked well to the root of the tree and were willing to wait with patience for the fruit to appear.

We demand the fruit immediately even though the root may be weak and knobby, or missing altogether. How can we ignore the fact that the bough that breaks off from the tree in a storm may bloom briefly, giving the impression that it is a healthy and fruitful branch, but its tender blossoms will soon perish and the bough itself will wither and die? There is no lasting life apart from the root.

Much that passes for Christianity today is the brief, bright effort of the severed branch to bring forth its fruit in its season. But the deep laws of life are against it. Preoccupation with appearances and a corresponding neglect of the out-of-sight root of the true spiritual life are prophetic signs which go unheeded.

September 13

Jesus Calls Us to His Rest: Meekness Is His Method

With all lowliness and meekness, with longsuffering, forbearing one another in love. Ephesians 4:2

Jesus calls us to His rest, and meekness is His method!

The meek man cares not at all who is greater than he, for he has long ago decided that the esteem of the world is not worth the effort. He develops toward himself a kindly sense of humor and learns to say, "Oh, so you have been overlooked? They placed someone else before you? They have whispered that you are pretty small stuff after all? And now you feel hurt because the world is saying about you the very things you have been saying about yourself? Only yesterday you were telling God that you were nothing, a mere worm of the dust. Where is your consistency? Come on, humble yourself, and cease to care what men may think!"

Rest is simply release from the heavy, crushing burden borne by mankind and the word Jesus used for 'burden' means a load carried or toil borne to the point of exhaustion. The 'rest' is not something we do—it is what comes to us when we cease to do.

The meek man is not a human mouse afflicted with a sense of his own inferiority. Rather he may be in his moral life as bold as a lion and as strong as Samson; but he has stopped being fooled about himself. He has accepted God's estimate of his own life. He knows he is as weak and helpless as God has declared him to be, but paradoxically, he knows at the same time that he is in the sight of God of more importance than angels. In himself nothing; in God, everything. He rests perfectly content to allow God to place His own values!

September 14

Prayer of Faith Lays Hold of God's Omnipotence

. . .In everything by prayer and supplication. . .let your requests be made known unto God. Philippians 4:6

To "accept the universe" does not mean that we are to accept evil conditions as inevitable and make no effort to improve them. So to teach would be to cancel the plain teachings of the Scriptures on that point.

Where a situation is contrary to the will of God, and there are clear promises concerning it in the Scriptures, it is our privilege and obligation to pray and labor to bring about a change. Should we become ill, for instance, we should not surrender to the illness as being inevitable and do nothing about it. Rather, we should accept it provisionally as the will of God for the time and seek His will about recovering our health.

While the prayer of faith enables us to lay hold of the omnipotence of God and bring about many wonderful changes here below, there are some things that not even prayer can change. These lie outside the field of prayer and must be accepted with thanksgiving as the wise will of God for us.

We should, for instance, accept the wisdom of God in nature. In the course of a lifetime there may be a thousand things we could wish had been different, but the word 'wish' is not in the Christian's vocabulary. The very word connotes a fretful rebellion against the ways of God in His universe.

Again, accept yourself. Apart from sin, which you have forsaken, there is nothing about yourself of which you need to be ashamed. Cease to vex yourself about anything over which you have no control. Keep your heart with all diligence and God will look after the universe!

September 15

A Jubilant Longing and Pining for God

But whosoever drinketh of the water that I shall give him shall never thirst; but the water that I shall give him shall be in him a well of water springing up into everlasting life. John 4:14

Almost every day of my life I am praying that "a jubilant pining and longing for God" might come back on the evangelical churches everywhere!

We do not need to have our doctrine straightened out; we are as orthodox as the Pharisees of old. But this longing for God that brings spiritual torrents and whirlwinds of seeking and self-denial—this is almost gone from our midst.

I believe that God wants us to long for Him with the longing that will become homesickness, that will become a wound to our spirits, to keep us always moving toward Him; always finding and always seeking; always having and always desiring!

So the earth becomes less and less valuable and heaven gets closer as we move into God and up into Christ.

Dare we bow our hearts and say, "Father, I have been an irresponsible, childish kind of Christian—more concerned with being happy than with being holy. O God, wound me with a sense of my own sinfulness. Wound me with compassion for the world, and wound me with love of Thee that will always keep me pursuing and always exploring and always seeking and finding!"

If you dare to pray that prayer sincerely and mean it before God, it could mean a turning point in your life. It could mean a great door of spiritual victory opened to you!

Jesus Taught the Moral Relation between Words and Deeds

The former treatise have I made, O Theophilus, of all that Jesus began both to do and teach, until the day in which he was taken up. . . . Acts 1:1, 2

I am afraid we modern Christians are long on talk and short on conduct. We use the language of power but our deeds are the deeds of weakness.

Our Lord and His apostles were long on deeds. The gospels depict a Man walking in power, "who went about doing good, and healing all that were oppressed of the devil; for God was with him."

The moral relationship between words and deeds appears quite plainly in the life and teachings of Christ.

In the Sermon on the Mount Christ placed doing before teaching: "Whosoever therefore shall break one of these least commandments, and shall teach men so, he shall be called the least in the kingdom of heaven: but whosoever shall do and teach them, the same shall be called great in the kingdom of heaven" (Matt. 5:19).

Since in one of its aspects religion contemplates the invisible it is easy to understand how it can be erroneously made to contemplate the unreal. The praying man talks of that which he does not see, and fallen human minds tend to assume that what cannot be seen is not of any great importance and probably not even real, if the truth were known.

So religion is disengaged from practical life and retired to the airy region of fancy where dwell the sweet insubstantial nothings which everyone knows do not exist but which they nevertheless lack the courage to repudiate publicly.

I could wish that this were true only of pagan religions; but candor dictates that I admit it to be true also of much that passes for evangelical Christianity .

September 17

Who Dares to Soften and Change Christ's Words

...By the resurrection of Jesus Christ; who is gone into heaven...angels and authorities and powers being made subject unto him. 1 Peter 3:21, 22

As believers, we should be warned that any appeal to the public in the name of Christ that rises no higher than an invitation to tranquility must be recognized as mere humanism with a few words of Jesus thrown in to make it appear Christian!

Strange, is it not, that we dare without shame to alter, to modulate the words of Christ while speaking for Christ to the very ones for whom He died?

Christ calls men to carry a cross; we call them to have fun in His name!

He calls them to forsake the world; we assure them that if they but accept Jesus the world is their oyster!

He calls them to suffer; we call them to enjoy all the bourgeois comforts modern civilization affords!

He calls them to self-abnegation and death; we call them to spread themselves like green bay trees or perchance even to become stars in a pitiful fifth-rate religious zodiac!

He calls them to holiness; we call them to a cheap and tawdry happiness that would have been rejected with scorn by the least of the Stoic philosophers!

Only that is truly Christian which accords with the spirit and teachings of Christ. Whatever is foreign to the Spirit of the Man of Sorrows and contrary to the teachings and practice of His apostles is un-Christian or anti-Christian, no matter whence it emanates!

Religious Teaching Gives Light: That Is Not Enough

Wherefore he saith, Awake thou that sleepest, and arise from the dead, and Christ shall give thee light. Ephesians 5:14

To find the way, we need more than light; we need also sight!

The Holy Scriptures are the source of moral and spiritual light. Yet I consider that I cast no aspersion upon the hallowed page when I say that its radiance is not by itself enough. Light alone is not sufficient.

The coming of knowledge is like the rising of the sun. But sunrise means nothing to the unseeing eye. Only the sighted benefit from the light of the sun.

Between light and sight there is a wide difference. One man may have light without sight; he is blind. Another may have sight without light; he is temporarily blind, but the coming of the light quickly enables him to see.

We have said this much to point out that religious instruction, however sound, is not enough by itself. It brings light, but it cannot impart sight. The text without the Spirit's enlightenment cannot save the sinner. Salvation follows a work of the Spirit in the heart. There can be no salvation apart from the truth but there can be, and often is, truth without salvation.

How many multiplied thousands have learned the catechism by heart and still wander in moral darkness because there has been no inward illumination! The Pharisees looked straight at the Light of the World for three years, but not one ray of light reached their inner beings. Light is not enough!

Truth Will Not Give Itself to a Rebel

. . .He that followeth me. . .shall have the light of life. John 8:12

Too many people consider Jesus Christ a 'convenience.' We make Him a lifeboat to get us to shore, a guide to find us when we are lost. We reduce Him simply to a Big Friend to help us when we are in trouble.

That is not biblical Christianity!

Jesus Christ is Lord, and when a man is willing to do His will, he is repenting and the truth flashes in. For the first time in his life, he finds himself willing to say, "I will do the will of the Lord, even if I die for it!"

Illumination will begin in his heart. That is repentance—for he has been following his own will and now decides to do the will of God.

Before the Word of God can mean anything inside of me there must be obedience to the Word. Truth will not give itself to a rebel. Truth will not impart life to a man who will not obey the light. If you are disobeying Jesus Christ you cannot expect to be enlightened spiritually.

No man can know the Son except the Father tell him. No man can know the Father except the Son reveal Him. I can know about God: that is the body of truth. But I cannot know God, the soul of truth, unless I am ready to be obedient.

True discipleship is obeying Jesus Christ and learning of Him and following Him and doing what He tells you to do, keeping His commandments and carrying out His will.

That kind of a person is a Christian—and no other kind is!

The Modern Cry: I Have a Right to Be Happy

Let your conversation be without covetousness; and be content with such things as ye have: for he hath said, I will never leave thee, nor forsake thee. Hebrews 13:5

A selfish desire for happiness is as sinful as any other selfish desire because its root is in the flesh which can never have any standing before God!

People are coming more and more to excuse every sort of wrongdoing on the grounds that they are "just trying to secure a little happiness!" That is the hedonistic philosophy of old Grecian days misunderstood and applied to everyday living in the twentieth century.

It destroys all nobility of character and makes milk-sops of all who consciously or unconsciously adopt it; but it has become quite the popular creed of the masses.

Now I submit that the whole hectic scramble after happiness is an evil as certainly as is the scramble after money or fame or success. It springs out of a vast misunderstanding of ourselves and of our true moral state.

The man who really knows himself can never believe in his right to be happy. A little glimpse of his own heart will disillusion him immediately so that he is more likely to turn on himself and own God's sentence against him to be just.

The doctrine of man's inalienable right to happiness is anti-God and anti-Christ, and its wide acceptance by society tells us a lot about that same society. No man should desire to be happy who is not at the same time holy. Seeking fully to know and do the will of God, he leaves to Christ the matter of how happy he should be!

A Word to Women: Seek the Inner Adorning

. . .Even the ornament of a meek and quiet spirit, which is in the sight of God of great price. 1 Peter 3:4

Certainly I am not going to try to fill the role of a feminine counselor, but I do want to remind you that the Apostle Peter, a great man of God, taught that true adorning is the lasting beauty that is within. Peter said that there is a glowing but hidden being of the heart, more radiant than all of the jewels that one can buy!

This ties in with the fact that a Christian woman should be very careful about the kind of person she sets up as a model of character and example in daily life. It is a sad thing to have our minds occupied with the wrong kind of people!

English history books will not report that Suzanna Wesley was one of the best-dressed women of her day or that she ever received a medal for social activity. But she was the mother of Charles and John Wesley, those princes of Christian song and theology. She taught her own family, and her spiritual life and example have placed her name high in God's hall of fame for all eternity.

So, if you want to take models to follow day by day, please do not take the artificial, globe-trotting females who are intent only upon themselves, their careers and their publicity! God help us all, men and women of whatever marital, social or domestic status, that we may do the will of God and thus win our crown!

God Would Save Us from Spiritual Delusion

Even him, whose coming is after the working of Satan with all power and signs and lying wonders. 2 Thessalonians 2:9

There are areas of Christian thought—and because of thought then also of life, where likenesses and differences are so difficult to distinguish that we are often hard put to escape complete deception!

Throughout the whole world error and truth travel the same highways, work in the same fields and factories, attend the same churches, fly in the same planes and shop in the same stores.

So skilled is error at imitating truth that the two are constantly being mistaken for each other. It takes a sharp eye these days to know which brother is Cain and which is Abel!

We must never take for granted anything that touches our soul's welfare. Isaac felt Jacob's arms and thought they were the arms of Esau. Even the disciples failed to spot the traitor among them; the only one of them who knew who he was was Judas himself. That soft-spoken companion with whom we walk so comfortably and in whose company we take such delight may be an angel of Satan, whereas that rough, plain-spoken man whom we shun may be God's very prophet sent to warn us against danger and eternal loss.

It is therefore critically important that the Christian take full advantage of every provision God has made to save him from delusion. The most important of these combine as a protective shield—faith, prayer, constant meditation on the Scriptures, obedience, humility, much serious thought and the illumination of the Holy Spirit.

September 23

A New Decalogue: Thou Shalt Not Disagree

Should a wise man utter vain knowledge?. . .Should he reason with unprofitable talk?. . . Job 15:3, 4

This above all others is the age of much talk!

Hardly a day passes that the newspapers do not carry one or another of the headlines "Talks to Begin" or "Talks to Continue." The notion back of this endless official chatter is that all differences between men result from their failure to understand each other!

This yen to confer has hit the church also, which is not strange since almost everything the church is doing these days has been suggested to her by the world. I observe with pained amusement how many "water boys" of the pulpit in their efforts to be prophets are standing up straight and tall and speaking out boldly in favor of ideas that have been previously fed into their minds by the psychiatrists, the sociologists, the novelists, the scientists and the secular educators.

A new Decalogue has been adopted by the neo-Christians of our day, the first word of which reads, "Thou shalt not disagree"; and a new set of Beatitudes too, which begins "Blessed are they that tolerate everything, for they shall not be made accountable for anything."

It is true that the blessing of God is promised to the peacemaker, for the ability to settle quarrels between members of God's family is a heavenly gift. That is one thing, but the effort to achieve unity at the expense of truth and righteousness is another. Darkness and light can never be brought together by talk. Some things are not negotiable!

Knowledge without Humility Turns to Vanity

He is proud, knowing nothing, but doting about questions and strifes of words. . . . 1 Timothy 6:4

A new school within evangelical Christianity has appeared in our time which appears to me to be in grave danger of producing a prime crop of intellectual snobs!

The disciples of this leaning are orthodox in creed, if by that we mean that they hold the fundamental tenets of the historical faith; but right there the similarity of their school to New Testament Christianity ends. Their spirit is quite other than the spirit of the Early Church.

This new breed of Christian may be identified by certain field marks. One is the habit of puffing out the chest and uttering a noise that sounds suspiciously like crowing. Another is the habit of nesting so high that ordinary Christians have difficulty in locating the aerie. Rarely is an original note sounded—each one waiting to hear what Barth or Brunner or Bultmann or Tillich has to say and then imitating it as nearly as possible, only transposing it into the orthodox key!

They are largely overlooking the fact that truth is not mental only—but moral. A theological fact becomes a spiritual truth only when it is received by a humble mind. The proud mind, however orthodox, can never know spiritual truth!

In the Scriptures knowledge is a kind of experience and wisdom has a moral content. Knowledge without humility is vanity. The religious snob is devoid of truth. Snobbery and truth are irreconcilable!

The Word of Authority by Which We Can Die

These all died in faith, not having received the promises, but having seen them afar off, and were persuaded of them. . . . Hebrews 11:13

There is not one word published on the North American continent today that I would want to die by!

If I knew that tomorrow evening was to be my last, and that I would never see another sunrise, there isn't a newspaper published anywhere in the world that I would want to see.

There hasn't been a book published this year that I would want to read. There hasn't been a word uttered in the United Nations that I would want to hear. There is no authority anywhere.

Everybody is writing and talking, but for dying men there is not one word of authority anywhere, except as you hear the sure, true, terrifying words of Jesus Christ! The only authoritative word ever published is that which comes from the Holy Scriptures.

"Holy" books that have been compounded out of all the high, fine, lofty thoughts of mankind since the beginning do not change the basic facts and the basic problems.

Jesus alone could teach: "I am the Light of the world and he that followeth me shall not walk in darkness."

You are responsible to the Light—and to the authority of the Word of God. You cannot hide behind differences of opinion, behind church politics, behind the philosophies of men. Neither can you hide behind this crazy relativity of morals now being taught in the schools.

If you quench the light, and dim it down, how great will be the darkness!

Christlike Conduct: The Goal of Christian Faith

Seest thou how faith wrought with his works, and by works was faith made perfect. James 2:22

Rightly understood, faith is not a substitute for moral conduct but a means toward it.

The tree does not serve in lieu of fruit but as an agent by which fruit is secured. Fruit, not trees, is what God has in mind in yonder orchard; so Christlike conduct is the end of the Christian faith! To oppose faith to works is to make the fruit the enemy to the tree; yet that is exactly what we have managed to do and the consequences have been disastrous!

In practice we may detect the subtle (and often unconscious) substitution when we hear a Christian assure someone that he will "pray over his problem," knowing full well that he intends to use prayer as a substitute for service. It is much easier to pray that a poor friend's needs may be supplied than to supply them! The mystical John noted the incongruity involved in substituting religion for action: "But whoso hath this world's good, and seeth his brother have need, and shutteth up his bowels of compassion from him, how dwelleth the love of God in him? My little children, let us not love in word, neither in tongue; but in deed and in truth."

A proper understanding of our spiritual foundation will destroy the false and artificial "either/or." Then we will have not less faith but more godly works; not less praying but more serving; not fewer words but more holy deeds; not weaker profession but more courageous possession; not a religion as a substitute for action but religion in faith-filled action! And what is that but to say that we will have come again to the teaching of the New Testament?

September 27

God's Spirit Bears Witness Within

Beware lest any man spoil you through philosophy and vain deceit,. . .after the tradition of men. . .and not after Christ. Colossians 2:8

When I was a young Christian I had my Bible and a hymnbook and a few other books, including Andrew Murray and Thomas a' Kempis and I got myself educated as well as I could by reading books. I read the philosophy of all the great minds—and many of those men did not believe in God, you know—and they did not believe in Christ.

I remember reading White's *Warfare of Science with Christianity*, and if any man can read that and still say he is saved, he isn't saved by his reading; he is saved by the Holy Ghost within him telling him that he is saved!

Do you know what I would do after I would read a chapter or two and find arguments that I could not possibly defeat? I would get down on my knees and with tears I would thank God with joy that no matter what the books said, "I know Thee, my Saviour and my Lord!"

I didn't have it in my head—I had it in my heart! There is a great difference, you see.

If we have it only in our heads, then philosophy may be of some help to us; but if we have it in our hearts, there is not much philosophy can do except stand aside reverently, hat in hand, and say, "Holy, holy, holy is the Lord God Almighty!"

In short, if you have to be reasoned into Christianity, some wise fellow can reason you out of it, as well!

We Should Always Seek to Know Christ Better

Seek ye the Lord, and his strength: seek his face evermore. Psalm 105:4

Are you aware that we have been snared in the coils of a modern spurious logic which insists that if we have found Christ we need no more seek Him?

This is set before us as the last word in orthodoxy, and it is taken for granted that no Bible-taught Christian ever believed otherwise. Thus the whole testimony of the worshipping, seeking, singing Church on that subject is crisply set aside!

The experiential heart-theology of a grand army of fragrant saints is rejected in favor of a smug interpretation of Scripture which would certainly have sounded strange to an Augustine, a Rutherford or a Brainerd.

In the midst of this great chill there are some, I rejoice to acknowledge, who will not be content with shallow logic. They will admit the force of the argument, and then turn away with tears to hunt some lonely place and pray, "O God, show me Thy glory!" They want to taste, to touch with their hearts, to see with their inner eyes the wonder that is God.

Complacency is a deadly foe of all spiritual growth. Acute desire must be present or there will be no manifestation of Christ to His people. He waits to be wanted!

Too bad that with many of us He waits so long, so very long, in vain!

A Tragedy: Believers Arguing about Christ's Return

For the Lord himself shall descend from heaven with a shout, with the voice of the archangel, and with the trump of God. . . . 1 Thessalonians 4:16

The believing Christian should be living in joyful anticipation of the return of Jesus Christ, and that is such an important segment of truth that the devil has always been geared up to fight it and ridicule it. In fact, one of his big successes is being able to get people to argue and get mad about the details of the Second Coming—rather than looking and waiting for it.

Suppose a man has been overseas two or three years, away from his family. Suddenly a cable arrives for the family with the message: "My work completed here; I will be home today."

After some hours he arrives at the front door with his bags. But in the house the family members are in turmoil. There has been a great argument as to whether he would arrive in the afternoon or evening and what transportation he would be using. So, no one is actually watching for his arrival.

You may say, "That is only an illustration."

But what is the situation in the various segments of the Christian community?

They are fighting with one another and glaring at each other. They are debating whether He is coming and how He is coming. That is the work of the devil—to make Christian people argue about the details of His coming so they forget the most important thing!

You Cannot Worship God without Loving Him

Keep yourselves in the love of God, looking for the mercy of our Lord Jesus Christ unto eternal life. Jude 21

Both the Old and New Testaments teach that the essence of true worship is the love of God.

Our Lord declared this to be the sum of the Law and the Prophets: "Thou shalt love the Lord thy God with all thy heart, and with all thy soul, and with all thy might."

Now, love is both a principle and an emotion; it is something both felt and willed. It is capable of almost infinite degrees. Love in the human heart may begin so modestly as to be hardly perceptible and go on to become a raging torrent that sweeps its possessor before it in total helplessness.

Something like this must have been the experience of the Apostle Paul, for he felt it necessary to explain to his critics that his apparent madness was actually the love of God ravishing his willing heart!

In the love which any intelligent creature feels for God there must always be a measure of mystery. It is even possible that it is almost wholly mystery, and that our attempt to find reasons is merely a rationalizing of a love already mysteriously present in the heart as a result of some secret operation of the Spirit within us.

We can be certain that it is quite impossible to worship God without loving Him. Scripture and reason agree to declare this. And God is never satisfied with anything less than all. This may not at first be possible, but the inward operations of the Holy Spirit will enable us in His time to offer Him our poured-out fullness of love!

October 1

Encouragement: The Eternal Nature of Our Father

The eternal God is thy refuge, and underneath are the everlasting arms. . . .
Deuteronomy 33:27

The eternal nature of our heavenly Father should humble us and encourage us, too. It should humble us when we remember how frail we are, how utterly dependent upon God, and it should encourage us to know that when everything else has passed we may still have God no less surely than before!

The remembrance of this could save nations from many tragic and bloody decisions. Were notes written by statesmen against the background of such knowledge they might be less inflammatory; and were kings and dictators to think soberly on this truth, they would walk softly and speak less like gods. After all, they are not really important and the sphere of their freedom is constricted more than they dream.

Shelley wrote of the traveler who saw in the desert two vast and trunkless legs of stone and nearby a shattered face half-buried in the sand. On the pedestal where once the proud image had stood were engraven these words: "My name is Ozymandias, king of kings: Look on my works, ye mighty, and despair."

And, says the poet, "Nothing else remains. Round the decay of that colossal wreck, boundless and bare the lone and level sands stretch far away."

Shelly was right except for one thing: Something else did remain! It was God. He had been there first to look in gentle pity upon the mad king who could boast so shamelessly in the shadow of the tomb. He was there when the swirling sands covered with a mantle of pity the evidence of human decay. God was there last!

October 2

Right Concept of Jesus—Savior and Judge

In the day when God shall judge the secrets of men by Jesus Christ, according to my gospel. Romans 2:16

What is your concept of Jesus Christ as Saviour and Judge?

If the "ten-cent-store Jesus" that is being preached by a lot of men, the plastic, painted Christ who has no spine and no justice and is pictured as a soft and pliable friend to everybody—if He is the only Christ there is, then we might as well close our books and bar our doors, and make a bakery or garage out of the church!

But that Christ that is being preached and pictured is not the Christ of God, nor the Christ of the Bible, nor the Christ we must deal with.

The Christ we must deal with will be the judge of mankind—and this is one of the neglected Bible doctrines in our day!

The Father judges no man. When the Lord, the Son of Man, shall come in the clouds of glory, then shall be gathered unto Him the nations, and He shall separate them.

God has given Him judgment, authority to judge mankind, so that He is both the Judge and Saviour of men.

That makes me both love Him and fear Him! I love Him because He is my Saviour and I fear Him because He is my Judge.

God Almighty is never going to judge the race of mankind and allow a mistake to enter. The judge must be one who has all wisdom. Therefore, I appeal away from St. Paul; I appeal away from Moses and Elijah; I appeal away from all men because no man knows me well enough to judge me, finally! Only Jesus Christ qualifies as one who is able to be the judge of all mankind.

October 3

God Was First to Say, "You Are My Friends"

Greater love hath no man than this, that a man lay down his life for his friends. John 15:13

The idea of the divine-human friendship originated with God. Had not God first said "Ye are my friends" it would be inexcusably brash for any man to say "I am a friend of God."

But since He claims us for His friends it is an act of unbelief to ignore or deny the relationship!

Even though radically different from each other, two persons may enjoy the closest friendship for a lifetime; for it is not a requisite of friendship that the participants be alike in all things; it is enough that they be alike at the points where their personalities touch. Harmony is likeness at points of contact, and friendship is likeness where hearts merge.

For this reason the whole idea of the divine-human friendship is logical enough and entirely credible. The infinite God and the finite man can merge their personalities in the tenderest, most satisfying friendship. In such relationship there is no idea of equality; only of likeness where the heart of man meets the heart of God!

This likeness is possible because God at the first made man in His own image and is now remaking men in the image that was lost by sin. Perfection lies on God's side but on man's side there are weaknesses of purpose, lack of desire and small faith.

In spite of human frailties we can grow in grace and move progressively toward a more perfect experiential union with God, exercising robust faith in the truths revealed in the Scriptures!

Spiritual Fruit Comes Only from Spiritual Life

For where your treasure is, there will your heart be also. Matthew 6:21

Water cannot rise above its own level, and neither can a Christian by any sudden, spasmodic effort rise above the level of his own spiritual life!

I have seen in my own experience how a man of God will let his tongue go all day in light, frivolous conversation; let his interest roam abroad among the idle pleasures of this world; and then under the necessity of preaching at night, seek a last minute reprieve just before the service by cramming desperately in prayer to put himself in a position where the spirit of the prophet will descend upon him as he enters the pulpit.

Men do not gather grapes of thorns, nor figs of thistles. The fruit of a tree is determined by the tree, and the fruit of life by the kind of life it is. What a man is interested in to the point of absorption both decides and reveals what kind of man he is; and the kind of man he is by a secret law of the soul decides the kind of fruit he will bear.

The catch is that we are often unable to discover the true quality of our fruit until it is too late!

Of what do we think when we are free to think of what we will?

What object gives us inward pleasure as we brood over it?

Over what do we muse in our free moments?

To what does our imagination return again and again?

When we have answered these questions honestly we will know what kind of persons we are, and when we have discovered what kind of persons we are we may deduce the kind of fruit we will bear. If we would do holy deeds we must be holy men and women!

October 5

Much of Our Praying Never Brings Anything Back

If ye abide in me, and my words abide in you, ye shall ask what ye will, and it shall be done unto you. John 15:7

In evangelical Christian circles, the question is often raised: "Why are there not more miracles and wonders wrought in our midst through faith?"

In our day everything seems to be commercialized, and I must say that I do not believe in wonders and miracles that are organized and incorporated!

"Miracles, Incorporated"—you can have it!

"Healing, Incorporated"—you can have that, too! And the same with "Evangelism, Incorporated"; you can have it all.

I have my doubts about some signs and wonders that have to be organized, that demand a letterhead and a president and a secretary and a big trailer with lights and cameras. God isn't in that!

But the man of faith can go alone into the wilderness and get on his knees and command heaven—God is in that!

The Christian who is willing to put himself in a place where he must get the answer from God and God alone—the Lord is in that!

But there is no use trying to cover up the fact that there is a great deal of praying being done among us that does not amount to anything—it never brings anything back! It is like sending a farmer into the field without a plow.

Little wonder that the work of God stands still!

Greatness among the Sons and Daughters of Faith

But so shall it not be among you: but whosoever will be great among you shall be your minister. Mark 10:43

From the words of Jesus to His disciples, we may properly conclude that there is nothing wrong with the desire to be great provided: (1) we seek the right kind of greatness; (2) we allow God to decide what greatness is; (3) we are willing to pay the full price that greatness demands, and (4) we are content to wait for the judgment of God to settle the whole matter at last!

It is vitally important, however, that we know what Christ meant when He used the word great in relation to men, and His meaning cannot be found in the lexicon or dictionary. Only when viewed in its broad theological setting is it understood aright. No one whose heart has had a vision of God, however brief or imperfect that vision may have been, will ever consent to think of himself as being great.

All this being true, still God Himself applies the word great to men, as when the angel tells Zacharias that the son who is to be born "shall be great in the sight of the Lord."

Obviously, there are two kinds of greatness recognized in the Scriptures: an absolute, uncreated greatness belonging to God alone, and a relative and finite greatness achieved by or bestowed upon certain friends of God and sons of faith, who by obedience and self-denial sought to become as much like God as possible.

It is obvious that Jesus was not impressed with the idea of greatness inherent in the political power and dominion held by "the princes of the Gentiles."

"It shall not be so among you!" He told his followers.

Learn the Truth about the Enemy of Your Soul

Lest Satan should get an advantage of us: for we are not ignorant of his devices. 2 Corinthians 2:11

The devil is declared in the Scriptures to be an enemy of God and of all good men. Because he is a spirit he is able to "walk up and down in the earth" at his pleasure.

While we must not underestimate the strength of our foe, we must at the same time recognize that we need not live in constant fear of him! If he cannot make skeptics of us he will make us devil-conscious and thus throw a permanent shadow across our lives, for there is but a hairline between truth and superstition.

We should learn the truth about the enemy, but we must stand bravely against every superstitious notion he would introduce about himself. The truth will set us free but superstition will enslave us!

The scriptural way to see things is to set the Lord always before us, put Christ in the center of our vision; and if Satan is lurking around he will appear on the margin only and be seen as but a shadow on the edge of the brightness. It is always wrong to invert this—to set Satan in the focus of our vision and push God out to the margin. Nothing but tragedy can come from such inversion!

The best way to keep the enemy out is to keep Christ in! The sheep need not be terrified by the wolf; they have but to stay close to the shepherd. The instructed Christian whose faculties have been developed by the Word and the Spirit will practice the presence of God moment by moment!

October 8

Cultivate Grace That Makes Holiness Attractive

For thou art not a God that hath pleasure in wickedness: neither shall evil dwell with thee. The foolish shall not stand in thy sight: thou hatest all workers of iniquity. Psalm 5:4, 5

God's Word is unusually plain in teaching us that the operations of grace within the heart of a believer will turn that heart away from sin and toward holiness; "For the grace of God that bringeth salvation hath appeared to all men, teaching us that, denying ungodliness and worldly lusts, we should live soberly, righteously, and godly, in this present world; looking for that blessed hope, and the glorious appearing of the great God and our Saviour Jesus Christ" (Titus 2:11-13).

I do not see how it could be plainer!

The same grace that saves teaches the believer inwardly, and its teaching is both negative and positive. Negatively it teaches us to deny ungodliness and worldly lusts. Positively it teaches us to live soberly, righteously and godly right here in this present world.

The man of honest heart will find no difficulty here. He has but to check his own bent to discover whether he is concerned about sin in his life more or less since the supposed work of grace was done. Anything that weakens his hatred of sin may be identified immediately as false to the Scriptures, to the Saviour and to his own soul.

Whatever makes holiness more attractive and sin more intolerable may be accepted as genuine!

Stop! God Wants More Than a Minute

. . .I count all things but loss for the excellency of the knowledge of Christ Jesus my Lord. . . . Philippians 3:8

A thousand distractions would woo us away from thoughts of God, but if we are wise we will sternly put them from us and make room for the King—and take time to entertain Him!

Progress in the Christian life is exactly equal to the growing knowledge we gain of the Triune God in personal experience. And such experience requires a whole life devoted to it and plenty of time spent at the holy task of cultivating God.

God can be known satisfactorily only as we devote time to Him.

Without meaning to do it we have written our serious fault into our book titles and gospel songs.

"A little talk with Jesus," we sing and we call our books "God's Minute," or something else as revealing.

The Christian who is satisfied to give God His "minute" and to have "a little talk with Jesus" is the same one who shows up at the evangelistic service weeping over his retarded spiritual growth and begging the evangelist to show him the way out of his difficulty!

Some things may be neglected with but little loss to the spiritual life, but to neglect communion with God is to hurt ourselves where we cannot afford it.

God will respond to our efforts to know Him. The Bible tells us how; it is altogether a matter of how much determination we bring to the holy task!

October 10

Choosing God's Will Does Not Deny Man's Free Will

. . .Paul answered,. . .I am ready. . .to die at Jerusalem for the name of the Lord Jesus. And when he would not be persuaded, we ceased, saying, The will of the Lord be done. Acts 21:13, 14

Someone has asked a thoughtful question: "When we pray 'Not my will, but Thine be done,' are we not voiding our will and refusing to exercise the very power of choice which is part of the image of God in us?"

The answer to that question is a flat No, but the whole thing deserves further explanation.

No act that is done voluntarily is an abrogation of the freedom of the will. If a man chooses the will of God he is not denying but exercising his right of choice. What he is doing is admitting that he is not good enough to desire the highest choice nor is he wise enough to make it, and he is for that reason asking Another who is both wise and good to make his choice for him. And for fallen man, this is the ultimate use he should make of his freedom of will!

Tennyson saw this and wrote of Christ,

Thou seemest human and divine,
The highest, holiest manhood, Thou;
Our wills are ours, we know not how;
Our wills are ours, to make them Thine.

There is a lot of sound doctrine in these words—"Our wills are ours, to make them Thine." The true saint acknowledges that he possesses from God the gift of freedom. He knows that he will never be cudgeled into obedience nor wheedled like a petulant child into doing the will of God; he knows that these methods are unworthy both of God and of his own soul!

Significant: The Low Level of Moral Enthusiasm

How shall we escape, if we neglect so great salvation?. . . Hebrews 2:3

In only one field of human interest do we Americans seem slow and apathetic: that is the field of personal religion.

Church people habitually approach the matter of their personal relation to God in a dull, halfhearted way which is altogether out of keeping with their general temperament and wholly inconsistent with the importance of the subject.

Dante, on his imaginary journey through hell, came upon a group of lost souls who sighed and moaned continually as they whirled about aimlessly in the dusky air. Virgil, his guide, explained that these were the "wretched people," the "nearly soulless," who while they lived on earth had not moral energy enough to be either good or evil. They had earned neither praise nor blame, and with them and sharing in their punishment were those angels who would take sides neither with God nor Satan.

The writer pictured the doom of all of the weak and irresolute crew to be suspended forever between a hell that despised them and a heaven that would not receive their defiled presence. Not even their names were to be mentioned again in heaven or earth or hell.

Was Dante saying in his own way what our Lord had said long before to the church of Laodicea: "I would thou wert cold or hot. So then because thou art lukewarm, and neither cold nor hot, I will spue thee out of my mouth"?

The low level of moral enthusiasm among us may have a significance far deeper than we are willing to believe!

October 12

Seeking Man's Favor: The Root of Religious Unbelief

How can ye believe, which receive honour one of another?. . . John 5:44

The whole course of our lives will be upset by failure to put God where He belongs. We exalt ourselves instead of God and the curse follows!

Consider the very disturbing question that Jesus asked of men when He was on earth: "How can ye believe, which receive honour of one another, and seek not the honour that cometh from God alone?"

If I understand this correctly, Christ taught here the alarming doctrine that the desire for honor among men made belief impossible!

Is this sin at the root of religious unbelief?

Could it be that those "intellectual difficulties" which men blame for their inability to believe are but smoke screens to conceal the real cause that lies behind them?

Was it this greedy desire for honor from man that made men into Pharisees and Pharisees into Deicides?

Is this the secret back of religious self-righteousness and empty worship? I believe it may be.

Men and women who will make the honest once-for-all decision to exalt and honor God and His Christ over all are precious to God above all treasures of earth or sea, for He knows that His honor is safe in such consecrated hands!

October 13

The Deadening Effect of Religious Make-Believe

Let. . .no man put a stumbling block or an occasion to fall in his brother's way. Romans 14:13

The deadening effect of religious make-believe on the human mind is beyond all describing.

What can the effect be upon the spectators who live day after day among the professed Christians who habitually ignore the commandments of Christ and live after their own private notions of Christianity?

Truth sits forsaken and grieves until her professed followers come home for a brief visit, but she sees them depart again when the bills become due. They protest great and undying love for her but they will not let their love cost them anything!

Will not those who watch us from day to day conclude that the whole thing is false?

Will they not be forced to believe that the faith of Christ is an unreal and visionary thing which they are fully justified in rejecting?

Certainly the non-Christian is not too much to be blamed if he turns disgustedly away from the invitation of the Gospel after he has been exposed for a while to the inconsistencies of those of his acquaintances who profess to follow Christ.

In that great and terrible day when the deeds of men are searched into by the penetrating eyes of the Judge of all the earth what will we answer when we are charged with inconsistency and moral fraud?

And at whose door will lie the blame for millions of lost men who while they lived on earth were sickened and revolted by the religious travesty they knew as Christianity?

October 14

A Great Loss: Power to Wage Spiritual Warfare

Moreover he must have a good report of them which are without; lest he fall into reproach and the snare of the devil. 1 Timothy 3:7

The Christian should always be aware that the devil's master strategy against us is to destroy our power to wage spiritual warfare! And he has been succeeding, we must add.

The average Christian these days is a harmless enough thing, God knows. He is a child wearing with considerable self-consciousness the harness of the warrior; he is a sick eaglet that can never mount up with wings; he is a spent pilgrim who has given up the journey and sits with a waxy smile trying to get what pleasure he can from sniffing the wilted flowers he has plucked by the way.

Such as these have been reached! Satan has gotten to them early.

By means of false teaching or inadequate teaching, or the huge discouragement that comes from the example of a decadent church, he has succeeded in weakening their resolution, neutralizing their convictions and taming their original urge to do exploits; now they are little more than statistics that contribute financially to the upkeep of the religious institution.

There can be complete victory for us if we will but take the way of the triumphant Christ, but too many have accepted the low-keyed Christian life as the normal one. That is all Satan wants. That will ground our power, stunt our growth and render us harmless to the kingdom of darkness—and we sons of eternity just cannot afford such a thing!

October 15

Christians Often Act Like They Are Bored with God

And they worshipped him, and returned to Jerusalem with great joy: and were continually in the temple, praising and blessing God. Amen. Luke 24:52, 53

One can only conclude that God's professed children are bored with Him, for they must be wooed to meeting with a stick of striped candy in the form of religious movies, games and refreshments.

It is scarcely possible in most places to get anyone to attend a meeting where the only attraction is God!

So we have the strange anomaly of orthodoxy in creed and heterodoxy in practice. The striped-candy technique has been so fully integrated into our present religious thinking that it is simply taken for granted. Its victims never dream that it is not a part of the teachings of Christ and His apostles.

Any objection to the carryings on of our present golden-calf Christianity is met with the triumphant reply, "But we are winning them!" And winning them to what? To true discipleship? To cross-carrying? To self-denial? To separation from the world? To crucifixion of the flesh? To holy living? To nobility of character? To a despising of the world's treasures? To hard self-discipline? To love for God? To total committal to Christ?

Of course the answer to all these questions is NO!

We are paying a frightful price for our religious boredom. And that at the moment of the world's mortal peril!

October 16

By God's Call the Minister Is a Man Apart

Let a man so account of us, as of the ministers of Christ, and stewards of the mysteries of God. 1 Corinthians 4:1

The Christian Church is God's witness to each generation, and her ministers are her voice. Through them she becomes vocal. By them she has spoken always to the world, and by them God has spoken to the Church herself.

The testimony of her godly laymen has ever been a mighty aid in the work she seeks to accomplish. But her laymen can never do, and assuredly are not called to do, the work of her ministers. By gift and calling the minister is a man apart.

To be effective the preacher's message must be alive; it must alarm, arouse, challenge; it must be God's present voice to a particular people. Then, and not till then, is it the prophetic word and the man himself a prophet.

To fulfill his calling the prophet must be under the constant sway of the Holy Ghost; and further, he must be alert to moral and spiritual conditions. All spiritual teaching should be related to life. It should intrude into the daily and private living of the hearers.

Without being personal, the true prophet will yet pierce the conscience of each listener as if the message had been directed to him alone. Really to preach the truth it is often necessary that the man of God know the people's hearts better than they themselves do!

Thus a minister is driven to God for wisdom. He must speak the mind of Christ and throw himself on the Holy Spirit for spiritual power and mental acumen equal to the task.

October 17

Weak Christianity Tends toward Humanism

. . .That your love may abound more and more in knowledge and in all judgment. . .that ye may be sincere and without offense till the day of Christ. Philippians 1:9, 10

I am in disagreement with many when I insist that the flaw in current evangelism lies in its humanistic approach. It struggles to be supernaturalistic but never quite makes it. It is frankly fascinated by the great, noisy, aggressive world with its big names, its hero worship, its wealth and its garish pageantry.

In this quasi-Christian scheme of things God becomes the Aladdin lamp who does the bidding of everyone that will accept His Son and sign a card. The total obligation of the sinner is discharged when he accepts Christ. After that he has but to come with his basket and receive the religious equivalent of everything the world offers and enjoy it to the limit.

Those who have not accepted Christ thus must be content with this world, but with the view held by many today the Christian gets this world with the one to come thrown in as a bonus!

This gross misapprehension of the truth is back of much of our present evangelical activity. It determines directions, builds programs, decides the content of sermons, fixes the quality of local churches and even of whole denominations, sets the pattern for religious writers.

This concept of Christianity is little more than weak humanism allied with weak Christianity to give it ecclesiastical respectability. It may be identified by its religious approach. Invariably it begins with man and his needs and then looks around for God; true Christianity reveals God as searching for man to deliver him from his ambitions!

Men Are Lost—But They Are Not Abandoned

And unto Adam he said. . .cursed is the ground for thy sake; in sorrow shalt thou eat of it all the days of thy life. Genesis 3:17

There is sound Bible reason to believe that nature itself, the brute creation, the earth and even the astronomical universe, have all felt the shock of man's sin and have been adversely affected by it.

When the Lord God drove out the man from the eastward garden and placed there cherubim and a flaming sword to prevent his return, the disaster was beginning to mount, and human history is little more than a record of its development.

It is not quite accurate to say that when our first parents fled from before the face of God they became fugitives and vagabonds in the earth; and it is certainly not true to say that they passed from the love and care of the One who had created them and against whom they had so deeply revolted. God never abandoned the creatures made in His image. Had they not sinned He would have cared for them by His presence; now He cares for them by His providence until a ransomed and regenerated people can look once more on His face (Rev. 21:3; 22:24).

Men are lost but not abandoned: that is what the Scriptures teach and that is what the Church is commissioned to declare.

In times of extraordinary crisis ordinary measures will not suffice. The world lives in such a time of crisis. Christians alone are in a position to rescue the perishing. We dare not settle down to try to live as if things were "normal."

Nothing is normal while sin and lust and death roam the world!

October 19

Seek More of God for Himself Alone

Or despiseth thou the riches of his goodness and forbearance and longsuf-fering; not knowing that the goodness of God leadeth thee to repentance?
Romans 2:4

Why should a man write and distribute a tract in-structing us on "How to Pray So God Will Send You the Money You Need"?

Any of us who have experienced a life and ministry of faith can tell how the Lord met our needs. Surely we believe that God can send money to His believing chil-dren—but it becomes a pretty cheap thing to get excited about the money and fail to give the glory to Him who is the Giver!

So, many are busy "using" God. Use God to get a job! Use God to give us safety! Use God to give us peace of mind! Use God to obtain success in business! Use God to provide heaven at last!

Brethren, we ought to learn—and learn it very soon—that it is much better to have God first and have God Himself even if we have only a thin dime than to have all the riches and all the influence in the world and not have God with it!

John Wesley believed that men ought to seek God alone because He is love. I think in our day we are in need of such an admonition as: "Seek more of God, and seek Him for Himself alone!"

If we become serious-minded about this, we would soon discover that all of the gifts of God come along with the knowledge and the presence of God Himself.

Mankind's Basic Need Remains Ever the Same

By terrible things in righteousness wilt thou answer us, O God of our salvation. . .which stilleth the noise of the seas, the noise of their waves, and the tumult of the people. Psalm 65:5, 7

Some earnest persons try to reason that since there is no stillness in this mechanized world, we must learn to get along without it.

This is the summation of their reasoning: we cannot hope to bring back the still waters and the quiet pastures where David once led his sheep. This rat race of civilization is too noisy for us to hear the still, small Voice, so we must learn to hear God speak in the earthquake and the storm. And if modern evangelism is geared to the tumult and the agitation of the times, why should anyone complain? Does it not represent an honest effort to be all things to all men that by any means some should be saved?

The answer is that the soul of man does not change fundamentally, no matter how external conditions may change!

The aborigine in his hut, the college professor in his study, the truck driver in the bedlam of city traffic have all the same basic need: to be rid of their sins, to obtain eternal life and to be brought into communion with God. Civilized noises and activities are surface phenomena, a temporary rash on the epidermis of the human race.

To attribute sound values to them and then to try to bring religion into harmony with them is to commit a moral blunder so huge as to stagger the imagination, and one for which we shall surely be paying long after this frenetic extravaganza we call civilization has ended in tragedy and everlasting grief!

October 21

We Look for Christ's Victory—Not Annihilation

They shall not hurt or destroy in all my holy mountain: for the earth shall be full of the knowledge of the Lord, as the waters cover the sea. Isaiah 11:9

No one with a trace of human pity can think of the effects of nuclear warfare without feeling utter abhorrence for such a thing and deepest compassion for those who may sometime be caught in its fiery hell.

Yet we Christians would be foolish to allow ourselves to be carried away by the ominous predictions of unbelieving men. We know well enough that nuclear energy is theoretically capable of wiping out every form of life on this planet, including mankind. But we also know that such a catastrophe will never occur. We further know that the earth will never be inhabited by a degenerate race of off-human mutants made so by huge overdoses of radiation.

First, the Holy Scriptures tell us what we could never learn in any other way: They tell us who we are and what we are, how we got here, why we are here and what we are required to do while we remain here. They trace our history from the beginning down to the present time and on into the centuries and millenniums ahead. They track us into the atomic age, through the space age and on into the golden age. They reveal that at an appropriate time direction of the world will be taken away from men and placed in the hands of the Man who alone has the wisdom and power to rule it!

The details are given in satisfying fullness in the writings of the holy prophets and apostles and in the words of Christ while He was yet among us.

The World Wants a Religious Touch in Its Schemes

Behold what manner of love the Father hath bestowed on us. . .therefore the world knoweth us not, because it knew him not. 1 John 3:1

Every once in a while some churchman in an acute attack of conscience does penance in public for Christianity's "failure" to furnish bold leadership for the world in this time of crisis.

Well, I am all for repentance if it is genuine, and I think the Church has failed, not by neglecting to provide leadership but by living too much like the world!

That, however, is not what the muddled churchman means when he bares his soul in public. Rather, he erroneously assumes that the Church of God has been left on earth to minister good hope and cheer to the world in such quantities that it can ignore God, reject Christ, glorify fallen human flesh and pursue its selfish ends in peace.

The Church has received no such commission from her Lord. Further, the world has never shown much disposition to listen to the Church when she speaks in her true prophetic voice. The attitude of the world toward the true child of God is precisely the same as that of the citizens of Vanity Fair toward Christian and his companion: "Therefore they took them and beat them, and besmeared them with dirt, and put them into the cage, that they might be made a spectacle to all men."

Christian's duty was not to "provide leadership" for Vanity Fair but to keep clean from its pollution and get out of it as fast as possible. He that hath ears to hear, let him hear!

The Strong Pull toward Church Complexity

For the fruit of the Spirit is in all goodness and righteousness and truth;
Proving what is acceptable unto the Lord. Ephesians 5:9, 10

Many church groups have perished from too much organization, even as others from too little. Wise church leaders will watch out for both extremes. A man may die as a result of having extremely low blood pressure as certainly as from having too high, and it matters little which takes him off. He is equally dead either way.

The important thing in church organization is to discover the scriptural balance between two extremes and avoid both!

It is painful to see a happy group of Christians, born in simplicity and held together by the bonds of heavenly love, slowly lose their simple character, begin to try to regulate every sweet impulse of the Spirit and slowly die from within.

Yet that is the direction almost all Christian denominations have taken throughout history, and in spite of the warnings set out by the Holy Spirit and the Scriptures of truth it is the direction almost all church groups are taking today.

Churches and societies founded by saintly men with courage, faith and sanctified imagination appear unable to propogate themselves on the same spiritual level beyond one or two generations. In all our fallen life, there is a strong gravitational pull toward complexity and away from things simple and real. There seems to be a kind of sad inevitability back of our morbid urge toward spiritual suicide!

October 24

Religion Should Be a Fount Not a Front

Take heed unto thyself, and unto the doctrine; continue in them: for in doing this thou shalt both save thyself, and them that hear thee. 1 Timothy 4:16

As students of God's Word, we should bear in mind that the burden of the Old Testament was the disparity between the external and the internal life of Israel and that much of the preaching of Christ was directed against the Jews for their failure to be inwardly what their outward profession proclaimed them to be.

Paul, too, warned of those who had but a form of godliness without the corresponding substance, and the history of the church provides all the proof we need that the temptation to make a "front" of religion is very real and very strong.

Probably the tendency to make a mere front of religion is strongest among persons engaged in professional Christian service, but the condition must not be accepted as inevitable. Our first responsibility is not to the public but to God and to our own souls!

Briefly, the way to escape religion as a front is to make it a fount! See to it that we pray more than we preach. Stay with God in the secret place longer than we are with men in the public place. Keep our hearts open to the inflowing Spirit. Cultivate the acquaintance of God more than the friendship of men and we will always have abundance of bread to give to the hungry!

In the Church: The Lordship of Christ in Control

. . .Ye were sealed with that holy Spirit of promise, which is the earnest of our inheritance until the redemption of the purchased possession unto the praise of his glory. Ephesians 1:13, 14

The nervous compulsion to get things done is found everywhere among us and right here is where the pragmatic philosophy comes into its own.

It asks no embarrassing questions about the wisdom of what we are doing or even about the morality of it.

It accepts our chosen ends as right and good and casts about for efficient means and ways to get them accomplished. When it discovers something that works, it soon finds a text to justify it, "consecrates" it to the Lord and plunges ahead. Next a magazine article is written about it, then a book, and finally the inventor is granted an honorary degree. After that, any question about the scripturalness of things or even the moral validity of them is completely swept away.

You cannot argue with success. The method works; ergo, it must be good!

The whole religious atmosphere around us is largely geared to pragmatic methodology. What shall we do to break its power over us?

The answer is simple. We must acknowledge the right of Jesus Christ to control the activities of His Church. The New Testament contains full instructions, not only about what we are to believe but what we are to do and how we are to go about doing it. Any deviation from those instructions is a denial of the Lordship of Christ!

When I Am Weak, Then Am I Strong

. . .For when I am weak, then am I strong. 2 Corinthians 12:10

Everything we need is found in Jesus Christ, the Son of God—and I think it is fair to say that we can never use all of the spiritual power and victory He is able to provide. He is all the guilty sinner needs and He is more than the fondest expectations of the loftiest saint!

If we are going to stand up for Jesus, it is good for us to remember how strong He is—and how weak we are! I settled this long ago. I tell you I have talked to God more than I have talked to anyone else and my conferences with Him have been longer than with anyone else.

I have told Him: "Now, Lord, if I say what I know in my heart I should say, and if I do what I know I should do, I will be in trouble with people and with groups."

Then after praying more, I have said: "Almighty Lord, I accept this with my eyes open! I will not run. I will not hide. I will dare to stand up because I am on your side—and I know that when I am weak, then I am strong!"

So, I don't let anyone praise me and I try not to pay attention to those who would blame me, for I am only a servant of the holiest man that ever walked the streets of Jerusalem—and they called Him a devil!

This is how I have learned to stand fast for Christ, and for all that He is to His own!

Prayer of Faith: Authority of God's Family

Praying always with all prayer and supplication in the Spirit. . .for all saints. Ephesians 6:18

Do you think the Christian Church genuinely believes God's promises that He will respond to our prayers raised to Him in true faith?

This matter of prayer really bears in on the great privileges of the common people, the children of God. No matter what our stature or status, we have the authority in the family of God to pray the prayer of faith, that prayer that can engage the heart of God and that can meet God's conditions of spiritual life and victory.

Our consideration of the power and efficacy of prayer enters into the question of why we are a Christian congregation and what we are striving to be and do.

Are we just going around and around—like a religious merry-go-round? Are we just holding on to the painted mane of the painted horse, repeating a trip of very insignificant circles to a pleasing musical accompaniment?

We are among those who believe in something more than holding religious services in the same old weekly groove. We believe that in an assembly of redeemed believers there should be marvelous answers to prayer.

We believe that God hears and actually answers our praying in the Spirit! Let it be said that one miraculous answer to prayer within a congregation will do more to lift and encourage and solidify the people of God than almost any other thing.

Answers to our prayers will lift up the hands that hang down in discouragement and strengthen the feeble spiritual knees!

October 28

Is It My Kingdom or God's Kingdom?

. . .For thine is the kingdom, and the power, and the glory, for ever. Amen.
Matthew 6:13

How many Christians are there who pray every Sunday in church, "Thy kingdom come. Thy will be done!" without ever realizing the spiritual implications of such intercession?

What are we praying for? Should we edit that prayer so that it becomes a confrontation: "My kingdom go, Lord; let Thy kingdom come!" Certainly His kingdom can never be realized in my life until my own selfish kingdom is deposed. It is when I resign, when I am no longer king of my domain that Jesus Christ will become king of my life.

This principle does not become practical and thus it does not become operative in the lives of many Christians. That is why I keep saying and teaching and hoping that this principle which is objective truth will become subjective experience in Christian lives. For any professing Christian who dares to say, "Knowing the truth is enough for me; I do not want to mix it up with my day-to-day life and experience," Christianity has become nothing but a farce and a delusion!

God is constantly calling for decisions among those in whom there is such great potential for displaying the life of Jesus Christ. Peace and power and fruitfulness can only increase according to our willingness to confess, "It is no longer I, but Christ that liveth in me!"

Christian Worship Is Not a Kind of Educated Magic

. . .Which worship God in the spirit, and rejoice in Christ Jesus, and have no confidence in the flesh. Philippians 3:3

A belief in magic and superstition was thought by the late Sir James G. Frazer to be the only truly universal faith, being accepted as it is in some form by all the peoples of the world.

The temptation to attribute supernatural powers, or at least moral qualities, to inanimate objects is one almost impossible to resist. It is as if the human mind wanted to have it so, and I am not sure but it does. Sin has done strange things to us!

Let it be said, then, that true Christian experience is direct knowledge of God. It is intimate fellowship between two personalities, God and the individual believer. The grounds of fellowship are mental, moral and spiritual, and these are precisely what material objects do not and cannot possess.

The union of the human soul with God in Christ establishes a personal relationship which cannot in any way be affected by material substances. The Church by pronouncing certain objects sacred, and attributing power to them, has turned from the pure freedom of the gospel to a kind of educated magic, far from New Testament truth and gravely injurious to the souls of men.

Our Lord swept aside material objects as having no spiritual significance, and placed the worship of God in the spirit, where it properly belongs. Our responsibility is to God and our fellowship is with Him. The Christian can simply have nothing to do with magic or superstition!

We Are Declared Not Guilty by the Highest Court

Put on the whole armour of God, that ye may be able to stand against the wiles of the devil. Ephesians 6:11

The Christian believer cannot be happy and victorious in the true liberty of the children of God if he is still quaking about his past sins.

God knows that sin is a terrible thing—yes, and the devil knows it, too! So the devil follows us around and as long as we will permit it, he will taunt us about our past sins.

As for myself, I have learned to talk back to him on this score.

I say, "Yes, Devil, sin is terrible—but I remind you that I got it from you! And I remind you, Devil, that everything good—forgiveness and cleansing and blessing—everything that is good I have freely received from Jesus Christ!"

Everything that is bad and that is against me I got from the devil—so why should he have the effrontery and the brass to argue with me about it? Yet he will do it because he is the devil, and he is committed to keeping God's children shut up in a little cage, their spiritual wings clipped.

Brethren, we have been declared "Not guilty!" by the highest court in all the universe. It is good to know that on the basis of grace as taught in the Word of God, when God forgives a man, He trusts him as though he had never sinned.

The Bible does not teach that if a man falls down, he can never rise again. The fact that he falls is not the most important thing—but rather that he is forgiven and allows God to lift him up! That is the basis of our Christian assurance and God wants us to be happy in it.

October 31

God Has Few Admirers among Christians Today

. . .He that dwelleth in love dwelleth in God, and God in him. 1 John 4:16

To love God because He has been good to us is one of the most reasonable things possible but the quality of our worship is stepped up as we move away from the thought of what God has done for us and nearer the thought of the excellence of His holy nature.

This leads us to admiration!

The dictionary says that to admire is "to regard with wondering esteem accompanied by pleasure and delight; to look at or upon with an elevated feeling of pleasure."

According to this definition, God has few admirers among Christians today.

Many are they who are grateful for His goodness in providing salvation. Testimony meetings are mostly devoted to recitations of incidents where someone got into trouble and got out again in answer to prayer. It is good and right to render unto God thanksgiving for all His mercies to us. But God's admirers—where are they?

The simple truth is that worship is elementary until it begins to take on the quality of admiration!

Just as long as the worshiper is engrossed with himself and his good fortune, he is a babe. We begin to grow up when our worship passes from thanksgiving to admiration. As our hearts rise to God in lofty esteem for that which He is, we begin to share a little of the selfless pleasure which is a portion of the blessed in heaven!

November 1

God Will Be All or He Will Be Nothing

Seek ye first the kingdom of God, and his righteousness; and all these things shall be added unto thee. Matthew 6:33

God is never found accidentally!

Whoever seeks other objects and not God is on his own; he may obtain those objects if he is able, but he will never have God.

Whoever seeks God as a means toward desired ends will not find God. The mighty God, the maker of heaven and earth, will not be one of many treasures, not even the chief of all treasures.

He will be all in all or He will be nothing!

His mercy and grace are infinite and His patient understanding is beyond measure, but He will not aid men in their selfish striving after personal gain. He will not help men to attain ends which, when attained, usurp the place He by every right should hold in their interest and affection.

Yet popular Christianity has as one of its most effective talking points the idea that God exists to help people to get ahead in this world. The God of the poor has become the God of an affluent society. We hear that Christ no longer refuses to be a judge or a divider between money-hungry brothers. He can now be persuaded to assist the brother that has accepted Him to get the better of the brother who has not!

The first and greatest commandment is to love God with every power of our entire being. Where love like that exists there can be no place for a second object. If we love God as much as we should surely we cannot dream of a loved object beyond Him which He might help us to obtain!

Having Faith in Faith Is Not Sufficient

Let us hold fast the profession of our faith without wavering; for he is faithful that promised. Hebrews 10:23

At first thought it may sound strange to you—but I cannot recommend that we have faith in "faith."

There is a good deal of preaching that is devoted only to faith. As a result, people have faith in "faith"—and are inclined to forget that our confidence is not in the power of faith but in the person and work of the Saviour, Jesus Christ.

We have full confidence in Jesus Christ—and that is the origin and source and foundation and resting place for all of our faith. In the kingdom of faith, we are dealing with Him, with God Almighty, the One whose essential nature is holiness, the One who cannot lie.

Our confidence rises as the character of God becomes greater and more beautiful and more trustworthy to our spiritual comprehension. The One with whom we deal is the One before whom goes faithfulness and truth.

Actually there is a great difference between believing God and having confidence in Him because of His character, instead of believing that the things of God can be proven and grapsed by human reason.

So, this is the confidence we have in Him. Faith mounts up on its long heavenly boots—up the mountain top, up toward the shining peaks, and says in satisfaction: "If God says it, I know it is so!"

It is the character of God Himself—the One who cannot lie—that gives us this confidence!

November 3

What Did Our Repentance Actually Mean to Us?

. . .The chastisement of our peace was upon him; and with his stripes we are healed. Isaiah 53:5

Have you ever really considered what it meant for Isaiah to report that "the chastisement of our peace was upon him"?

A chastisement fell upon Jesus so that we as individual humans could experience peace with God if we so desired. How few there are who realize that it is this peace—the health and prosperity and welfare and safety of the individual—which restores us to God!

But the chastisement was upon Him. Rebuke, discipline and correction—these are found in chastisement. He was beaten and scourged in public by the decrees of the Romans. They whipped and punished Him in full view of the jeering public, and His bruised and bleeding and swollen person was the answer to the peace of the world and to the peace of the human heart.

We who are forgiven and justified sinners sensed in our own repentance only a token of the wounding and chastisement which fell upon Jesus Christ as He stood in our place and in our behalf. A truly penitent man does not feel that he can actually dare to ask God to let him off—but peace has been established! The blows fell on Him!

Isaiah sums up his message of a substitutionary atonement with the good news that "with his stripes we are healed."

November 4

Fear of the Lord: Cannot Be Induced by Threats

No man can come to me, except the Father which hath sent me draw him. . . . John 6:44

The efforts of liberal and borderline modernists to woo men to God by presenting the soft side of religion is an unqualified evil because it ignores the very reason for our alienation from God in the first place!

It seems to be an obvious fact that until a man has gotten into trouble with his own heart he is not likely to get out of trouble with God.

Cain and Abel are solemn examples of this truth. Cain brought a present to One whom he assumed to be pleased with him. Abel brought a sacrifice to One who he knew could not accept him as he was. His trembling heart told him to find a place to hide. Cain's heart did not tremble—he was well satisfied with himself.

The fear of God would have served Cain well in that critical moment for it would have changed the whole character of his offering and altered the entire course of his life for the better.

As indispensable as is the terror of the Lord, we must always keep in mind that it cannot be induced by threats made in the name of the Lord. Hell and judgment are realities, and they must be preached in their biblical context as fully as the Bible teaches them, but they cannot induce that mysterious thing we call the fear of the Lord.

The Holy Spirit alone can induce this emotion in the human breast. It is a feeling rather than idea: it is the deep reaction of a fallen creature in the presence of the holy Being the stunned heart knows is God!

November 5

Christ Opens Our Hearts to Grasp the Truth

Then opened he their understanding, that they might understand the scriptures. Luke 24:45

The disciples of Jesus were instructed in the Scriptures. Christ Himself had taught them out of the Law of Moses and the Prophets and the Psalms; yet it took a specific act of inward "opening" before they could grasp the truth!

The Apostle Paul discovered very early in his ministry that, as he put it, "not all men have faith." And he knew why: "But if our gospel be hid, it is hid to them that are lost: in whom the god of this world hath blinded the minds of them which believe not, lest the light of the glorious gospel of Christ, who is the image of God, should shine unto them" (2 Cor. 4:3, 4).

Satan has no fear of the light as long as he can keep his victims sightless. The uncomprehending mind is unaffected by truth. The intellect of the hearer may grasp saving knowledge while yet the heart makes no moral response to it.

A classic example of this is seen in the meeting of Benjamin Franklin and George Whitefield. In his autobiography, Franklin recounts how he listened to the mighty preaching of the great evangelist. Whitefield talked with Franklin personally about his need of Christ and promised to pray for him. Years later Franklin wrote rather sadly that the evangelist's prayers must not have done any good, for he was still unconverted.

Why? Franklin had light without sight. To see the Light of the World requires an act of inward enlightenment wrought by the Spirit. We must pit our prayer against that dark spirit who blinds the hearts of men!

November 6

The Pattern of Unbelief: Begins at the Bible

It is a fearful thing to fall into the hands of the living God. Hebrews 10:31

The present refusal of so many religious teachers to accept the doctrine of the wrath of God is part of a larger pattern of unbelief that begins with doubt concerning the veracity of the Christian Scriptures.

Let a man question the inspiration of the Scriptures and a curious, even monstrous, inversion takes place: thereafter he judges the Word instead of letting the Word judge him; he determines what the Word should teach instead of permitting it to determine what he should believe; he edits, amends, strikes out, adds at his pleasure; but always he sits above the Word and makes it amenable to him instead of kneeling before God and becoming amenable to the Word!

The tender-minded interpreter who seeks to shield God from the implications of His own Word is engaged in an officious effort that cannot but be completely wasted.

Why such a man still clings to the tattered relics of religion it is hard to say. The manly thing would be to walk out on the Christian faith and put it behind him along with other outgrown toys and discredited beliefs of childhood, but this he rarely does. He kills the tree but still hovers pensively about the orchard hoping for fruit that never comes!

Sinning in the Name of the Sinless One

Love suffereth long and is kind; doth not behave itself unseemly, seeketh not her own. . . 1 Corinthians 13:4, 5

Religious acts done out of low motives are twice evil—evil in themselves and evil because they are done in the name of God!

This is equivalent to sinning in the name of the sinless One, lying in the name of One who cannot lie and hating in the name of the One whose nature is love.

Christians, and especially very active ones, should take time out frequently to search their souls to be sure of their motives.

Many a solo is sung to show off; many a sermon is preached as an exhibition of talent; many a church is founded as a slap at some other church.

Even missionary activity may become competitive, and soul winning may degenerate into a sort of brush-salesman project to satisfy the flesh.

A good way to avoid the snare of empty religious activity is to appear before God every once in awhile with our Bibles open to the thirteenth chapter of First Corinthians. This passage, though rated one of the most beautiful in the Bible, is also one of the severest to be found in Sacred Writ.

The apostle takes the highest religious service and consigns it to futility unless it is motivated by love. Lacking love, prophets and teachers, orators, philanthropists and martyrs are sent away without reward.

To sum it up, we may say simply that in the sight of God we are judged not so much by what we do as by our reasons for doing it!

November 8

Good News: He Cares for You

Casting all your care upon him; for he careth for you. 1 Peter 5:7

I have noticed in recent years that many of the Lord's people—not just ministers and missionaries—tend more and more to become a nervous and harried people.

I don't claim to know everything about it. I only claim that there is hope and relief for the children of God in these terrible days, for Paul wrote to the Philippians and said, "Be anxious for nothing—the peace of God can keep your hearts and minds!"

How are we going to escape fear, when there are legitimate dangers that lie all around us?

Here's what the man of God says: "Don't be anxious—but in everything by prayer and supplication with thanksgiving let your requests be made known unto God and the peace of God which passeth all understanding shall keep your hearts and minds through Christ Jesus."

So, Someone who is able is looking after us!

The Bible says, "He careth for you." Jesus our Lord, says, "Your Father knows what you have need of before you ask Him." And Jesus said, "Let not your heart be troubled." And in all your afflictions, He was afflicted, the Word says.

Remember that peace of heart does not come from denying that there is trouble, but comes from rolling your trouble on God. By faith you have the right to call on One who is your brother, the Son of Man, who is also the Son of God. And if He is going to look after you, why should you worry at all!

Would You Settle for an Absentee God?

Hear now this, O foolish people, and without understanding; which have eyes and see not, which have ears and hear not; Fear ye not me? saith the Lord: will ye not tremble at my presence?. . . Jeremiah 5:21, 22

"There are over many who have much knowledge and little virtue," said the blind saint, Malaval, "and who often speak of God while rarely speaking to Him."

The Bible teaches plainly enough the doctrine of the divine omnipresence, but for the masses of professed Christians this is the era of the Absentee God. Most Christians speak of God in the manner usually reserved for a departed loved one, rarely as of one present; but they do not often speak to Him.

Truth is always better than error, and with the inspired Scriptures before us we need not think wrongly about such an important matter as this. We can know the truth if we will.

An Absentee God is among other things inadequate!

He does not meet the needs of the being called man. As a baby is not satisfied away from its mother, and as life on earth is impossible without the sun, so human beings need a present God, and they can be neither healthy nor satisfied without Him.

Surely God would not have created us to be satisfied with nothing less than His presence if He had intended that we should get on with nothing more than His absence.

No. The Scriptures and moral reason agree that God is present!

November 10

Conversion: Beginning of a Journey

And they continued stedfastly in the apostles' doctrine and fellowship, and in breaking of bread, and in prayers. Acts 2:42

Conversion for the early New Testament Christians was not a destination; it was the beginning of a journey. And right there is where the biblical emphasis differs from ours.

Today, all is made to depend upon the initial act of believing. At a given moment a "decision" is made for Christ, and after that everything is "automatic." Such is the impression inadvertently created by our failure to lay a scriptural emphasis in our evangelistic preaching. We of the evangelical churches are almost all guilty of this lopsided view of the Christian life.

In our eagerness to make converts we allow our hearers to absorb the idea that they can deal with their entire responsibility once and for all by an act of believing. This is in some vague way supposed to honor grace and glorify God, whereas actually it is to make Christ the author of a grotesque, unworkable system that has no counterpart in the Scriptures of truth.

In the Book of Acts, faith was for each believer a beginning, not an end; it was a journey, not a bed in which to lie while waiting for the day of our Lord's triumph. Believing was not a once-done act; it was more than an act, it was an attitude of heart and mind which inspired and enabled the believer to take up his cross and follow the Lamb whithersoever He went.

"They continued," says Luke, and is it not plain that it was only by continuing that they could confirm their faith?

Our Lord Still Demands New Testament Standards

That ye might walk worthy of the Lord unto all pleasing, being fruitful in every good work, and increasing in the knowledge of God. Colossians 1:10

Not the naked Word only but the character of the witness determines the quality of the Christian convert. The church can do no more than transplant herself. What she is in one land she will be in another. A crab apple does not become a Grimes Golden by being carried from one country to another.

God has written His law deep into all life; everything must bring forth after its kind!

It would appear logical that a subnormal, powerless church would not engage in missionary activity, but again the facts contradict the theory. Christian groups that have long ago lost every trace of moral fire nevertheless continue to grow at home and reproduce themselves in other lands.

There is a weakness too in world missionary activity carried on by the evangelical wing of the church. That weakness is the naive assumption that we have only to reach the last tribe with our brand of Christianity and the world has been evangelized! This is an assumption that we dare not make.

Evangelical Christianity is now tragically below the New Testament standard. Worldliness is an accepted part of our way of life. Our religious mood is social instead of spiritual. We have lost the art of worship. We are not producing saints. We carry on our religious activities after the methods of the modern advertiser. Our literature is shallow and our hymnody borders on sacrilege. And scarcely anyone appears to care!

November 12

Loving the Lord: Not Easy in Today's World

. . .If a man love me, he will keep my words; and my Father will love him, and we will come to him. . . . John 14:23

The gravest question any of us face is whether we do or do not love the Lord!

Too much hinges on the answer to pass the matter off lightly, and it is a question that no one can answer for another. Not even the Bible can tell the individual man that he loves the Lord; it can only tell him how he can know whether or not he does. It can and does tell us how to test our hearts for love as a man might test ore for the presence of uranium, but we must do the testing.

If we lived in a spiritual Utopia where every wind blew toward heaven and every man was a friend of God we Christians could take everything for granted, counting on the new life within us to cause us to do the will of God without effort and more or less unconsciously. Unfortunately, we have opposing us the lusts of the flesh, the attraction of the world and the temptations of the devil. These complicate our lives and require us often to make determined moral decisions on the side of Christ and His commandments.

When with honesty and serious minds we ask ourselves, "Do I love the Lord, or no?", there will likely be any number of personal workers standing by to quote convenient texts to prove that we do.

But our Lord told His disciples that love and obedience were organically united, that the keeping of His sayings would prove that we love Him. This is the true test of love and we will be wise to face up to it!

November 13

A Dangerous Philosophy: Success Is Everything

For the wrath of God is revealed from heaven against all ungodliness and unrighteousness of men, who hold the truth in unrighteousness. Romans 1:18

The philosophy of pragmatism—basically, the doctrine of the utility of truth, is having a powerful influence upon Christianity in the latter half of the twentieth century.

For the pragmatist there are no absolutes, nothing is absolutely good or absolutely true. Truth and morality float on a sea of human experience.

For the pragmatist, truth is to use. Whatever is useful is true for the user, though for someone else it may not be useful, so not true. The truth of any idea is its ability to produce desirable results. If it can show no such results it is false. This is pragmatism stripped of its jargon!

We live in a day when no one wants to argue with success. It is useless to plead for the human soul, to insist that what a man can do is less important than what he is!

The spectacular drama of successful deeds leaves the beholder breathless—deeds you can see. So who cares about ideals and character and morals? These things are for poets, nice old ladies and philosophers—"let's get on with the job!"

The weakness of all this in the church is its tragic shortsightedness. It never takes the long view of religious activity, but goes cheerfully on believing that "because it works it is both good and true." It is satisfied with present success and shakes off any suggestion that its works may go up in smoke in the day of Christ!

We Still Want to Boss Our Own Lives

Quench not the Spirit. 1 Thessalonians 5:19

"Doesn't everybody desire to be filled with the Holy Spirit?" I have been asked, and the answer is "No."

I suppose many people desire to be full but not many desire to be filled. I want to responsibly declare that before you can be filled with the Spirit, you must desire to be—and some people do not desire to be filled.

We ought to be very plain in our teaching that Satan has tried to block every effort of Christ's Church to receive from the Father her divine and blood-bought patrimony that the Holy Spirit should fill His Church and that He should fill individuals who make up His Church.

It is plain in the Scriptures that the gentle and good Holy Spirit wants to fill us and possess us if we are Christians. This Spirit is like Jesus—pure, gentle, sane, wise and loving.

He wants to possess you so that you are no longer in command of the little vessel in which you sail. You may be a passenger on board, or one of the crew, but you definitely are not in charge. The Spirit of God is now in command of the vessel.

The reason we object to it being that way is because we were born of Adam's corrupted flesh. We want to boss our own lives. That is why we ask: Are you sure that you want to be possessed by the blessed Spirit of the Father and of the Son? Are you ready and willing for your personality to be taken over by someone who is like this?

The Devotional Life Is Almost Crowded Out

And that ye study to be quiet, and to do your own business. . .That ye may walk honestly toward them that are without. . . . 1 Thessalonians 4:11, 12

We Christians must simplify our lives or lose untold treasures on earth and in eternity!

Modern civilization is so complex as to make the devotional life all but impossible, multiplying distractions and beating us down by destroying our solitude.

"Commune with your own heart upon your bed and be still" is a wise and healing counsel, but how can it be followed in this day of the newspaper, the telephone, the radio and the television? These modern playthings, like pet tiger cubs, have grown so large and dangerous that they threaten to devour us all. No spot is now safe from the world's intrusion.

One way the civilized world destroys men is by preventing them from thinking their own thoughts. Our "vastly improved methods of communication" of which the shortsighted boast so loudly now enable a few men in strategic centers to feed into millions of minds alien thought stuff, ready-made and predigested.

The need for solitude and quietness was never greater than it is today. Even the majority of Christians are so completely conformed to this present age that they, too, want things the way they are.

However, there are some of God's children who have had enough. They want to relearn the ways of solitude and simplicity and gain the infinite riches of the interior life. They want to discover the blessedness of what has been called "spiritual aloneness"—a discipline that will go far in making us acquainted with God and our own souls!

November 16

Morality by Public Pressure Is Not Morality

For so is the will of God, that with well doing ye may put to silence the ignorance of foolish men. 1 Peter 2:15

Carnal fear may take either of two opposite directions. It may make us afraid to do what we know we should do, or afraid not to do what we have reason to think people expect us to do.

There is a foolish consistency which brings us into bondage to the consciences of other people, but this morality by public pressure is not pure morality at all. At best it is a timid righteousness of doubtful parentage; at worst it is the child of weakness and fear.

A free Christian should act from within with a total disregard for the opinions of others. If a course is right he should take it because it is right, not because he is afraid not to take it. Any act done because we are afraid not to do it is of the same moral quality as the act that is not done because we are afraid to do it.

The way to escape this double snare is simple. Make a complete surrender to God; love Him with all your heart and love every man for His sake. Determine to obey your own convictions as they crystallize within yourself as a result of unceasing prayer and constant study of God's Word. After that you may safely ignore the expectations of your friends as well as the criticisms of your enemies. You will experience first the shocked surprise of the regimented army of lock-step believers, then their grudging admiration!

The Church Can Claim a Heavenly Origin

And I say unto thee,. . .upon this rock I will build my church; and the gates of hell shall not prevail against it. Matthew 16:18

The highest expression of the will of God in this age is the Church which He purchased with His own blood.

According to the Scriptures the Church is the habitation of God through the Spirit, and as such is the most important organism beneath the sun. She is not one more good institution along with the home, the state, and the school; she is the only one that can claim a heavenly origin!

The Church is found wherever the Holy Spirit has drawn together a few persons who trust Christ for their salvation, worship God in spirit and have no dealings with the world and the flesh. The members may by necessity be scattered and separated by distance and circumstances, but in every true member of the Church is the homing instinct and the longing of the sheep for the fold and the shepherd.

Give a few real Christians half a chance and they will get together and organize and plan regular meetings for prayer and worship and Bible study, and try as far as possible to spread the saving gospel to the lost world.

Such groups are cells in the Body of Christ, and each one is a true church, a real part of the greater Church. It is in and through these cells that the Spirit does His work on earth. Whoever scorns the local church scorns the Body of Christ.

The Church is still to be reckoned with—"The gates of hell shall not prevail against her."

November 18

Figures of Speech Are Not Christian Doctrine

Fear not little flock; for it is your Father's good pleasure to give you the kingdom. Luke 12:32

Some time ago I heard a man attempt to pour ridicule upon the custom of pastoral preaching. He made a strong point that after conversion, a person should go out at once and begin to win souls, not go to church and hear preaching.

For illustration, he reasoned that a farmer candles his eggs once, not every week, and sends them to market.

But there was one very serious weakness in the argument: Christ did not say to Peter, "Candle my eggs"; He said, "feed my sheep."

Christians are not eggs to be candled; they are sheep to be fed!

Feeding sheep is not a job to be gotten over with once and for all; it is a loving act to be repeated at regular intervals as long as the sheep live. Peter well understood His Lord's meaning and years later admonished certain elders of the church to "feed the flock of God which is among you." Not one word did he say about candling eggs!

Figures of speech should illustrate truth, not originate **it**. Christians are living creatures dependent on food, **and** must be fed well and often if they are to remain **healthy**. Our Lord selected the figure of sheep because it **accords** with the facts. The figure of eggs does not.

Beware the man who makes a figure of speech teach doctrine. There's something better in the Bible than figures of speech to be twisted to fit our own prejudices!

It Is Best to Cooperate with the Inevitable

I will cry unto God most high; unto God that performeth all things for me.
Psalm 57:2

A simple-hearted man was once asked how he managed to live in such a state of constant tranquility even though surrounded by circumstances anything but pleasant.

His answer was as profound as it was simple: "I have learned to cooperate with the inevitable!"

The idea here set forth is so wise and practical that it is hard to see how we Christians have managed to overlook it so completely in our everyday living. That we do overlook it is shown by our conduct and conversation. Some of us "kick against the pricks" for a lifetime, all the while believing that we are surrendered to the will of God.

What wicked men do should not disturb the good man's tranquility. The inner world consists of our thoughts and emotions, presided over by our will. While we cannot determine circumstances we can determine our reaction to them. And that is where the battle is to be fought and victory won!

This is not to teach fatalism or to deny the freedom of the human will. Quite the contrary, it is to assert that freedom unequivocally.

Though we cannot control the universe, we can determine our attitude toward it. We can accept God's will wherever it is expressed. If my will is to do God's will, then there will be no controversy with anything that comes in the course of my daily walk. Let God make the alterations as He may see fit, either by His own sovereign providence or in answer to believing prayer!

November 20

Tearless Teachers Have Harmed Us

Serving the Lord with all humility of mind, and with many tears, and temptations. . . . Acts 20:19

It is not a reassuring thought that the writings of the grief-stricken prophets are often pored over by persons whose interests are curious merely and who never shed one tear for the woes of the world.

They have a prying inquisitiveness about the schedule of future events, forgetting apparently that the whole purpose of Bible prophecy is to prepare us morally and spiritually for the time to come.

The doctrine of Christ's return has fallen into neglect, on the North American continent at least, and as far as I can detect, today exercises little power in the lives of the rank and file of Bible-believing Christians. For this there may be a number of contributing factors; but the chief one is, I believe, the misfortune suffered by prophetic truth when men without tears undertook to instruct us in the writings of the tear-stained prophets. Big crowds and big offerings resulted until events proved the teachers wrong on too many points.

Another field where tearless men have done us untold harm is in prayer for the sick. Thankfully, there have always been reverent, serious men who felt it their sacred duty to pray for the sick that they might be healed in the will of God. But when tearless promoters took up the doctrine it was turned into a lucrative racket. Smooth, persuasive men used superior salesmanship methods to make impressive fortunes out of their campaigns—and this in the name of the Man of Sorrows who had not where to lay His head!

God Knows the Potential of the Human Soul

If we confess our sins, he is faithful and just to forgive us our sins, and to cleanse us from all unrighteousness. 1 John 1:9

Only man was created in God's own image, according to the Scriptures.

I know that I take a chance of being misunderstood when I state that man was more like God than any other creature ever created. Because of the nature of man's creation, there is nothing in the universe so much like God as the human soul.

Even in the face of man's sin and lost condition, there is still that basic potential in the soul and nature of man that through grace can become more like God than anything in the universe.

There is no question about man's sin—therefore there is no question about his being lost. A man is lost if he is not converted—overwhelmed in the vast darkness of emptiness!

Man was created to know God but he chose the gutter. That is why he is like a bird shut away in a cage or like a fish taken from the water. That is the explanation of man's disgraceful acts—war and hate, murder and greed, brother against brother!

Is there still a good word for man in his lost condition?

Is there an answer for man in whom there is that instinctive groping and craving for the lost image and the knowledge of the Eternal Being?

Yes, the positive answer is in the Word of God, teaching the sinner-man that it is still possible for him to know God. It all has to do with forgiveness and grace and regeneration and justification in Jesus Christ!

November 22

A Thankful Heart Cannot Also Be Cynical

Giving thanks always for all things unto God and the Father in the name of our Lord Jesus Christ. Ephesians 5:20

Let me recommend the cultivation of the habit of thankfulness as an effective cure for the cynical, sour habits of fault-finding among Christian believers.

Thanksgiving has great curative power. The heart that is constantly overflowing with gratitude will be safe from those attacks of resentfulness and gloom that bother so many religious persons. A thankful heart cannot be cynical!

Please be aware that I am not recommending any of the "applied psychology" nostrums so popular in liberal circles. We who have been introduced to God through the miracle of the new birth realize that there is good scriptural authority for the cultivation of gratitude as a cure for spiritual sourness. Further, experience teaches us that it works!

We should never take any blessing for granted, but accept everything as a gift from the Father of Lights. We should write on a tablet, one by one, the things for which we are grateful to God and to our fellow men.

Personally, I have gotten great help from the practice of talking over with God the many kindnesses I have received. I like to begin with thanking Him for His thoughts of me back to creation; for giving His Son to die for me when I was still a sinner; for giving the Bible and His blessed Spirit who inwardly gives us understanding of it. I thank Him for my parents, teachers, statesmen, patriots.

I am grateful to God for all of these and more—and I shall not let God forget that I am!

November 23

The Bible World: Still the Warm, Living World

Study to show thyself approved unto God, a workman that needeth not to be ashamed, rightly dividing the word of truth. 2 Timothy 2:15

When reading the Scriptures the sensitive person is sure to feel the marked difference between the world as the Bible reveals it and the world as conceived by religious people today. And the contrast is not in our favor!

The world as the men and women of the Bible saw it was a personal world, warm, intimate, populated. Their world contained first of all the God who had created it, who still dwelt in it as in a sanctuary and who might be discovered walking among the trees of the garden if the human heart were but pure enough to feel and human eyes clear enough to see. There were also present many beings sent of God to be ministers to them who were the heirs of salvation. They also recognized the presence of sinister forces which it was their duty to oppose and which they might conquer by an appeal to God in prayer.

Jacob saw a ladder set up on the earth with God standing above it and the angels ascending and descending upon it. Abraham and Balaam and Manoah and how many others met the angels of God and conversed with them. Moses saw God in the bush; Isaiah saw Him high and lifted up and heard the antiphonal chant filling the temple.

Christians today think of the world in wholly different terms—a world cold and impersonal and completely without inhabitants except for man. The blind eyes of modern Christians cannot see the invisible but that does not destroy the reality of the spiritual creation. If we will believe we may even now enjoy the presence of God and the ministry of His heavenly messengers.

November 24

Our Humor Should Not Lead to Foolish Talk

Be ye therefore followers of God, as dear children;. . .neither filthiness, nor foolish talking, nor jesting,. . .but rather giving of thanks. Ephesians 5:1, 4

Few things are as useful in the Christian life as a gentle sense of humor and few things are as deadly as a sense of humor out of control.

Many lose the race of life through frivolity. Paul is careful to warn us. He says plainly that the Christian's characteristic mood should not be one of jesting and foolish talking but rather one of thanksgiving. It is significant that the apostle classifies levity along with uncleanness, covetousness and idolatry.

Now obviously an appreciation of the humorous is not an evil in itself. When God made us He included a sense of humor as a built-in feature, and the normal human being will possess this gift in some degree at least. The source of humor is the ability to perceive the incongruous.

Humor is one thing but frivolity is quite another. Cultivation of a spirit that can take nothing seriously is one of the great curses of society, and within the church it has worked to prevent much spiritual blessing that otherwise would have descended upon us. We have all met those people who will not be serious. They meet everything with a laugh and a funny remark. This is bad enough in the world, but positively intolerable among Christians.

I see no value in gloom and no harm in a good laugh. My plea is for a great seriousness which will put us in mood with the Son of Man and with the prophets and apostles, that we may attain that moral happiness which is one of the marks of spirituality.

The Church Must Look First to Christ

And are built upon the foundation of the apostles and the prophets, Jesus Christ himself being the chief corner stone. . .in whom ye also are builded together for an habitation of God through the Spirit. Ephesians 2:20, 22

The first look of the Church is toward Christ, who is her Head, her Lord and her All!

After that she must be self-regarding and world-regarding, with a proper balance between the two.

By self-regarding I do not mean self-centered. I mean that the Church must examine herself constantly to see if she be in the faith; she must engage in severe self-criticism with a cheerful readiness to make amends; she must live in a state of perpetual penitence, seeking God with her whole heart; she must constantly check her life and conduct against the Holy Scriptures and bring her life into line with the will of God.

By world-regarding I mean that the Church must know why she is here on earth; that she must acknowledge her indebtedness to all mankind (Rom. 1:14, 15); that she must take seriously the words of her Lord, "Go ye into all the world, and preach the gospel to every creature" and "Ye shall be witnesses unto me both in Jerusalem, and in all Judaea, and in Samaria, and unto the uttermost part of the earth."

The task of the Church is twofold: to spread Christianity throughout the world and to make sure that the Christianity she spreads is the pure New Testament kind. To spread an effete, degenerate brand of Christianity to pagan lands is not to fulfill the commandment of Christ or discharge our obligation to the heathen!

November 26

Christian Reproof: With Kindness and Charity

Brethren, if a man be overtaken in a fault, ye which are spiritual, restore such a one in the spirit of meekness. Galatians 6:1

It is quite natural, and even spiritual, to feel sorrow and heaviness when we see the professed followers of Christ walking in the ways of the world. Our first impulse may be to go straight to them and upbraid them indignantly, but such methods are seldom successful. The heat in our spirit may not be from the Holy Spirit, and if it is not then it can very well do more harm than good.

Satan has achieved a real victory when he succeeds in getting us to react in an unspiritual way toward sins and failures in our brethren. We cannot fight sin with sin or draw men to God by frowning at them in fleshly anger, "for the wrath of man worketh not the righteousness of God."

Often acts done in a spirit of religious irritation have consequences far beyond anything we could have guessed. Moses allowed himself to become vexed with Israel and in a fit of pique smote the rock. With the same stroke he closed the land of promise against him for the rest of his life.

It is not an easy task to stand for God as we should in our generation and yet maintain a spirit of kindliness toward the very ones we are sent to reprove—but it is not impossible! In this as in everything else, Christ is our perfect example and He can do the impossible if we but yield and obey. He will surely show us how to oppose with kindness and reprove with charity and the power of the Holy Spirit within will enable us to follow His blessed example!

November 27

The Holy Spirit Is at Hand to Help You

But why dost thou judge thy brother?. . . for we shall all stand before the judgment seat of Christ. Romans 14:10

God in love and wisdom has given us in His Holy Spirit every gift and power and help that we need to serve Him. We do not have to look around for some other way!

The most solemn aspect of this is our individual responsibility. The Bible teaches that a day is coming when we must all appear before the judgment seat of Christ; that everyone faces a review of the things done in the body, whether good or bad.

In that day we will be fully exposed and the things that we have done in our own strength and for our own glory will be quickly blown away, like worthless straw and stubble, forever separated from the kind of deeds and ministries which were wrought by the Spirit and which are described as eternal treasures in the sight of God, gold and silver and precious stones that the fire cannot harm.

In that day, all that is related to the work of the flesh will perish and pass away, and only that which has been wrought by the Spirit of God will remain and stand.

Do you dare to accept the fact that the sovereign God has designed to do all of His work through spiritually gifted men and women? Therefore, He does all of His work on earth through humble and faithful believers who are given spiritual gifts and abilities beyond their own capacities.

It was the promise of Christ that "you shall receive power" through the ministry of the Holy Spirit—and along with power the bestowment of sweet graces and pleasant fruits of godliness when He is allowed to gain control of our persons!

November 28

The Ministry: Actually a Perilous Profession

. . .For the accuser of our brethren is cast down, which accused them before our God day and night. And they overcame him by the blood of the Lamb, and by the word of their testimony. . . . Revelation 12:10, 11

The clergyman is considered one of the best actuarial risks any insurance company can handle—from the standpoint of physical hazard.

Yet, the ministry is one of the most perilous of professions!

The devil hates the Spirit-filled minister with an intensity second only to that which he feels for Christ Himself. The source of this hatred is not difficult to discover. An effective, Christlike minister is a constant embarrassment to the devil, a threat to his dominion, a rebuttal of his best arguments and a dogged reminder of his coming overthrow. No wonder he hates him!

Satan knows that the downfall of a prophet of God is a strategic victory for him, so he rests not day or night devising hidden snares and deadfalls for the ministry. Perhaps a better figure would be the poison dart that only paralyzes its victim, for I think that Satan has little interest in killing the preacher outright.

An ineffective, half-alive minister is a better advertisement for hell than a good man dead!

So, the preacher's dangers are likely to be spiritual rather than physical, though sometimes the enemy works through bodily weakness to get to the preacher's soul!

Spiritual Twins: Holiness and Happiness

But rejoice, inasmuch as ye are partakers of Christ's sufferings: that when his glory shall be revealed, ye may be glad also with exceeding joy. 1 Peter 4:13

I want to bring you my postulate that most present-day Christians live sub-Christian lives. As a result, Christianity has been watered down until the solution is so weak that if it were poison it would not hurt anyone and if it were medicine it would not cure anyone!

Most Christians are not joyful persons because they are not holy persons, and they are not holy persons because they are not filled with the Holy Spirit, and they are not filled with the Holy Spirit because they are not separated persons.

The Spirit cannot fill whom He cannot separate, and whom He cannot fill, He cannot make holy, and whom He cannot make holy, He cannot make happy!

My postulate further insists that the average modern Christian is not Christlike. The proof of this is apparent in the disposition that we find among the children of God. They have moral weaknesses and suffer frequent defeats. They have a dulled understanding and often live far below the standard of the Scriptures and thus outside the will of God.

To be honest, let us admit that the application of the gospel is being pulled down to the standard of the most carnal, the cheapest saintling hanging on by the teeth anywhere in the kingdom of God!

November 30

Nothing Can Hinder God or a Good Man

If any man will to do His will, he shall know of the doctrine, whether it be of God. . . . John 7:17

The notion that hostile persons or unfavorable circumstances can prevent the will of God from being fulfilled in a human life is altogether erroneous.

Nothing, no one, can hinder God or a good man!

It is one of the glories of the Christian faith that it can be present in effective power regardless of whether or not the moral and political environment is favorable to it. We recall that H. G. Wells once said that he personally believed Buddhism to be the best religion, but admitted that it could flourish only in countries having a warm climate!

If true religion consisted in outward practices, then it could be destroyed by laws forbidding those practices. But if the true worshiper is one who worships God in spirit and in truth, how can laws or jails or abuses or deprivations prevent the spiritual man from worshiping?

Let a man set his heart only on doing the will of God and he is instantly free! No one can hinder him. It is only when we introduce our own will into our relation to God that we get into trouble. When we weave into the pattern of our lives threads of our own desires we instantly become subject to hindrances from the outside.

The essence of spiritual worship is to love supremely, to trust confidently, to pray without ceasing and to seek to be Christlike and holy, doing all the good we can for Christ's sake.

How impossible for anyone to hinder that kind of "practice"!

Jesus Asks Us to Love the Unlovely

No man hath seen God at any time. If we love one another God dwelleth in us, and his love is perfected in us. 1 John 4:12

In his earthly ministry, our Lord Jesus loved babies, publicans, harlots and sick people—and He loved them spontaneously and individually!

The person who claims to follow Christ cannot afford to do otherwise.

A peril always confronting the minister is that he may come unconsciously to love religious and philosophic ideas rather than saints and sinners. It is altogether possible to feel for the world of lost men the same kind of detached affection that the naturalist Fabre, say, felt for a hive of bees or a hill of black ants. They are something to study, to learn from, possibly even to help, but nothing to weep over or die for!

Where this attitude prevails it soon leads to a stilted and pedantic kind of preaching. The minister assumes that his hearers are as familiar with history, philosophy and theology as he is, so he indulges in learned allusions, makes casual references to books and writers wholly unknown to the majority of people who listen to him, and mistakes the puzzled expression on the faces of his parishioners for admiration of his brilliance!

Why religious people continue to put up with this sort of thing, as well as to pay for it and support it, is beyond me. I can only add it to the long list of things I do not and probably never will understand.

God's Promise Will Outlive Man's Violence

Ye therefore, beloved, seeing ye know these things before, beware lest ye also, being led away with the error of the wicked, fall from your own stedfastness. 2 Peter 3:17

Those who still read and trust their Bibles in the midst of the nuclear age have found a great truth and a message the rest of the world does not know: after the war lords have shot their last missile and dropped their last bomb there will still be living men inhabiting this globe!

After the world has gone through the meat grinder of Armageddon the earth will still be inhabited by men; not by biological freaks, but by real people like you and me.

If the world can escape annihilation only by adopting the ethics of Jesus, as some think, we may as well resign ourselves to the inevitable explosion, for a huge block of the earth's population is controlled by Communists whose basic ideology is violently anti-Christian and who are determined to extirpate every trace of Christianity from among them. Other large blocks are non-Christian and grimly set to remain so.

The West, it is true, pays lip service to Christianity, but selfishness, greed, ambition, pride and lust rule the rulers of these lands almost to a man. While they will now and then speak well of Christ, yet the total quality of their conduct leaves little doubt that they are not much influenced by His teachings.

All this being true, still we Christians can sing at the foot of the threatening volcano. Things have not gotten out of hand. However bad they look, the Lord sitteth king forever and reigneth over the affairs of men!

Holiness and Worship Come before Power

. . .He that soweth to the Spirit shall of the Spirit reap life everlasting.
Galatians 6:8

To teach that the filling with the Holy Spirit is given the Christian to provide "power for service" is to teach truth, but not the whole truth!

Power for service is but one effect of the experience, and I do not hesitate to say that it is the least of several effects. Contrary to the popular belief, "to serve this present age" is not the Christian's first duty nor the chief end of man.

The primary work of the Holy Spirit is to restore the lost soul to intimate fellowship with God through the washing of regeneration. To accomplish this He first reveals Christ to the penitent heart (1 Cor. 12:3). He then goes on to illuminate the newborn soul with brighter rays from the face of Christ (John 14:26; 16:13-15) and leads the willing heart into depths and heights of divine knowledge and communion. Remember, we know Christ only as the Spirit enables us and we have only as much of Him as the Holy Spirit imparts!

God wants worshipers before workers; indeed the only acceptable workers are those who have learned the lost art of worship. It is inconceivable that a sovereign and holy God should be so hard up for workers that He would press into service anyone who had been empowered regardless of his moral qualifications. The very stones would praise Him if the need arose and a thousand legions of angels would leap to do His will!

Gifts and power for service the Spirit surely desires to impart; but holiness and spiritual worship come first!

December 4

God Was Never the Author of Disorder

For by him all things were created, that are in heaven, and that are in earth, visible and invisible. . .and he is before all things, and by him all things consist. Colossians 1:16, 17

Everywhere I look in the created world I see God—and my soul is delighted!

I look into a dry, old book that looks like a telephone directory gone mad—we call it a lexicon—and I find that in the New Testament the word "world" means "an orderly arranged system, highly decorative, which is tended, cared for and provided for."

Anyone who knows God, even slightly, would expect God to make an orderly world because God Himself is the essence of order. God was never the author of disorder—whether it be in society, in the home, or in the mind or body of man.

I have noticed that some people let themselves go to seed in a number of ways, thinking it makes them more spiritual—but I disagree. I think it is proper to comb your hair, if you have any! I do not think it is a mark of deep inward spirituality for a man to forget that a soiled shirt is easily cleaned and that baggy trousers were originally meant to have an orderly crease. God is not grieved when His Christian children take a little time every day for neatness and cleanness.

Neither do I think that our Lord is grieved by a service of worship in which we know what we are going to sing and what we are going to preach—because God is a God of order!

Submerge Our Wills in the Will of God

...O my Father, if it be possible, let this cup pass from me: nevertheless not as I will but as thou wilt. Matthew 26:39

Where there is no freedom of choice there can be neither sin nor righteousness, because it is of the nature of both that they be voluntary.

However good an act may be, it is not good if it is imposed from without. The act of imposition destroys the moral content of the act and renders it null and void!

Sin is the voluntary commission of an act known to be contrary to the will of God. Where there is no moral knowledge or where there is no voluntary choice, the act is not sinful; it cannot be, for sin is the transgression of the law and transgression must be voluntary.

Lucifer became Satan when he made his fateful choice: "I will ascend above the heights of the clouds; I will be like the most High." Clearly here was a choice made against light. Both knowledge and will were present in the act.

Conversely, Christ revealed His holiness when He cried in His agony, "Not my will, but thine, be done." Here was a deliberate choice made with the full knowledge of the consequences. Here two wills were in temporary conflict, the lower will of the Man who was God and the higher will of the God who was Man, and the higher will prevailed.

Here also was seen in glaring contrast the enormous difference between Christ and Satan; and that difference divides saint from sinner and heaven from hell. The secret of saintliness is not the destruction of the will—but the submergence of it in the will of God!

December 6

Hope: The Atmosphere of the Entire Bible

Which hope we have as an anchor of the soul, both sure and stedfast, and which entereth into that within the veil. Hebrews 6:19

In the New Testament, the word "hope" becomes one of the great words that Christ gave us. It was a word often used before but it has received new and wonderful meaning because the Saviour took it into His mouth.

Hope is the music, the drift and direction of the whole Bible. It sets the heartbeat and atmosphere of the Bible, meaning as it does desirable expectation and pleasurable anticipation!

Human hopes will fail and throw us down. But the Christian's hope is alive. The old English word "lively" meant what the word "living" means now; the word coming from God Himself for it is the strongest word in the Bible for life. It is the word used of God Himself when it says He is the Living God. So it is that God takes a Christian's hope and touches it with Himself and imparts His own "livingness" to the hope of the believer.

The true Christian hope is a valid hope! We have been born of God. There has been a new creation. No emptiness there, no vanity, no dreams that can't come true.

We have no great place of beauty in this world—Taj Mahal, Buckingham Palace or the White House—that can compare with the glory that belongs to the true child of God who has known the major miracle, who has been changed by an inward operation of supernatural grace unto an inheritance, a living hope!

Your expectation should rise and you should challenge God, and begin to dream high dreams of faith and spiritual anticipation. Remember, you cannot out-hope the living God!

December 7

God Has an Interest in Making Us Righteous

Not by works of righteousness which we have done, but according to his mercy he saved us, by the working of regeneration, and renewing of the Holy Ghost. Titus 3:5

A whole new generation of Christians has come up believing that it is possible to "accept" Christ without forsaking the world.

But what saith the Holy Ghost? "Ye adulterers and adulteresses, know ye not that the friendship of the world is enmity with God? whosoever therefore will be a friend of the world is the enemy of God" (James 4:4), and "If any man love the world, the love of the Father is not in him" (1 John 2:15).

This requires no comment, only obedience.

It is an error to assume that we can experience justification without transformation. Justification and regeneration are not the same; they may be thought apart in theology but they can never be experienced apart in fact!

When God declares a man righteous He instantly sets about to make him righteous.

The error today is that we do not expect a converted man to be a transformed man, and as a result of this error our churches are full of substandard Christians. Many of these go on day after day assuming that salvation is possible without repentance and that they can find some value in religion without righteousness.

A revival is, among other things, a return to the belief that real faith invariably produces holiness of heart and righteousness of life!

December 8

Supernatural Grace: God Works the Miracle

. . .He that believeth on me, the works that I do shall he do also; and greater works than these shall he do; because I go to my Father. John 14:12

I don't mind telling you that it is my earnest faith that all that is worthwhile in Christianity is a miracle!

The trappings and paraphernalia and outward dressings of Christianity are unnecessary—we could get along nicely without them.

But there is a series of miracles, throbbing and beating within the divine message of God, and within the hearts of those who believe truly—and that's about all there is to the Christian faith.

When Peter wrote that God "according to his abundant mercy hath begotten us again unto a living hope by the resurrection of Jesus Christ from the dead," he arrived at a major miracle of the New Testament.

Peter was witnessing about a major miracle, that is, being born again—begotten again! Supernatural grace has been the teaching of the Christian Church from Pentecost to the present hour.

It is sad that some men are being forced from their pulpits because they have insisted upon preaching the supernatural quality of the acts of God. We stand with them in the belief that pure religion is a continuing perpetuation of a major miracle, and we cannot settle for just the mental quality of things.

The new birth is the creating of a new man in the heart, where another man has been. It is the putting of a new man in the old man's place, and we are born anew! It is a vital and unique work of God in human nature.

Waves of Glory: Now Few and Far Between

. . .Ask, and ye shall receive, that your joy may be full. John 16:24

There seems to be a chilling and paralyzing fear of holy enthusiasm among the people of God in our day.

We try to tell how happy we are—but we remain so well controlled that there are very few waves of glory among us!

Some go to the ball game and come back whispering because they are hoarse from shouting and cheering. But no one in our day ever goes home from church with a voice hoarse from shouts brought about by a manifestation of the glory of God among us.

Actually, our apathy about praise in worship is like an inward chill in our beings. We are under a shadow and we are still wearing the grave clothes. You can sense this in much of our singing in the contemporary church. Perhaps you will agree that in most cases it is a kind of plodding along, without the inward lift of blessing and victory, resurrection joy and overcoming in Jesus' name.

Why is this?

It is largely because we are looking at what we are, rather than responding to who Jesus Christ is!

We have often failed and have not been overcomers because our trying and striving have been in our own strength. This leaves us very little to sing about!

Brethren, human activity and human sweat and tears work not the victory of Christ! It took the sweat and tears and blood of the Lord Jesus Christ. It took the painful dying and the victorious resurrection and ascension to bring us the victory. Jesus Christ is our Overcomer!

God Will Know When to Exalt Us

Humble yourselves in the sight of the Lord, and he shall lift you up. James 4:10

Christians have often asked: "Must I humble myself and meekly accept every situation in life?"

I think this is the answer: As Christians, we must never violate morals or truth in humility.

If in humbling ourselves we compromise the truth, we must never do it. If it means a compromise of morality, we must never do it.

I am confident that no man or woman is ever called of God to degrade himself or herself, either morally or in truth. But we do have a calling from God to humble ourselves under His mighty hand—and let the other party do the rock-throwing!

In this call to His people for true humility, God adds the promise that He will exalt us in due time! "Due time." It will be the time that God knows is best suited to perfect us and a time that will bring honor to God and the most good to men. That is "due time."

It may be that in God's will He will expect us to wait a long time before He can honor us or exalt us. But God knows what is best for each of us in His desire to make us the kind of saints that will glorify and honor Him in all things!

It is well for us to remember here that Jesus willingly humbled himself under the hand of men and so He humbled Himself under the hand of God!

Losing God amid the Wonders of His Word

. . .To be conformed to the image of his Son, that he might be the firstborn among many brethren. Romans 8:29

The doctrine of justification by faith—a biblical truth, and a blessed relief from sterile legalism and unavailing self-effort—has in our time fallen into evil company and been interpreted by many in such a manner as actually to bar men and women from the knowledge of God.

The whole transaction of religious conversion has been made mechanical and spiritless. Faith may now be exercised without a jar to the moral life and without embarrassment to the Adamic ego. Christ may be "received" without creating any special love for Him in the soul of the receiver. The man is "saved" but he is not hungry or thirsty after God!

The modern scientist has lost God amid the wonders of this world; we Christians are in real danger of losing God amid the wonders of His Word! We have almost forgotten that God is a Person and, as such, can be cultivated as any person can.

God is a Person and in the deep of His mighty nature He thinks, wills, enjoys, feels, loves, desires and suffers as any other person may. In making Himself known to us He stays by the familiar pattern of personality.

Religion, so far as it is genuine, is in essence the response of created personalities to the Creating Personality, God, so "This is life eternal, that they might know thee the only true God, and Jesus Christ, whom thou hast sent."

Spiritual Pride: Asking God Once Is Enough

Continue in prayer, and watch in the same with thanksgiving. Colossians 4:2

I have met Christians who insist that it is wrong to pray for the same thing twice, the reason being that if we truly believe when we pray we have the answer the first time; any second prayer betrays the unbelief of the first!

There are three things wrong with this teaching. One is that it ignores a large body of Scripture; the second is that it rarely works in practice, even for the saintliest soul; and the third is that, if persisted in, it robs the praying man of two of his mightiest weapons in his warfare with the flesh and the devil—intercession and petition.

For let it be said without qualification that the effective intercessor is never a one-prayer man, neither does the successful petitioner win his mighty resources in his first attempt!

It must be noted that such a teaching will very often result in an unconscious spiritual pride.

One has but to note the smug smile of superiority on the face of the one-prayer Christian to sense that there is a lot of pride behind the smile. While other Christians wrestle with God in an agony of intercession they sit back in humble pride waiting it out. They do not pray because they have already prayed. The devil has no fear of such Christians. He has already won over them, and his technique has been false logic.

Spiritual Priority: The Missionary Obligation

But ye shall receive power, after that the Holy Ghost is come upon you: and ye shall be witnesses unto me. . .unto the uttermost part of the earth. Acts 1:8

The popular notion that the first obligation of the Christian Church is to spread the gospel to the uttermost parts of the earth is false!

Her first obligation is to be spiritually worthy to spread the gospel.

Our Lord said "Go ye" but He also said "Tarry ye," and the tarrying had to come before the going. Had the disciples gone forth as missionaries before the day of Pentecost it would have been an overwhelming spiritual disaster, for they could have done no more than make converts after their own likeness, and this would have altered for the worse the whole history of the Western world and had consequences throughout the ages to come.

Theoretically the seed, being the Word of God, should produce the same kind of fruit regardless of the spiritual condition of those who scatter it; but it does not work that way! The identical message preached to the heathen by men of differing degrees of godliness will produce different kinds of converts and result in a quality of Christianity varying according to the purity and power of those who preach it.

Christianity will always reproduce after its kind. A worldly minded, unspiritual church, when she crosses the ocean to give her witness to peoples of other tongues and cultures, is sure to bring forth on other shores a Christianity much like her own!

December 14

We Should Yearn to Be More Like Jesus

Surely the righteous shall give thanks unto thy name: the upright shall dwell in thy presence. Psalm 140:13

There should be a holy quality, a mysterious and holy Presence within the fellowship of Christian believers!

If we are what we ought to be in Christ and by His Spirit, if the whole sum of our lives beginning with the inner life is becoming more Godlike and Christlike, I believe something of God's divine and mysterious quality and Presence will be upon us!

I have met a few of God's saints who appeared to have this holy brightness upon them, but they did not know it because of their humility and gentleness of spirit. I do not hesitate to confess that my fellowship with them has meant more to me than all of the teaching I have ever received. I do stand deeply indebted to every Bible teacher I have had through the years, but they did little but instruct my head. The brethren I have known who had this strange and mysterious quality and awareness of God's Person and Presence instructed my heart!

Do we understand what a gracious thing it is to be able to say of a man, a brother in the Lord, "He is truly a man of God"? He does not have to tell us that, but he lives quietly and confidently day by day with the sense of this awe-inspiring Presence that comes down on some people and means more than all the glib tongues in the world!

Oh, that we might yearn for the knowledge and Presence of God in our lives from moment to moment!

December 15

Wise Christians Use Every Means of Grace

That being justified by his grace, we should be made heirs according to the hope of eternal life. Titus 3:7

Every human being is in a state of passing from what he was to what he is to be—and this is as true of the Christian as of every other person.

The new birth does not produce the finished product. The new thing that is born of God is as far from completeness as the new baby born into this world an hour ago.

That new human being, the moment he is born, is placed in the hands of powerful molding forces that go far to determine whether he shall be an upright citizen or a criminal. The one hope for him is that he can later choose which forces shall shape him, and by the exercise of his own power of choice he can place himself in the right hands.

It is not otherwise with the Christian. He can fashion himself by placing himself in the hands first of the supreme Artist, God, and then by subjecting himself to such holy influences and such formative powers as shall make him into a man of God.

Or he may foolishly trust himself to unworthy hands and become at last a misshapen and inartistic vessel, of little use to mankind and a poor example of the skill of the heavenly Potter.

The wise Christian will take advantage of every proper means of grace: he has but to cooperate with God in embracing the good. God Himself will do the rest!

December 16

Christians Need Each Other

But with the precious blood of Christ, as of a lamb without blemish and without spot. 1 Peter 1:19

In the Lord's instructions to Israel concerning the preparation for the Passover in Egypt we clearly see a foreshadowing of the communal quality of the Christian life: "Take every man a lamb, according to the house of your fathers."

A lamb for an house—the chosen lamb of that particular family. But when John the Baptist appeared, he said, "Behold the Lamb of God." A lamb for each family was one thing—but they were all pointing to this great Lamb, which was not Israel's lamb at all, but the Lamb of God!

Yes, there is a blessed communal quality in the Christian faith and I add that "communal" is a beautiful word that has been ruined for us by communism. There is a sense in which the people of the Lord are a people apart, belonging to each other in a sense in which they do not belong to anyone else.

I do not hesitate to say that Christians belong to each other more than they belong to their country. I will also say to you, good wives and husbands in the faith, that you belong to Jesus Christ first and to husbands and wives second.

And to you who have Christian children, that those children belong to God first, and to you second. This is where we stand for we belong to each other in the communal family of God first!

As believers we discover there is a kingdom within the kingdoms of this world. A new people within the old. A royal priesthood, a holy nation, a chosen generation—Christians sharing together in the Lamb of God, precious to one another!

December 17

The Sleeping Church Cannot Resist Her Enemies

Knowing the time, that now it is high time to awake out of sleep. . .let us therefore cast off the works of darkness, and let us put on the armour of light. Romans 13:11, 12

Some day the Church can relax her guard, call her watchmen down from the wall and live in safety and peace—but not yet, not yet!

All that is good in the world stands as a target for all that is evil and manages to stay alive only by constant watchfulness and the providential protection of Almighty God.

The Church lives in a hostile world. Within and around her are enemies that not only could destroy her, but are meant to and will unless she resists force with yet greater force. The Christian would collapse from sheer external pressure were there not within him a counterpressure sufficiently great to prevent it. The power of the Holy Spirit is, therefore, not optional but necessary. Without it the children of God simply cannot live the life of heaven on earth. The hindrances are too many and too effective!

A church is a living organism and is subject to attack from such enemies as prey on living things. The human body can fight its enemies even while it is asleep, but the Church cannot. She must be awake and determined—or she cannot win.

She must recognize her enemies for what they are and she must resist them: Unbelief, Complacency, Self-righteousness, Fear of Man, Love of Luxury, Secret Sympathy with the world, Self-confidence, Pride and Unholy thoughts. These we must resist with every power within us, looking unto Jesus, author and finisher of our faith!

December 18

Let Us Not Substitute Organization for Life

For this cause left I thee in Crete, that thou shouldest set in order the things that are wanting, and ordain elders in every city, as I had appointed thee. Titus 1:5

I have been for years much distressed about the tendency to overorganize the Christian community, and I have for that reason had it charged against me that I do not believe in organization. The truth is quite otherwise!

A certain amount of organization is necessary everywhere throughout the created universe and in all human society. Without it there could be no science, no government, no family unit, no art, no music, no literature, no creative activity of any kind.

The man who would oppose all organization in the church must needs be ignorant of the facts of life. Art is organized beauty; music is organized sound; philosophy is organized thought; science is organized knowledge; government is merely society organized.

And what is the true Church of Christ but organized mystery?

The throbbing heart of the Church is life—in the happy phrase of Henry Scougal, "the life of God in the soul of man." This life, together with the actual presence of Christ within her, constitutes the Church a divine thing, a mystery, a miracle! Yet without substance, form and order this divine life would have no dwelling place, and no way to express itself to the community.

There is real danger in the efforts of some to substitute organization for life, so that while they have a name to live they are spiritually dead. Let us be reminded that there is no such thing as life apart from the medium through which it expresses itself!

December 19

Our Goal: Do All to the Glory of God

. . . Therefore glorify God in your body, and in your spirit, which are God's.
1 Corinthians 6:20

As Christian believers, we must practice living to the glory of God, actually and determinedly, for Paul's exhortation to "do all to the glory of God" is more than pious idealism!

It is an integral part of the sacred revelation and is to be accepted as the very Word of Truth. It opens before us the possibility of making every act of our lives contribute to the glory of God. Lest we should be too timid to include everything, Paul mentions specifically eating and drinking. This humble privilege we share with the beasts that perish. If these lowly animal acts can be so performed as to honor God, then it becomes difficult to conceive of one that cannot.

The New Testament accepts as a matter of course that in His incarnation our Lord took upon Him a real human body, and no effort is made to steer around the downright implications of such a fact.

The Lord Jesus lived in that body here among men and never once performed a non-sacred act! His presence in human flesh sweeps away forever the evil notion that there is about the human body something innately offensive to the Deity.

God created our bodies, and we do not offend Him by placing the responsibility where it belongs. He is not ashamed of the work of His own hands!

December 20

God Knows How Much Pressure We Can Take

Looking unto Jesus. . . .who for the joy that was set before him endured the cross, despising the shame. . . . Hebrews 12:2

Those who have gone through some "long night of the soul" realize that there is a limit to man's ability to live without joy!

Even Christ could endure the cross only because of the joy set before Him.

The strongest steel breaks if kept too long under unrelieved tension. Believe it that God knows exactly how much pressure each one of us can take! He knows how long we can endure the night, so He gives the soul relief, first by welcome glimpses of the morning star and then by the fuller light that harbingers the morning.

Slowly you will discover God's love in your suffering. Your heart will begin to approve the whole thing. You will learn from yourself what all the schools in the world could not teach you—the healing action of faith without supporting pleasure!

You will feel and understand the ministry of the night; its power to purify, to detach, to humble, to destroy the fear of death, and what is more important to you at the moment, the fear of life. And you will learn that sometimes pain can do what even joy cannot, such as exposing the vanity of earth's trifles and filling your heart with longing for the peace of heaven!

What I write here is in no way original. This has been discovered anew by each generation of Christian seekers and is almost a cliche' of the deeper life. A few will understand—and they will constitute the hard core of practicing saints so badly needed at this serious hour if New Testament Christianity is to survive to the next generation!

December 21

Growing Love for Our Fellow Christians

By this shall all men know that ye are my disciples, if ye have love one to another. John 13:35

Sometimes an earnest Christian will, after some remarkable spiritual encounter, withdraw himself from his fellow believers and develop a spirit of faultfinding.

This is a dangerous state of mind, and the more dangerous because it can justify itself by the facts—it may easily be true that the professed Christians with whom he is acquainted are worldly and dull and without spiritual enthusiasm. It is not that he is mistaken in his facts that proves him to be in error, but that his reaction to the facts is of the flesh! His new spirituality has made him less charitable, and we must be cautioned that any religious experience that fails to deepen our love for our fellow Christians may be safely written off as spurious.

The Apostle John makes love for our fellow Christians to be a test of true faith, insisting that as we grow in grace we grow in love toward all of God's people: "Every one that loveth him that begat loveth him also that is begotten of him" (1 John 5:1). This means simply that if we love God we will love His children. All true Christian experience will deepen our love for other Christians!

Therefore we conclude that whatever tends to separate us in person or in heart from our fellow Christians is not of God, but is of the flesh or of the devil. Conversely, whatever causes us to love the children of God is likely to be of God!

December 22

God Himself Awaits Our Response to His Presence

Blessed are the pure in heart: for they shall see God. Matthew 5:8

A spiritual kingdom lies all about us, enclosing us, embracing us, altogether within reach of our inner selves, waiting for us to recognize it. God Himself is here waiting for our response to His Presence. This eternal world will come alive to us the moment we begin to reckon upon its reality.

As we begin to focus upon God the things of the spirit will take shape before our inner eyes. Obedience to the word of Christ will bring an inward revelation of the Godhead (John 14:21-23).

This is not by any trick of the imagination. May we not safely conclude that, as the realities of Mount Sinai were apprehended by the senses, so the realities of Mount Zion are to be grasped by the soul? The soul has eyes with which to see and ears with which to hear!

Such an inward revelation of the Godhead will give acute perception enabling us to see God even as is promised to the pure in heart. A new God-consciousness will seize upon us and we shall begin to taste and hear and inwardly feel the God who is our life and our all.

There will be seen the constant shining of the light that lighteth every man that cometh into the world. More and more, as our faculties grow sharper and more sure, God will become to us the great All, and His Presence the glory and wonder of our lives! This is what will make heaven more real to us than any earthly thing has ever been.

December 23

A Blessed Fact: God Has Never Been Silent

God. . .hath in these last days spoken unto us by his Son, whom he hath appointed heir of all things. . . . Hebrews 1:1, 2

I think it may be accepted as axiomatic that God is constantly trying to speak to man. He desires to communicate Himself, to impart holy ideas to those of His creatures capable of receiving them. The Second Person of the Godhead is called the Word of God, that is, the mind of God in expression.

Are you aware that many Christians appear to believe that God spoke the Holy Scriptures into being and then lapsed into silence, a silence that will not be broken until God calls all men before Him into judgment? If that is true, we have the Bible as a deposit of embalmed truth which scribe and theologian must decipher as they can.

This view is extremely injurious to the Christian's soul, for it holds that God is no longer speaking, and thus we are shut up to our intellects for the understanding and apprehension of truth. According to this notion the human mind becomes the final arbiter of truth as well as the organ for its reception into the soul.

Now, the blessed fact is that God is not silent and has never been silent, but is speaking in His universe. The written Word is effective because, and only because, the Living Word is speaking in Heaven and the Living Voice is sounding in the earth! "And it is the Spirit that beareth witness, because the Spirit is truth. For there are three that bear record in heaven, the Father, the Word, and the Holy Ghost: and these three are one" (1 John 5:6, 7).

December 24

The Root of All Theology and Truth

He came. . . . John 1:11

"He came"—these two simple words are at the root of all theology and of all truth!

Before Christ came in the incarnation, there had been only the eternal past. Then from the time of creation, we have such hints as "In the beginning he was God" and "In him was light" and "all things were made by him" and "In him was life."

Now it says, "He came!"

We are struck by the wonder of these simple words.

All of the pity that God is capable of feeling, all of the mercy that God is capable of showing, and all of the redeeming love and grace that He could pour out of His divine being—all are at least suggested in the fact that Jesus came!

Then too, all of the hopes and longings and aspirations and dreams of immortality that lie in the human breast had their fulfillment in these two words, "He came!"

The message is more profound than all philosophy. It may be a superlative statement, but I believe it to be a balanced and accurate statement, to insist that the impact of these two words, understood in their high spiritual context, is wiser than all of man's learning.

Because He is "the true light that lighteth every man that cometh into the world," man's long night of darkness is dispelled. We celebrate with Milton the delight that "This is the happy morn wherein the Son of heaven's eternal king, of wedded maid and virgin mother born, our great redemption from above did bring!"

December 25

Compassion: In Christ It Was Fully Perfected

And of some have compassion, making a difference: and others save with fear. . . . Jude 22, 23

The word compassion is a vital New Testament word. Do you realize that compassion is an emotional identification, and that Jesus Christ had that in full perfection?

The man who has this wound of compassion is a man who suffers along with other people. Jesus Christ our Lord can never suffer to save us any more. This He did, once and for all, when He gave Himself without spot through the Holy Ghost to the Father on Calvary's cross.

He cannot suffer to save us but He still must suffer to win us. He does not call His people to redemptive suffering for that is impossible; it could not be. Redemption is a finished work!

But He does call His people to feel along with Him and to feel along with those that rejoice and those that suffer. He calls His people to be to Him the kind of an earthly body in which He can weep again and suffer again and love again. For our Lord has two bodies!

One is the body He took to the tree on Calvary; that was the body in which He suffered to redeem us. But He has a body on earth now, composed of those who have been baptized into it by the Holy Ghost at conversion. Paul said he was glad that he could suffer for the Colossians and fill up the measure of the afflictions of Christ in his body for the Church's sake.

It is in that body now, on earth, that Christ would suffer to win men!

December 26

Sinful Men May Now Become One with God

Whereby are given unto us exceeding great and precious promises: that by these ye might be partakers of the divine nature. . . . 2 Peter 1:4

Here is the whole final message of the New Testament: Through the atonement in Jesus' blood sinful men may now become one with God!

Deity indwelling men! That is Christianity in its fullest effectuation, and even those greater glories of the world to come will be in essence but a greater and more perfect experience of the soul's union with God.

Deity indwelling men! That, I say, is Christianity and no man has experienced rightly the power of Christian belief until he has known this for himself as a living reality.

Everything else is preliminary to this! Incarnation, atonement, justification, regeneration; what are these but acts of God preparatory to the work of invading and the act of indwelling the redeemed human soul? Man who moved out of the heart of God now moves back into the heart of God by redemption!

God who moved out of the heart of man because of sin now enters again His ancient dwelling to drive out His enemies and once more make the place of His feet glorious!

That visible fire on the day of Pentecost had for the Church a deep and tender significance, for it told to all ages that they upon whose heads it sat were men and women apart. The mark of the fire was the sign of divinity; they who received it were forever a peculiar people, sons and daughters of the Flame.

Singing and Praise: Silence and Worship

Be silent, O all flesh, before the Lord: for he is raised up out of his holy habitation. Zechariah 2:13

There is a notion widely held among Christians that song is the highest possible expression of the joy of the Lord in the soul of a man or woman.

That idea is so near to being true that it may seem spiritually rude to challenge it. However, it does need to be brought to the test of the Scriptures and Christian testimony.

Both the Bible and the testimony of a thousand saints show that there is experience beyond song. There are delights which the heart may enjoy in the awesome presence of God which cannot find expression in language: they belong to the unutterable elements in Christian experience. Not many enjoy them because not many know that they can.

The whole concept of ineffable worship has been lost to this generation of Christians. Our level of life is so low that no one expects to know the deep things of the soul until the Lord returns. So, we cheer ourselves by breaking into song.

Far be it from me to discourage the art of singing. Creation itself took its rise in a burst of song; Christ rose from the dead and sang among His brethren. But still there is something beyond song!

When the Holy Spirit is permitted to exercise His full sway in a redeemed heart there will likely be voluble praise first; then, when the crescendo rises beyond the ability of studied speech to express, comes song. When song breaks down under the weight of glory, then comes silence where the soul, held in deep fascination, feels itself blessed with an unutterable beatitude!

December 28

Know the Lord as Perfectly as Possible

The throne of God and of the Lamb shall be in it; and his servants shall serve him: and they shall see his face. . . . Revelation 22:3, 4

If God is the Supreme Good then our highest blessedness on earth must lie in knowing Him as perfectly as possible!

The ultimate end to which redemption leads is the immediate sight of the ever-blessed Godhead. In our present state we cannot with our natural eyes look upon God, for it is written, "Thou canst not see my face: for there shall no man see me, and live" (Exod. 33:20).

When the work of Christ has been completed in His people, however, it will be possible, even natural, for redeemed men to behold their Redeemer. This is stated plainly by the Apostle John: "But we know that, when he shall appear, we shall be like him: for we shall see him as he is" (1 John 3:2).

This rapturous experience has been called the Beatific Vision and will be the culmination of all possible human blessedness. It will bring the glorified saint into a state of perpetual bliss which to taste for even one moment will banish forever from his mind every memory of grief or suffering here below.

I suppose the vast majority of us must wait for the great day of the Lord's coming to realize the full wonder of the vision of God Most High. In the meantime, we are, I believe, missing a great measure of radiant glory that is ours by blood-covenant and available to us in this present world if we would but believe it and press on in the way of holiness.

The Perfume of Remembered Blessing

For in him dwelleth all the fulness of the Godhead bodily, and ye are complete in him. . . . Colossians 2:9, 10

Christ is so many wonderful things to His people and brings to them such a wealth of benefits as the mind cannot comprehend nor the heart find words to express!

Bernard of Clairvaux speaks in his writings of a "perfume compounded of the remembered benefits of God."

Such fragrance is all too rare!

Every follower of Christ should be redolent of such a perfume; for have we not all received more from God's kindness than our imagination could have conceived before we knew Him and discovered for ourselves how rich and how generous He is?

That we have received of His fullness grace for grace no one will deny, but the fragrance comes not from the receiving but from the remembering.

Ten lepers received their health—that was the benefit. One came back to thank his benefactor—that was the perfume!

Unremembered benefits, like dead flies, may cause the ointment to give forth a stinking savor.

Remembered blessings, thankfulness for present favors and praise for promised grace blend like myrrh and aloes and cassia to make a rare bouquet for the garments of the saints. With this perfume David also anointed his harp and the hymns of the ages have been sweet with it.

We are reminded that much of the Bible is devoted to prediction. Nothing God has yet done for us can compare with all that is written in the sure word of prophecy. And, nothing He has done or may yet do for us can compare with what He is and will be to us!

December 30

A Daily Prayer: Even So Come, Lord Jesus

He which testifieth these things saith, Surely I come quickly. Amen. Even so, come, Lord Jesus. Revelation 22:20

The people of God ought to be the happiest people in all the wide world!

Fellow Christian, consider the source of our joy and delight: redeemed by the blood of the Lamb, our yesterdays behind us, our sin under the blood forever and a day, to be remembered against us no more forever!

God is our Father, Christ is our Brother, the Holy Ghost our Advocate and Comforter!

Our Brother has gone to the Father's house to prepare a place for us, leaving with us the promise that He will come again!

Don't send Moses, Lord, don't send Moses! He broke the tables of stone.

Don't send Elijah for me, Lord! I am afraid of Elijah—he called down fire from heaven.

Don't send Paul, Lord! He is so learned that I feel like a little child when I read his epistles.

O Lord Jesus, come yourself! I am not afraid of Thee. You took the little children as lambs to your fold. You forgave the woman taken in adultery. You healed the timid woman who reached out in the crowd to touch You. We are not afraid of You!

Even so, come, Lord Jesus!

Come quickly!

December 31

Subject Index

Since dates rather than page numbers designate each devotional selection, the subject and Scripture indexes use the number of the month rather than the name of the month; therefore, 1/2 means January 2.

January

God Is Always First—and Will Surely Be Last	1/1
Jesus Christ Is All That the Godhead Is	1/2
Holy Spirit: God in Contact with His Creatures	1/3
The Spirit of Man Makes Him a Human Being	1/4
Do Not Mistake the True Meaning of the Cross	1/5
The Bible: More Than a Volume of Facts	1/6
The Flock of God: Safe in Jesus Christ	1/7
True Worship: Fully Seeking the Lord We Adore	1/8
Believe the Right Thing about the Right Person	1/9
Everyone Must Pray as if He Alone Could Pray	1/10
A Calamity: Accepting This World as Our Home	1/11
Satan Would Bind Us in Our Own Grave Clothes	1/12
Learn to Love God for Himself Alone	1/13
Feeling Right: Not the Same as Being Right	1/14
The World Changes—But Not the Human Race	1/15
The Grace of God Cannot Be Extinguished	1/16
Man's Fall Created a Perpetual Moral Crisis	1/17
The True Christian Is the Practicing Christian	1/18
Obedience: The Final Test of Love for Christ	1/19
Wisdom: Knowing the True Fear of the Lord	1/20
Unsung but Singing: The Unappreciated Christian	1/21
Getting Glory for God—or for Ourselves?	1/22
Our Lord the Object of Faith for Salvation	1/23
Walking a Tightrope between Two Kingdoms?	1/24
Old Things Pass—All Things Become New	1/25
Faith Rests upon the Character of God	1/26
Knowing God: Goal of All Christian Doctrine	1/27
God's Will: Less of Me, More of Him	1/28
Discipleship: Saying Goodbye to World's Toys	1/29
The Humble Man Says: "The Mistakes Are Mine"	1/30
Teach the Bible with High Moral Obligation	1/31

February

God's Boundless Power Is All around Us	2/1

Faith Must Rest in the Adequacy of Christ   2/2
To Be Christlike: Walk in the Spirit   2/3
We Are Loved of God—for Jesus' Sake   2/4
Christ's Victory Rightfully Belongs to Us   2/5
God Tells Us in the Bible What He Is Like   2/6
A Compromise: "The Church Must Change"   2/7
Encounter with God Brings Wonder and Awe   2/8
True Faith Is Accompanied by Expectation   2/9
Prayer Is Never a Substitute for Obedience   2/10
Our Heavenly Abode: Part of God's Goodness   2/11
The Devil Hates Everything Dear to God   2/12
Divine Love: Necessity for the Church on Earth   2/13
Bad Dispositions: "The Vice of the Virtuous"   2/14
Tragedy: Men Do Not Know That God Is Here   2/15
Secular Men Confuse Truths with "Truth"   2/16
Live for Christ? Then Die with Him First   2/17
The Christian Life Cannot Feed on Negatives   2/18
Question: How Much More Could I Have Done?   2/19
Stricter Discipline for God's Willing Children   2/20
"Create in Me a Clean Heart, O God"   2/21
Only Servants of Truth Can Know the Truth   2/22
Keys to Greatness: Submission and Service   2/23
God Will Not Play along with Adam   2/24
The Early Disciples Burned with an Inward Fire   2/25
The Importance of Right Relationship with God   2/26
Test Your Conduct: What Are Your Motives?   2/27
Rationalism: A Danger in Today's Christianity   2/28
Faith in God Never Adds up to Gullibility   2/29

March
God Expects Gratitude when He Gives Us Gifts   3/1
Jesus Christ Is Every Man's Contemporary   3/2
Spiritual Excellence: Freedom in the Spirit   3/3
Sinful Man: Uncomfortable in God's Presence   3/4
Christianity Is What Christ Says It Is   3/5
You Will Find Christ Everywhere in the Bible   3/6
The Christian Message: Prophetic, Not Diplomatic   3/7
A Great Need among Us: More Reverence   3/8
Christ Established True Values for the Human Race   3/9
Effective Prayer: Letting All Our Pretenses Go   3/10
Anticipation of Heaven: More Than Eschatology   3/11
The Delusive Glory of This World's Kingdoms   3/12

Christ Died Even for Those Who Hated Him   3/13
Men Will Not Praise You for Genuine Spirituality   3/14
God's Voice Still Entreats Lost Mankind   3/15
Truth Addresses Itself to the Total Man   3/16
No One for Whom Christ Died Is Worthless   3/17
A Bible Fact: A Regenerated Man Knows God   3/18
A Selfish Lust: Man's Desire for First Place   3/19
Jesus Christ: Our Chief Joy and Delight   3/20
God Blesses His Children for Holy Intentions   3/21
God Is Glorified in Our Moral Victories   3/22
The True Minister: Man of God Speaking to Men   3/23
God Is Not Dependent on Our Human Success   3/24
Concept of the Trinity: Infinite Love Poured Out   3/25
Jesus Knows All about You—and Still Loves You   3/26
The New Man in Christ Is a Perpetual Miracle   3/27
It Is Modern Man Himself Who Is the Dreamer   3/28
True Wisdom: Listening to the Words Jesus Spoke   3/29
Believing: Directing the Heart's Attention to Jesus   3/30
Salvation: A Right Relation between God and Man   3/31

April
No Burial in Sight for the Faith of Our Fathers   4/1
By Creation, We Have the Capacity to Know God   4/2
Plan of Redemption: God Has Not Abandoned Man   4/3
Worth of a Soul: God Gave His Only Son   4/4
God Shares His Good Pleasure with His Own   4/5
All Had a Share in Putting Jesus on the Cross   4/6
Our Lord Jesus Was Bruised for Our Iniquities   4/7
We Are Amazed That God Has Forgiven Us   4/8
The Christian: Citizen of Heaven Living on Earth   4/9
A Beautiful Reality: We Do Love Christ,   4/10
   Never Having Seen Him
On Earth, Only Man Has Capacity for Worship   4/11
Believe What God Says He Will Do for Us   4/12
Christ's Call: Leave the Old, Begin the New   4/13
Generally, We Pray Only as Well as We Live   4/14
Christianity Is No Longer Producing Saintliness   4/15
There Is a Finality in the Biblical Revelation   4/16
View God's Wrath in the Light of His Holiness   4/17
The Cross You Bear Is Yours—Not Christ's   4/18
A Fallacy: To Think That Time Is a Great Healer   4/19
A High Privilege: God Counts Us His Friends   4/20

We Do Not Despise God-given Emotions   4/21
A Blessing: The Unchanging Faithfulness of God   4/22
The Word of God: Shortest Route to Spiritual Peace   4/23
Letting the Will Be the Master of the Heart   4/24
The Preacher: Servant of the Lord and the People   4/25
Today, Ask God to Remove Every False Trust   4/26
Christian Couples: Heirs Together of the Grace of Life   4/27
Happiness: Your Whole Ambition to Be Like Jesus   4/28
Sensitive to Religion—but Living like the Devil   4/29
Revival Blessings Flow from God's Promises   4/30

May
God Spoke—and It Was Done   5/1
Holy, Holy, Holy: Kneel at Jesus' Feet   5/2
Christ Does in Us What We Cannot Do   5/3
Let Nothing Keep Us from Communion with God   5/4
Man, Though Guilty, Is Offered God's Mercy   5/5
Lean Back on the Keeping Power of God   5/6
Prayerful Thoughts of God Are Never a Burden   5/7
Most Important: Your Names Written in Heaven   5/8
Place the Greatest Value on Godliness   5/9
It Is Not Fanatical to Love God Supremely   5/10
Human Suffering: Learn What God Says about It   5/11
Many Christians Still Taking the Broad Road   5/12
The Erotic Is Rapidly Displacing the Spiritual   5/13
Our Thoughts Reveal What We Are Becoming   5/14
The Characteristic of the Prophet Is Always Love   5/15
Polite Society: "Religion Must Not Get Personal"   5/16
A Silent Christian: Is That Possible?   5/17
God Does Not Have Power: God Is Power   5/18
The Great Unseen Reality Is God Himself   5/19
God Would Impart Himself with His Gifts   5/20
No Task Is Too Big If God Is in It   5/21
Hope in Ethics: Utterly Unrealistic and Naive   5/22
God Stands Ready to Confirm Our Faith in Him   5/23
Find Something Better Than Spiritual Curiosity   5/24
God's Plain, Good People: Always a Benediction   5/25
Are You a Settled and Contented Christian?   5/26
Primary Meaning of Pentecost: Christ Is Exalted   5/27
The Holy Spirit Is to Us All Jesus Would Be   5/28
The Holy Spirit: More Than a Poetic Yearning   5/29
Spirit Led, We Will Obey the Word of God   5/30

Think of the Holy Spirit as a Moral Flame   5/31

June
God Would Produce Christ's Beauty in Our Lives   6/1
Christ Bridged the Gulf between God and Man   6/2
Our Richest Treasure: Inner Knowledge of God   6/3
Attitude of Worship: Everywhere, All the Time   6/4
Believe That God Is Infinitely Generous   6/5
God's Spirit Is a Gentle, Loving Spirit   6/6
True Faith Must Influence Our Daily Living   6/7
A Spiritual Rule: Hot Furnace, Cool Chimney   6/8
We All Stand Daily in the Mercy of God   6/9
Spiritual Authority: The Word and the Testimony   6/10
The Wickedness of Unbelief: Making God a Liar   6/11
Faith Understands: God Framed the Worlds   6/12
God's Right: To Ask Obedience of His Creatures   6/13
Life's Greatest Honor: Following Christ's Call   6/14
Everything God Does Is Worthy of Our Praise   6/15
Scriptural Guidance: Believers May Test Themselves   6/16
A Possibility: To Mean Right and Still Go Wrong   6/17
My and Mine: Symptoms of Our Deep Disease   6/18
The True Christian: Still an Enigma to the World   6/19
The Whole Universe Is Alive with God's Life   6/20
Poets Admire Nature: Prophets Look to the Creator   6/21
Christians Drawn by This Present World's Charms   6/22
The Profane Man: He Rules out God Completely   6/23
Do Not Laugh at Something God Takes Seriously   6/24
Right Thinking Spiritually Will Bring Right Living   6/25
God Does Not Have to Be Persuaded to Bless Us   6/26
Be Completely Honest with God When You Pray   6/27
Christian Responsibility Is a Day-by-Day Reality   6/28
Sad But True: Many Know God Only by Hearsay   6/29
Do We Really Long for Our Lord to Come?   6/30

July
God Is Always at the Controls of the Universe   7/1
Unchanging: The Love and Compassion of Christ   7/2
The Nature of True Worship: Wholly Spiritual   7/3
Wrong Choices May Imperil Our Freedom   7/4
God Never Violates Our Freedom of Choice   7/5
Great Bible Saints: Enraptured Lovers of God   7/6
The Cross We Bear Must Be Assumed Voluntarily   7/7

We Reduce Truth to a Code—and Die Spiritually   7/8
Spirit Taught: The Result Is Spiritual Illumination   7/9
Humility: A Blessed Thing If You Can Find It   7/10
Self Does Not Die without Our Full Consent   7/11
Our Position: Believing God, Defying the Devil   7/12
Many Practice Fraud upon Their Own Souls   7/13
The Praying Man: Purity and Honesty Are Essential   7/14
Believe It: Christ, the Just, Died for the Unjust   7/15
If We Confess: Straight, Plain Bible Teaching   7/16
The High Casualty Rate among Christians   7/17
Who Sets the Moral Pace for Us Today?   7/18
God's True Prophets Never Applied for the Job   7/19
Faith Is More Than Believing the Evidence   7/20
Christian Experience: Encounter with God   7/21
By Its Very Nature, Love Must Be Voluntary   7/22
Seek God's Glory and Purity   7/23
The Foolish Man: No Store of Eternal Treasure   7/24
Many Never Cross over into God's Promised Land   7/25
Our First Service for God: Inward Devotion   7/26
Absence of Repentance Brings Spiritual Uncertainty   7/27
Faith and Holiness Linked to Christ's Return   7/28
Wrong Desires Pervert Our Moral Judgments   7/29
Our View of God's Presence Is Not Pantheism   7/30
Christ's Words Are for the Children of God   7/31

August
Contemplating the Sweet Mystery of the Godhead   8/1
Many Spiritual Blessings in Christ Go Unclaimed   8/2
Spiritual Radiance Comes from an Inner Witness   8/3
Faith: Our Minds Brought into Accord with Truth   8/4
The Devil Never Forgives Those Who Escape Bondage   8/5
Deliverance: Saved from the World's Nervous Scramble   8/6
Love Must Leave When Resentment Moves In   8/7
True Believers Do Not Shy Away from Obedience   8/8
Our Final Accountability Will Be to Our Maker   8/9
Spiritual Receptivity May Be Increased by Exercise   8/10
Bold Men Needed in the Warfare of the Soul   8/11
Church Must Discern between Popularity and Greatness   8/12
The Glory of the Cross: Atonement and Forgiveness   8/13
God Still Speaks through Those Who Can Weep   8/14
Explore God's High Purposes in Salvation   8/15
There Are No Shortcuts to a Godly Life   8/16

God's Love: A Quality That Cannot Be Defined 8/17
The True Christian Is a Saint in Embryo 8/18
The Example of Jesus: Hold No Grudges 8/19
We Can Sanctify the Ordinary Each Day 8/20
We Have within Us the Spirit of Optimism 8/21
The Quality of True Faith Is Moral, Not Mental 8/22
Men in Love with Sin Do Not Receive Christ 8/23
We Make Religion Easy for the Moral Rebel 8/24
We Must Surrender: God Must Have His Way 8/25
We Settle for Words: Deeds Are Too Costly 8/26
Religious Work Should Be Most Open to Inspection 8/27
Caution: Our Ego Will Try to Act Spiritual 8/28
Our Lord Looks for Heavenly Minded Christians 8/29
The Bible Is Not Addressed to Just Anybody 8/30
Simple Rules for the Christian in Discouragement 8/31

September
God Is the Most Winsome of All Beings 9/1
There Is Delight in True Service for God 9/2
Do Not Hope to Win the Lost by Being Agreeable 9/3
Our Moral Climate Does Not Encourage Faith 9/4
Capacity to Think: God Wants You to Understand 9/5
In God's Plan the Doctrine of Faith Is Central 9/6
A Minister Must Not Be a Privileged Idler 9/7
Good Literature: Responsibility of Christian Home 9/8
Without Divine Illumination, Theology Is Dead 9/9
Unbelief: A Luxury No Man or Woman Can Afford 9/10
Bible History: Be Careful Whose Advice You Follow 9/11
Redemption: A Moral Restoration to the Divine Image 9/12
More Concern Today for Fruit Than for the Root 9/13
Jesus Calls Us to His Rest: Meekness Is His Method 9/14
Prayer of Faith Lays Hold of God's Omnipotence 9/15
A Jubilant Longing and Pining for God 9/16
Jesus Taught the Moral Relation between Words
    and Deeds 9/17
Who Dares to Soften and Change Christ's Words? 9/18
Religious Teaching Gives Light: That Is Not Enough 9/19
Truth Will Not Give Itself to a Rebel 9/20
The Modern Cry: I Have a Right to Be Happy 9/21
A Word to Women: Seek the Inner Adorning 9/22
God Would Save Us from Spiritual Delusion 9/23
A New Decalogue: Thou Shalt Not Disagree 9/24

Knowledge without Humility Turns to Vanity   9/25
The Word of Authority by Which We Can Die   9/26
Christlike Conduct: The Goal of Christian Faith   9/27
God's Spirit Bears Witness Within   9/28
We Should Always Seek to Know Christ Better   9/29
A Tragedy: Believers Arguing about Christ's Return   9/30

October
You Cannot Worship God without Loving Him   10/1
Encouragement: The Eternal Nature of Our Father   10/2
Right Concept of Jesus—Savior and Judge   10/3
God Was First to Say, "You Are My Friends"   10/4
Spiritual Fruit Comes Only from Spiritual Life   10/5
Much of Our Praying Never Brings Anything Back   10/6
Greatness among the Sons and Daughters of Faith   10/7
Learn the Truth about the Enemy of Your Soul   10/8
Cultivate Grace That Makes Holiness Attractive   10/9
Stop! God Wants More Than a Minute   10/10
Choosing God's Will Does Not Deny Man's Free Will   10/11
Significant: The Low Level of Moral Enthusiasm   10/12
Seeking Man's Favor: The Root of Religious Unbelief   10/13
The Deadening Effect of Religious Make-Believe   10/14
A Great Loss: Power to Wage Spiritual Warfare   10/15
Christians Often Act Like They Are Bored with God   10/16
By God's Call, the Minister Is a Man Apart   10/17
Weak Christianity Tends toward Humanism   10/18
Men Are Lost—But They Are Not Abandoned   10/19
Seek More of God for Himself Alone   10/20
Mankind's Basic Need Remains Ever the Same   10/21
We Look for Christ's Victory—Not Annihilation   10/22
The World Wants a Religious Touch in Its Schemes   10/23
The Strong Pull toward Church Complexity   10/24
Religion Should Be a Fount Not a Front   10/25
In the Church: The Lordship of Christ in Control   10/26
When I Am Weak, Then I Am Strong   10/27
Prayer of Faith: Authority of God's Family   10/28
Is It My Kingdom or God's Kingdom?   10/29
Christian Worship Is Not a Kind of Educated Magic   10/30
We Are Declared Not Guilty by the Highest Court   10/31

November
God Has Few Admirers among Christians Today   11/1

God Will Be All or He Will Be Nothing   11/2
Having Faith in Faith Is Not Sufficient   11/3
What Did Our Repentance Actually Mean to Us?   11/4
Fear of the Lord: Cannot Be Induced by Threats   11/5
Christ Opens Our Hearts to Grasp the Truth   11/6
Pattern of Unbelief: Begins at the Bible   11/7
Sinning in the Name of the Sinless One   11/8
Good News Today: He Cares for You   11/9
Would You Settle for an Absentee God?   11/10
Conversion: Beginning of a Journey   11/11
Our Lord Still Demands New Testament Standards   11/12
Loving the Lord: Not Easy in Today's World   11/13
A Dangerous Philosophy: Success Is Everything   11/14
We Still Want to Boss Our Own Lives   11/15
The Devotional Life Is Almost Crowded Out   11/16
Morality by Public Pressure Is Not Morality   11/17
The Church Can Claim a Heavenly Origin   11/18
Figures of Speech Are Not Christian Doctrines   11/19
It Is Best to Cooperate with the Inevitable   11/20
Tearless Teachers Have Harmed Us   11/21
God Knows the Potential of the Human Soul   11/22
A Thankful Heart Cannot Also Be Cynical   11/23
The Bible World: Still the Warm, Living World   11/24
Our Humor Should Not Lead to Foolish Talk   11/25
The Church Must Look First to Christ   11/26
Christian Reproof: With Kindness and Charity   11/27
The Holy Spirit Is at Hand to Help You   11/28
The Ministry: Actually a Perilous Profession   11/29
Spiritual Twins: Holiness and Happiness   11/30

December
Nothing Can Hinder God or a Good Man   12/1
Jesus Asks Us to Love the Unlovely   12/2
God's Promises Will Outlive Man's Violence   12/3
Holiness and Worship Come before Power   12/4
God Was Never the Author of Disorder   12/5
Submerge Our Wills in the Will of God   12/6
Hope: The Atmosphere of the Entire Bible   12/7
God Has an Interest in Making Us Righteous   12/8
Supernatural Grace: God Works the Miracle   12/9
Waves of Glory: Now Few and Far Between   12/10
God Will Know When to Exalt Us   12/11

Losing God amid the Wonders of His Word   12/12
Spiritual Pride: Asking God Once Is Enough   12/13
Spiritual Priority: The Missionary Obligation   12/14
We Should Yearn to Be More Like Jesus   12/15
Wise Christians Use Every Means of Grace   12/16
Christians Need Each Other   12/17
The Sleeping Church Cannot Resist Her Enemies   12/18
Let Us Not Substitute Organization for Life   12/19
Our Goal: Do All to the Glory of God   12/20
God Knows How Much Pressure We Can Take   12/21
Growing Love for Our Fellow Christians   12/22
God Himself Awaits Our Response to His Presence   12/23
A Blessed Fact: God Has Never Been Silent   12/24
The Root of All Theology and Truth   12/25
Compassion: In Christ It Was Fully Perfected   12/26
Sinful Men May Now Become One with God   12/27
Singing and Praise: Silence and Worship   12/28
Know the Lord as Perfectly as Possible   12/29
The Perfume of Remembered Blessings   12/30
A Daily Prayer: Even So Come, Lord Jesus   12/31

Scripture Index

Genesis
1:26, 27 ...... 4/11
1:31 .... 7/1
3:9 .... 3/4
3:17 .... 10/19
28:16 .... 2/15

Exodus
3:6 .... 7/21
3:11 .... 7/19

Deuteronomy
1:6, 8 .... 6/3
33:27 .... 10/2

Job
15:3, 4 .... 9/24

Psalms
5:1, 4 .... 1/27
5:4, 5 .... 10/9
5:11 .... 7/6
32:11 .... 3/20
42:2 .... 8/10
46:10 .... 3/2
50:12 .... 7/30
57:2 .... 11/20
62:11 .... 5/18
65:5, 7 ...... 10/21
66:18 .... 4/14
73:25 .... 4/5
95:6 .... 1/8
105:4 .... 9/29
107:43 .... 6/5
119:11 .... 7/31
140:13 ...... 12/15

Proverbs
1:7 .... 1/20
3:19 .... 2/16
12:3 .... 9/13
12:15 .... 9/11
15:26 .... 9/8

16:5 .... 3/17
16:16 .... 8/25

Isaiah
11:9 .... 10/22
12:2 .... 8/31
26:3 .... 9/5
40:8 .... 8/30
42:16 .... 8/22
53:4 .... 8/13
53:5 ...... 4/7, 11/4

Jeremiah
5:21, 22 ..... 11/10
17:9 .... 4/26
20:12 .... 6/27

Daniel
12:3 .... 4/9

Zechariah
2:13 .... 12/28

Matthew
4:10 .... 3/12
5:6 ...... 6/26, 7/29
5:8 .... 12/23
6:13 .... 10/29
6:21 .... 10/5
6:33 .... 11/2
7:21 .... 2/10
9:36 .... 4/21
10:22 .... 9/4
11:29 .... 1/30
16:18 .... 11/18
16:26 .... 4/4
16:27 .... 6/30
19:22 .... 9/10
19:25 .... 7/17
19:26 .... 5/21
20:26, 27 ..... 2/23
23:28 .... 3/10
24:35 .... 5/4

24:50, 51 ..... 1/14
25:34 .... 5/22
26:39 .... 12/6
28:18 .... 3/26
28:20 .... 8/21

Mark
12:44 .... 2/19
10:28 .... 4/13
10:43 .... 10/7
15:39 .... 3/19

Luke
10:42 .... 7/26
12:19 .... 6/23
12:20 .... 7/24
12:32 .... 11/19
14:11 .... 7/10
18:1 .... 1/10
18:8 .... 4/29
23:34 .... 8/19
24:11 .... 5/16
24:45 .... 11/6
24:52, 53 .... 10/16

John
1:1 .... 5/1
1:11 .... 12/25
1:36 .... 3/30
3:3 .... 2/21
3:8 .... 2/22
3:19 .... 8/23
3:36 .... 4/17
4:14 .... 9/16
4:24 .... 6/15
5:44 .... 10/13
6:44 .... 11/5
6:60 .... 3/29
7:17 ..... 7/22, 12/1
7:19 .... 2/28
7:28 .... 7/8
8:12 .... 9/20
8:29 .... 1/24

8:54 .... 3/21
10:10 .... 5/24
12:26 .... 8/12
12:36 .... 5/10
13:35 .... 12/22
14:1 .... 5/19
14:12 .... 12/9
14:21 .... 1/19
14:23 ...11/13, 7/23
15:7 .... 10/6
15:13 .... 10/4
15:26 .... 1/3
16:13 .... 5/29
16:13, 14 ..... 2/3
16:15 .... 4/2
16:24 .... 12/10
17:17 .... 3/16
17:24 .... 8/29

Acts

1:1, 2 .... 9/17
1:8 .... 12/14
2:3 .... 2/6
2:32 .... 5/23
2:36 .... 5/27
2:42 .... 11/11
3:14, 15 ..... 2/27
3:19 .... 4/12
4:12 .... 3/13
5:3 .... 8/5
5:41 .... 8/24
9:6 .... 4/19
10:36 .... 1/23
11:24 .... 5/25
20:19 .... 11/21
20:24 .... 8/11
21:13, 14 ... 10/11
27:25 .... 3/18

Romans

1:18 .... 11/14
2:4 .... 10/20
2:15 .... 6/24
2:16 .... 10/3
3:4 .... 7/20

3:26 .... 7/15
5:1 .... 9/6
5:6 .... 5/5
5:8 .... 2/4
5:19 .... 1/17
6:8 .... 2/17
6:13 .... 1/31
6:22 .... 8/8
8:6 .... 3/22
8:6, 9 .... 5/31
8:14 .... 3/27
8:16 .... 2/26
8:19, 22 ..... 3/15
8:29 .... 12/12
8:32 .... 5/9
10:10 .... 5/17
11:33 .... 8/1
12:2 .... 4/28
12:21 .... 2/14
13:11, 12 ... 12/18
14:10 .... 11/28
14:12 .... 8/9
14:13 .... 10/14
15:13 .... 1/9

1 Corinthians

1:17 .... 3/7
1:25 .... 2/2
1:30 .... 1/2
2:5 .... 9/9
2:11 .... 1/4
2:12 .... 6/8
3:18, 19 ..... 4/25
4:1 .... 10/17
4:5 .... 6/28
6:20 .... 12/20
8:6 .... 3/6
9:27 .... 9/7
10:31 .... 1/22
13:4, 5 ...... 11/8
14:40 .... 8/27
15:3 .... 7/16
15:9, 10 ..... 4/8
15:58 .... 5/8
16:13 .... 9/3

2 Corinthians

2:11 .... 10/8
3:17 .... 3/3
4:7 .... 1/25
5:1 .... 2/11
5:18 .... 6/2
9:8 .... 5/20
9:15 .... 3/1
12:9 .... 8/20
12:10 .... 10/27

Galatians

2:20 .... 6/7
4:7 .... 6/20
4:8 .... 6/21
5:17 .... 7/11
5:24 ..... 7/25, 4/18
6:1 .... 11/27
6:8 .... 12/4
6:14 .... 1/5

Ephesians

1:3 .... 8/2
1:13, 14 ..... 10/26
1:19, 20 ...... 2/1
2:9 .... 8/28
2:13 .... 3/31
2:20, 22 .... 11/26
3:19 .... 9/2
4:2 .... 9/14
4:13 .... 4/23
4:14 .... 2/29
4:15 .... 6/19
4:17 .... 1/15
4:18 .... 7/9
4:23, 24 ...... 6/1
5:1, 4 .... 11/25
5:9, 10 ...... 10/24
5:14 .... 9/19
5:18 .... 5/28
5:19 .... 1/21
5:20 .... 11/23
6:11 .... 10/31
6:18 .... 10/28

Philippians

1:9, 10 .... 10/18
1:11 .... 1/28
1:20 .... 2/9
1:20, 21 ...... 1/26
1:29 .... 7/7
2:5 .... 2/24
2:7 .... 7/2
2:9 .... 6/14
3:3 .... 10/30
3:8 .... 10/10
3:13 .... 2/18
3:14 .... 8/16
4:4 .... 4/30
4:6 .... 9/15
4:8 .... 5/14

Colossians

1:10 .... 11/12
1:16, 17 ...... 12/5
2:8 .... 9/28
2:9, 10 ...... 12/30
3:1 .... 4/24
3:2 .... 3/5
3:4 .... 5/3
3:13 .... 8/7
3:17 .... 6/4
4:2 .... 12/13

1 Thessalonians

2:4 .... 3/14
2:8 .... 5/15
4:11, 12 ..... 11/16
4:16 .... 9/30
5:5, 6 .... 3/28
5:19 .... 11/15

2 Thessalonians

2:9 .... 9/23
3:5 .... 8/4
3:16 .... 9/12

1 Timothy

1:14 .... 1/16
3:7 .... 10/15
3:16 .... 4/3

4:16 .... 10/25
6:4 .... 9/25
6:6, 7 .... 6/18

2 Timothy

1:10 .... 8/18
2:1 .... 7/4
2:15 .... 11/24
2:25 .... 7/27
3:16 .... 1/6
4:3, 4 .... 2/7
4:5 .... 3/23

Titus

1:5 .... 12/19
1:9 .... 6/25
2:12 .... 5/13
3:5 .... 12/8
3:7 .... 12/16

Hebrews

1:1, 2 .... 12/24
2:1 .... 4/16
2:3 .... 10/12
2:17 .... 2/5
2:18 .... 5/11
4:16 .... 6/9
6:1 .... 5/26
6:19 .... 12/7
9:28 .... 3/9
10:23 .... 11/3
10:31 .... 11/7
10:36 .... 8/6
11:3 .... 6/12
11:13 .... 9/26
11:16 .... 3/11
12:2 .... 12/21
12:11 .... 2/20
12:23 .... 4/1
12:28 .... 3/8
13:5 .... 9/21
13:8 .... 4/22
13:21 .... 8/15

James

1:12 .... 1/29

2:1 .... 5/2
2:22 .... 9/27
2:23 .... 4/20
4:3 .... 7/14
4:7 .... 7/12
4:9 .... 8/14
4:10 .... 12/11
5:16 .... 5/7

1 Peter

1:2 .... 3/25
1:5 .... 5/6
1:7, 8 .... 4/10
1:8 .... 2/25
1:19 .... 12/17
2:15 .... 11/17
2:19 .... 6/17
2:21 .... 7/18
3:4 .... 9/22
3:7 .... 4/27
3:18 .... 4/6
3:21, 22 ..... 9/18
4:13 .... 11/30
5:2, 4 .... 1/7
5:6 .... 3/24
5:7 .... 11/9

2 Peter

1:3 .... 1/18
1:4 .... 12/27
2:1 .... 6/10
2:19 .... 6/22
3:17 .... 12/3
3:18 .... 4/15

1 John

1:3 .... 9/1
1:8 .... 7/13
1:9 .... 11/22
2:15 .... 1/11
3:1 .... 10/23
3:2 .... 7/28
3:8 ...... 1/12, 2/12
3:10 .... 6/29
3:16 .... 8/17
3:18 .... 8/26

3:24 .... 8/3
4:1 .... 6/16
4:12 .... 12/2
4:16 .... 11/1
4:19 .... 1/13
5:6 .... 5/30
5:10 .... 6/11

2 John
7 .... 5/12

Jude
21 .... 10/1
22, 23 .... 12/26

Revelation
1:8 .... 1/1
1:17 .... 2/8
3:20 .... 7/3
3:21 .... 6/6
3:21, 22 ...... 2/13

12:10, 11 .... 11/29
22:3, 4 .... 12/29
22:14 .... 6/13
22:17 .... 7/5
22:20 .... 12/31